Craft Galleries Guide

A Selection of British Galleries and their Craftspeople

SIXTH EDITION
2002

Compiled and edited by
Caroline Mornement

BCF Books

Craft Galleries Guide

A Selection of British Galleries
and their Craftspeople

Contents

Contents

Logos used on title pages:

 0% Galleries who are part of an interest free credit scheme

 Full disabled access

Partial disabled access

 * Galleries in all 6 editions

5

Foreword by Sir Terence Conran

Craftsmanship is very important to the future of this country and is often the spawning ground for the development of small, high quality enterprises. With the increase in mass production and global business it is difficult to find individuality as one shops the world. The craftsman can and does offer this much sought after quality in his or her work.

One of the things that this country seems to have forgotten is the pleasure of making things. During the Thatcher years there was a belief that we could exist by service industries alone and that manufacturing was dead in the water.

Thank goodness there seems to be a realisation that clever and talented creative people can make things that the world admires and acquires. Much of this change in attitude comes from the combination of aesthetic and practical sensibilities of designers and craftsmen working together or quite often when these skills are combined in the same person.

The problem that the craft industry faced in the past was the belief that you could simply continue to produce the same traditional products, with no reference to the huge changes in taste or style of life that have occurred throughout the world in the last fifty years. Of course, there are certain traditional products and methods of manufacture that are still as relevant to life today as they ever were, but the really exciting challenge for craftsmen is to use their talents to make things that are truly innovative and suit a contemporary style of life and that are useful as well as decorative. Whilst making things by hand and as one offs, rather as an artist would paint a picture or make a sculpture is still an important area of craftsmanship, I believe that there is also a new understanding that craft need not rely on skilled hands alone and that modern technology can also be harnessed to produce quality and individuality by using the brain rather than the hand or best of all, a combination of the two.

In this way products of high quality and individuality can be offered at a price that more people can afford and therefore help to democratise the crafts and allow people to choose things that will enhance their lives and which they are proud to own.

The craft industries throughout the world have suffered from endless amounts of tourist junk sold as 'craft' in souvenir shops in seaside resorts, airports and tourist destinations. These products are usually made in low cost labour places such as the Philippines or Thailand and are as different to the things you will find in this book as night is to day. Nevertheless, the undiscerning customer is confused. The craft retailers have an important job to do in the education of the customer and craftspeople need to find ways to produce things at a price that does not inhibit the customers' purchase.

P.S. I used to use Lucie Rie pots in the kitchen every day, they cost four shillings and sixpence.

Sir Terence Conran

Photo courtesy of the Crafts Council

Large white stoneware bowl by Lucie Rie
Dated 1969 - Diam 254mm

Editor's View

I am delighted that Sir Terence Conran has written the foreword this year, helping to celebrate the 10th anniversary of the *Craft Galleries Guide* in high-profile style.

Looking back over the six editions, it certainly feels as if we've all come a very long way. The book is now over four times longer than the first edition, with more than 130 galleries represented, but there is still along way to go to achieve the comprehensive coverage that has always been my goal.

I would like to say a special 'thank you' to the seven galleries who have appeared in every edition (spot the* on their title pages).

With all the problems imposed by the Foot and Mouth crisis, which coincided with the production of this editon, I am delighted to have over 40 new galleries participating. Not all are recently launched some, like Primavera, have been established for many years and have set the standard for others to follow. However, there are a number of very new, enthusiastic galleries with no track record as yet. It will be interesting to watch their progress, we wish them well.

I am continually amazed at the number of top quality makers in this country. Back in 1991, when compiling the first edition, I remember a gallery owner saying, "we won't take part as there won't be enough different makers to go around". Well there are nearly 600 in this book, with more graduating each year.

This year for the first time, we introduce a new section, 'Signpost', a guide to new makers, as yet unattached to galleries.Turn to page 385 to see a selection of their untapped talent.

Finally, I hope that this book will encourage you to go out and see for yourselves the fascinating work being shown at galleries throughout the UK. Buying crafts is now easier than ever before thanks largely to the 0% interest schemes available through many galleries (page 9).

Caroline Mornement

0% Interest Schemes

Buying a piece of contemporary craft is often a spontaneous decision. People usually pre-plan the purchase of a new freezer or sofa, thus having their finances organised. Where art is concerned they often find themselves taken by surprise when the desire to buy a piece of craft hits them, and they may not have the funds ready and available.

Now this problem can be solved with very little trouble, via the interest free schemes running successfully at many galleries throughout the UK.

In 1983 the Welsh Arts Council introduced a strikingly simple but effective scheme to encourage art and craft lovers to become active buyers. They set up **'Collectorplan'**, a self financing purchasing scheme to provide interest free loans for the purchase of contemporary arts and crafts on sale in selected galleries throughout Wales.

This idea has now been taken up by nearly all the English Regional Arts Boards, who have each introduced their own particular version, with minor differences, except South West Arts and Southern Arts who have combined together to run **'ARTCred'**. The London, Scottish and Irish Boards do not yet run schemes.

'Owning a piece of art is satisfying, isn't it ..'
From ArtCred leaflet, given on completion of payment.

* All request 10% of the purchase price to be paid at the beginning of the payment period (10 months, although a couple extend this to 12 months).

* Staff at participating galleries will give the buyer application forms which are then sent to the RAB, who will normally deal with the paperwork within a few days, max two weeks. Written quotations can be requested.

* The item can be collected once the loan is approved, unless it is part of an exhibition.

0% Interest Schemes

The main terms are similar for all:

* Loans are available for anyone over 18 years, who has a bank or building society account from which to operate standing orders.

* They cover purchases from £60 - £1000, with three RABs offering loans for purchases up to a maximum of £2000.

These schemes have been highly successful in encouraging sales. As Aileen Hamilton of the Grace Barrand Centre says,"The part payment scheme gives the public a wonderful opportunity to own a piece of art or craft, by spreading the cost, interest free! Everyone benefits, the Artist, the Gallery and the lucky purchaser. It has made a big difference to our sales".

Many buyers have found that this method gives them the confidence and funds to start building a collection of craft, and return for further loans time after time. Jackie Blunt at Ferrers Gallery agrees "We have found that many of our customers use the scheme regularly to 'collect' and from the Galleries' point of view it is easy to administrate".

*Enthusiastic buyers from the SWA **Art**Cred leaflet*

Photos: John Martin

Art Buyers Credit ABC
'Brings works of art within your reach'
W. Midlands Arts - 0121 631 3121

Art£oan -
'Buy your art in pieces'
Yorkshire Arts - 01924 455 555

ifree/art
'Enjoy the art of individualism for ifree'
East England Arts - 01223 215 355

pART payment -
'The easy way to own art and crafts at home'
South East Arts - 01892 507 257

Art Purchase Plan
Northern Arts - 0191 255 8500

Acquire
'Create your own gallery at home !'
East Midlands Arts - 01509 218 292

ArtCred
'How to Buy Art'
South West & Southern Arts - 01392 218188

TAPS
'How to TAP into Art'
North West Arts - 0161 834 6644

Collectorplan
Arts Council of Wales - 02920 376 532

interest free loans
to buy art or craft*

ArtCred

With an **Art**Cred interest free loan you can borrow from £90 to £2,000 towards buying art and craft at any of 48 specially approved **Art**Cred member galleries from Buckinghamshire to Cornwall.

southwest arts

For full details of the scheme and a list of galleries contact: ArtCred Co-ordinator, South West Arts Trading Company Ltd, Bradninch Place, Gandy Street, Exeter EX4 3LS
Tel: 01392 218188 E-mail: artcred@swa.co.uk www.swa.co.uk/artcred
ArtCred is run by South West Arts Trading Company Ltd on behalf of Southern Arts and South West Arts

0% apr

*Subject to age and status. Written quotations available on request.

Artwork shown is illustrative

From top left: Jelly Leg'd Chicken Gallery, Reading. Bluestone Gallery, Devizes. Carrying A Fallen Angel by Louise McClary. Rearing Horse by Heather Jansch

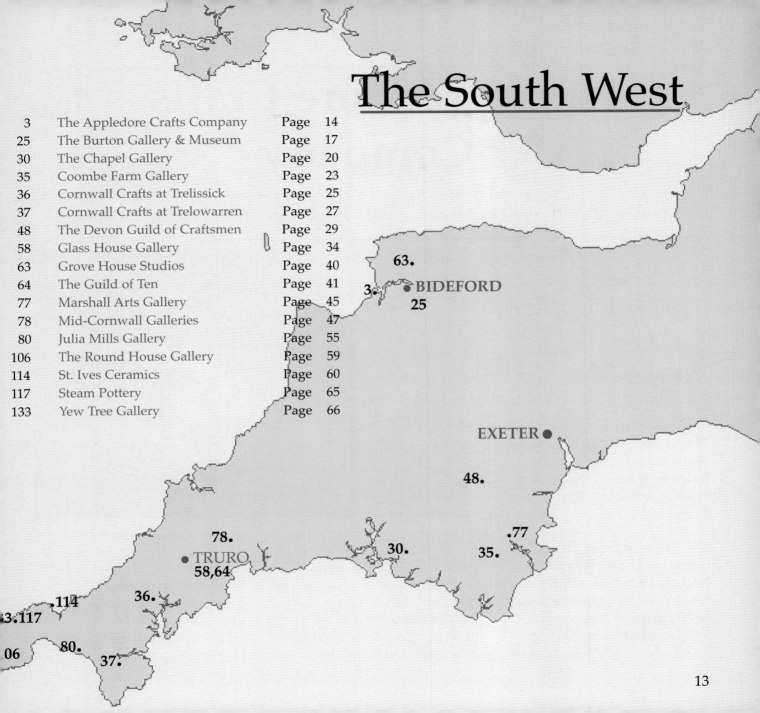

The South West

63.

3. ● BIDEFORD
25

EXETER ●

48.

78.
● TRURO
58,64

30.

35.

.77

36.

.114

3.117

06

80.

37.

13

The Appledore Crafts Company

5 Bude Street, Appledore, Devon EX39 1PS. Telephone: 01237 423547

Open 7 days a week 10am - 6pm (Easter - October) Wednesday - Sunday 10am - 4pm (Winter)

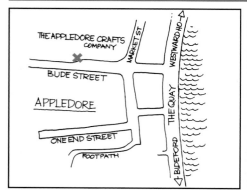

Bob Seymour

The Appledore Crafts Company was founded in 1991 by fourteen of North Devon's leading artists and it continues to thrive.

The gallery is staffed by the members, so that helpful and informed advice is always on hand. An ever-changing display of ceramics, metalwork, jewellery, photography, painting, textiles, lighting and wood-carving is enhanced by the work of carefully selected guest exhibitors throughout the year. We also feature a choice of contemporary furniture, with the work of three cabinet makers. The gallery is situated in one of the narrow streets typical of this unspoiled fishing village on the River Torridge. It has an historic past and is a haven for artists and craftspeople, many of whom live and work in the village and exhibit in the galleries here.

14

The Appledore Crafts Company

Penny Laird

Other members, not
shown here:
Rupert Ashmore, Kim
Woodward and Tony
Worthington

Jo Davies

Terry Sawle

Malcolm Vaughan

The Appledore Crafts Company

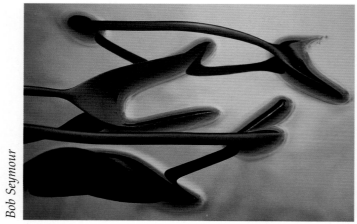

Bob Seymour

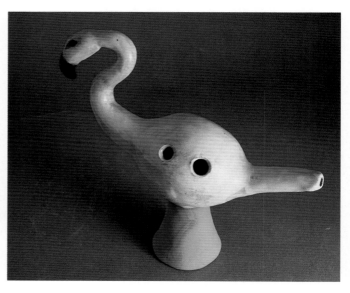

Bob Seymour   *Right:* Len Stevens

Eleanor Bartleman

Bill & Peach Shaw

0% The Burton Art Gallery & ♿ Museum

Kingsley Road, Bideford, North Devon EX39 2QQ. Telephone: 01237 471455 Fax: 01237 473813
Open April - October: Tuesday - Saturday 10am - 5pm, Sunday 2 - 5pm
November - March: Tuesday - Saturday 10am - 4pm, Sunday 2pm - 4pm

Overlooking the historic port of Bideford and set in Victoria Park, the Burton Art Gallery was originally built in 1951 to house the work and collections of local watercolour artist Hubert Coop. Coop was joined in the venture by local dignitary Thomas Burton and the gallery commemorates the life of Burton's daughter, Mary, herself an artist. In 1994 the gallery was reopened after a complete refurbishment and extension.

Known as one of the Westcountry's premier centres for art, the Burton boasts three galleries, which house a regular change-over of National, touring and local exhibitions. Two museum areas show some of the finest examples of North Devon slipware, along with other local artifacts. A workshop, shop, coffee

shop and of course the craft gallery completes the facilities on offer. A specially commissioned stained glass window, created by local

maker Robert Paterson, in memory of his father James, illuminates one end of the craft gallery. Running the length of the main gallery and with the natural light flooding in from Victoria Park, this space is an excellent showground for craftmakers from all over Devon and the West Country.

We are delighted to be able to display an eclectic range of craft from ceramics to textiles, wood carving to woven silks, large metal work to pieces of jewellery, to name but a few. Exhibitions during the year showcase the work of groups and individual makers. Reflecting the craftsmanship of the stained glass window, all works exhibited here are selected for their quality and originality.

The Burton Art Gallery & Museum

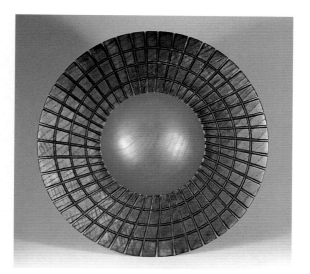

Top Left:
Bill & Peach Shaw

Top right:
Paul Anderson

Left: Mike Wilson

Right: Taja

The Burton Art Gallery & Museum

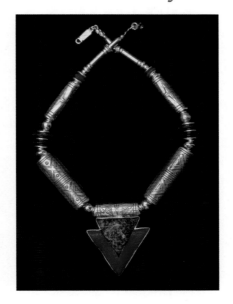

Rachel & Mary Sumner

Anne Farag

Clive Bowen

Veronica Gould

Roger Copple

The Chapel Gallery

The National Trust, Saltram House, Plympton, Plymouth, Devon PL7 1UH.
Telephone & Fax: 01752 347852 Email: DSARGX@SMTP.NTRUST.ORG.UK
Email: chapelgallery@hotmail.com Website: www.nationaltrust.org.uk
Open Sunday - Thursday 11.30 - 4.30pm 2nd April - 31st October. From 1st November - 20th December open every day, except Friday, Saturday 11am - 4pm

The Chapel Gallery is set within the beautiful thirty acres of Grade II listed gardens that make up part of the Saltram Estate, owned by The National Trust in South Devon. The Gallery itself is located to the North West of the Georgian Mansion; which has a past history of the Arts with a collection that includes works by the painter Sir Joshua Reynolds and the Furniture Maker Thomas Chippendale.

The Chapel Gallery continues the tradition of supporting the Contemporary Applied Arts with a series of Seasonal Exhibitions in the Lower Gallery, where the vaulted ceiling and huge gothic windows give natural light and lend a beautiful backdrop to the varied crafts shown. These include Ceramic Sculptures, Ceramics, Pottery, Jewellery, Baskets, Textiles, Furniture, Automata, Woodturning, Papier Maché, Glass, Etchings and Paintings. The Upper Gallery shows a programme of themed and solo exhibitions by artists and makers from around the United Kingdom, but

The Chapel Gallery

predominantly those within the South West, throughout the year. Exhibitions are extended into the gardens and within the listed buildings such as the 17th century Orangery, where themes and artist's work are shown in harmony with the surroundings.

Through the Chapel Gallery, Makers come together to show their crafts and skills at the annual 'Garden' and 'Yuletide Crafts Fairs', which are held within the Saltram Estate enabling collectors old and new to meet, learn and buy direct from the varied makers showing.

The Chapel Gallery is open throughout the year. For further opening details and Exhibitions, Listings or Events, please contact the Chapel Gallery.

The Chapel Gallery - Saltram House
From a wood engraving by Pam Pebworth

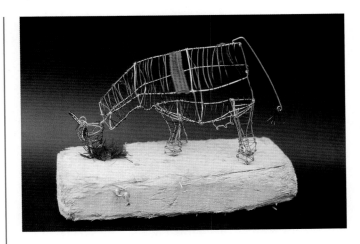

Amanda Bates

The style of my work has developed from an interest in children's toys and folk art from around the world, particularly items that involve automata and moving parts. Having obtained a degree that involved working in wood, metal, ceramics and textiles, my work often uses a variety of materials - the majority are made using wire, driftwood and some textile elements.

The humourous characteristics of animals and the way they move are the main focus of the kinetic sculptures. I work from a shed in my garden in Wilton, near Salisbury and so am often influenced by the animals in the surrounding countryside and the ducks that freely wander the streets of Wilton. The work is exhibited frequently throughout the country and in Europe.

Les Grimshaw

Les Grimshaw graduated as a fashion designer and then trained as a jeweller before working as a technician and teaching jewellery at Plymouth College of Art and Design. More recently he has produced his own range of gold, and silver and gold jewellery, selling to galleries in Devon and Cornwall.

Les has developed and refined his technique of fusing metals and creating textures and designs that bring out the richness of different coloured golds when combined together. His pieces are often set with diamonds.

For his silver jewellery, Les uses processes of reticulation and oxidizing which give an individual look and colour to each piece. He also includes yellow or red gold in many of his silver rings and earrings.

Les now devotes himself solely to his jewellery making, and as well as supplying galleries, also works to private commission.

Nic Collins

Blandine Anderson
The Chapel Gallery

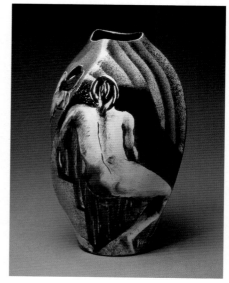

Paul Jackson

Coombe Farm Gallery

Dittisham, near Dartmouth, South Devon TQ6 OJA. Telephone: 01803 722352
Email: mark@rileyarts.com   Website: www.rileyarts.com
Open Daily 10am - 5pm (Closed on Sundays)

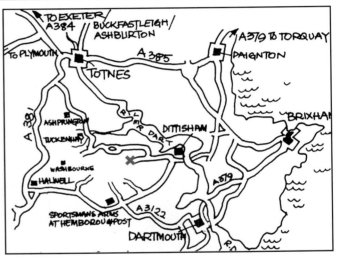

Situated in the beautiful countryside and rolling hills of South Devon, Coombe Farm Gallery opened her doors in 1993. The gallery is part of the Coombe Farm Studios complex which was established by Paul Riley and his family in 1983 for the teaching of Fine Arts and Crafts.

The gallery exhibits a wide range of media including ceramics, mirrors, prints, collages, furniture, glass, jewellery, sculptural ceramics, wood, photographs and textiles. We display work by leading artists and makers predominantly from the West Country. Our exhibition programme includes four themed exhibitions a year in which we also include work from talented makers from Britain and abroad.

Pauline Lee

My work with clay began fifteen years ago, fuelled by a pressing urge toward creative self expression and as a complementary activity to home and children. In no time I was hooked and my dream was to become a ceramicist.

I studied at Plymouth Art College for two years then set up a studio in Devon and I was away ! During a period of intense experiment, I found that I loved handbuilding as it allowed my imagination and intuition to flow.

Throughout my life my passion has been for nature and the inherent nature within things and I now live and work in the beautiful and inspiring Dart Valley on Dartmoor National Park. I work with white stoneware clay and the pieces are washed with oxides, stains and slips to bring them to life.

On a good day, building a torso vase with pinched, rolled and textured clay that develops organically is the most natural and engaging experience.

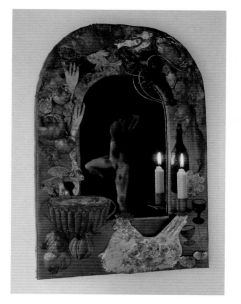

Burr Elm Form Nick Agar,
Patinated Copper Mirror
Tina Riley,
Mohican Perfume Bottles
Susan Nixon and Allister Malcolm

Cornwall Crafts at Trelissick

Trelissick Gardens, Feock, Truro, Cornwall TR3 6QL. Telephone: 01872 864084
Email: info@cornwallcrafts.co.uk Website: www.cornwallcrafts.co.uk
Open same hours as National Trust, seven days a week, mid February - 23rd December

The Cornwall Crafts Association was formed in 1973, to support craftworkers living and working in the county. Its aims to encourage high standards of workmanship and design and to sell the work of over 150 selected makers.

In a unique partnership between the C.C.A. and the National Trust, Trelissick Gallery was opened in 1988 amidst four hundred acres of parkland, gardens and woods at Trelissick Gardens.

This fine gallery is housed on two floors of a beautifully converted nineteenth century barn. Craftwork is well displayed on one floor, and paintings, prints and sculpture are shown on the other. The gallery plays an important role in promoting both art and crafts in Cornwall.

Open from mid - February until 23rd December, the programme includes three exhibitions of members work, workshops and demonstrations. During the last year, over one hundred and fifty craftworkers have exhibited at the gallery.

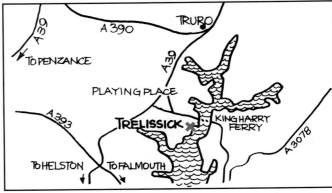

Geoffrey Bickley

I observe birds in their natural habitat and my aim is not to carve an exact likeness of a bird but to capture its essence.

When I draw the shape of a bird, I like to portray it in different poses and so create a shoreline, or a group picture. I find carving like this enables my work to flow.

I work mostly with reclaimed materials using pine for the majority of my carvings.

J.Watton F.R.P.S.

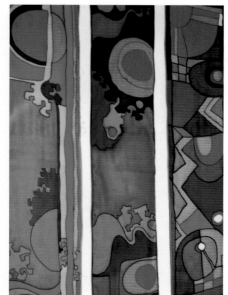

Lorna Wiles

Lorna Wiles has been fortunate that she has, for the past thirty years, been able to live and work in her native Cornwall using her close proximity to vast beaches and coastal ruggednesss as constant visual reference for her ever changing textile prints.

Expanding print-paste, brilliant reactive dyes and devore techniques used boldly on wall hangings, scarves, cushions and table linen are just part of her creative output.

Her paintings are very textured, using various media depicting meticulously observed sea, rocks and pools, in soft natural colours; a total contrast to her textiles.

As well as supplying several Galleries in Cornwall, Lorna has her own gallery in Crantock showing the work of several young talented artists.

Cornwall Crafts at Trelowarren

Trelowarren, Mawgan, Helston, Cornwall TR12 6AF. Telephone: 01326 221567
Email: info@cornwallcrafts.co.uk Website: www.cornwallcrafts.co.uk
Open March, April, May & October 10.30 am - 5pm , Tuesday - Sunday & Bank Holidays,
June - September 10.30am - 5.30 pm daily.

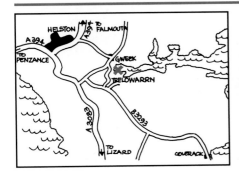

The Georgian stable block on the historic Trelowarren Estate is the home of the Cornwall Crafts Association's principal gallery. Since 1978 the Association has held regular exhibitions of work by makers living in Cornwall interspersed by exhibitions from outside the county.

The Association's programme also includes workshops, seminars and social events.

An annually rotated committee of selectors ensures that all work shown is of the highest standard.

Future exhibitions will continue to cover a wide area of quality crafts reflecting the standard of work being produced in a part of the country with a strong craft tradition, while at the same time acknowledging the adventurous work being produced by new makers.

Cornwall Crafts at Trelowarren

27

Adela M. Powell

The work is hand-built using a variety of techniques, clays and glazes. My main passion is texture but I also enjoy using colour.

The forms I make are mainly sculptural and often vessel related. Inspiration comes from many sources including abstract art, rocks, erosion, prehistoric caves, drawings and artefacts, rusty metal, peeling paint and so on. My main difficulty is in creating the right forms with which to respond to these inspirations whilst exploring the possiblities of clay as a material in its own right.

The work often fails technically or aesthetically (or both!) but clay has such wonderful properties I am unable to abandon it as a medium through which to communicate. The good pieces are, however, hard won !

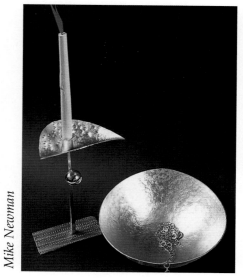

Mike Newman

Jack Trowbridge

Jane Blonder

Julia Mills

28

The Devon Guild of Craftsmen

0%

Riverside Mill, Bovey Tracey, Devon TQ13 9AF. Telephone: 01626 832223 Fax: 01626 834220
Email: devonguild@crafts.org.uk Website: www.crafts.org.uk
Open 10am - 5.30pm (7 days a week all year, except Winter Bank Holidays)

On the banks of the River Bovey, in the centre of the little town of Bovey Tracey on the eastern fringes of Dartmoor, stands the attractive Grade II listed Riverside Mill which is the permanent home of the Devon Guild of Craftsmen.

Established in 1955 in order to encourage a wide appreciation of crafts and to promote the highest standards of craftsmanship and design amongst craftsmen and women in the South West, the Devon Guild is now a registered charity. It has a selected membership of over two hundred and thirty makers who include such internationally renowned craftsmen as the potter David Leach and furniture maker Alan Peters.

Since the move to Riverside Mill over fifteen years ago, the Devon Guild has established one of the most exciting craft venues in the South West. With a regular annual programme of six own and touring craft shows, and Members' solo exhibitions, which attract over one hundred thousand visitors a year.

There is also a shop, which is on the National List of Craft Shops and Galleries, with permanent and

Bim

changing displays of Members' work for sale, including ceramics, furniture, prints, textiles, jewellery and woodwork.

The Gallery Café is well known for its delicious home cooked food including vegetarian dishes, excellent cakes and local wines which can also be enjoyed outside in the courtyard during the summer.

The Devon Guild of Craftsmen also has an active education and outreach programme organising craftspeople to work in schools as part of its Big Hand, Little Hand scheme. It also organises demonstrations and other craft related events both at Riverside Mill and elsewhere.

The Devon Guild now has a Commissions resource, a Wedding List Service, and is an ArtCred gallery offering interest free loans subject to status.

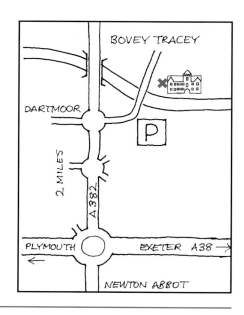

Claire Attridge

David Gilliland

Following her illustration degree, Claire worked on projects from cookery books to monthly magazines.

In 1992, wanting a change of direction, she started making Papier Maché, finding it a wonderfully versatile and expressive medium. It was immediately apparent that texture and surface pattern, which had been important elements in her illustration, would become intrinsic parts of her three dimensional work.

By combining a long standing fascination with found natural objects and hand made papers, she also began to make her own papers, using plant fibres, seeds, and leaves. Claire started using layering, but is now experimenting more with paper pulp.

Recent one-off pieces are more concerned with the relationship between interior and exterior form as well as pure surface decoration.

Ann Powell

Ann was born in Devon and brought up on a farm on the northern edge of Dartmoor, an area which still provides the inspiration for much of her work. Organic flowing forms, the translucent colours of semi-precious stones, rainbow hues of opals and subtle contrasts of silver and gold, along with river pearls and mother-of-pearl bring richness and variety to Ann's jewellery.

All her work is made by hand with particular attention to fine detail. No casting is involved, so each piece is unique.

Her aim is to create jewellery which is feminine and exciting, believing it equally important that it is both comfortable and a joy to wear.

Ann's work has been commissioned by clients in America, Canada, Australia, Japan and Europe, and exhibited throughout Britain and in Canberra, Australia.

Penny Simpson

I started making pots whilst living in Japan - inspired by the wonderful food, so beautifully presented and by the living tradition in the many pottery-making areas.

I then trained at Dartington Pottery and set up my own workshop and showroom at Moretonhampstead in Devon.

My continuing love of food and cooking has kept me interested in making pots for everyday use. I use red earthenware clay with poured or brushed slip and incised decoration.

Recently, I have developed an interest in designing and making tiles. I decorate the tiles using similar techniques to those developed on the pots. I enjoy designing schemes to suit a particular kitchen or bathroom. Photographs of commissions can be seen at the Devon Guild of Craftsmen. I am also a member of The Craft Potters Association.

Peet Leather

My work springs from the subconscious - days by a river, up a mountain, on a beach.

In retrospect I recognise the past elements of my life that influence what I create, my textile designer mother, the Yorkshire coastline with its rich tide of rubbish to ignite the imagination, walking the Pennines and the Scottish Highlands, teenage years at jumble sales transforming bargains into a unique wardrobe, dancing late into the night, colour, music, performances and visual arts, working in costume for theatre and fancy dress and fifteen years of intense city life all play their part.

The conscious element is to take waste materials and give them new life through my work - inspiration always takes me by surprise.

Debby Mason

Specialising in marine life etchings, her recent work is inspired by her love of the sea and the diversity of life it contains. Seahorses and Sea dragons are particular favourites. As a qualified diver, she feels privileged to be able to come face to face with the subjects of her art. Delicate, often fragile, colourful, always fascinating, the hidden life beneath the sea is brought vividly to life in her pictures.
Etching is the perfect medium for her with its fineness of line and the ability to lend itself to the meticulous detail of the underwater creatures that attract her to them as subjects.

Although Debby has dived in many exotic places, she still regards her home waters off Plymouth Sound as amongst the best.

The Devon Guild of Craftsmen

Carl Hahn

Light, form, substance, memory, landscape; my signature piece has become this chest of drawers, beautifully photographed by Richard Davies. The beach by Dungeness nuclear power station is, I am told, frequently rebuilt to protect its unlovely neighbour from the seas' repeated onslaughts. The lighting is artificial, a portable flash on a dark and stormy day, as chunks of foam the size of dinner plates flew about our ears, driven over the machine made shingle bank by the force of the wind off the sea. I became temporarily airborne carrying the largest drawer back to the van it was so wild.

Simple image, complex process, both appropriate and analogous to the work I do.

I make for galleries and individuals and exhibit widely with work in numerous private collections on four continents.

Bruce Chivers

Bruce's work revolves around simple forms handthrown in porcelain, utilising both high-fired and 'Raku' techniques.

'Raku' allows him the opportunity to embrace the element of surprise. The spontaneity of the flame plays an integral role in the formation of the glaze surfaces.

The copper, under reducing conditions, pools magically to create unique visual pieces; where seeing and knowing become as important as the making.

Bruce is a full member of both The West Country Potters Association and Craft Potters Association of Great Britain.

He exhibits and lectures extensively throughout the UK and abroad.

Glass House Gallery

112 Kenwyn Street, Truro, Cornwall TR1 3DJ. Telephone & Fax: 01872 262376
Website: www.glass-house-gallery.co.uk

Open Monday - Friday 10am - 5.15pm, Saturday 10am - 5.30pm throughout the year

The Glass House Gallery, housed in a converted stable block in the Specialist Quarter of Truro, is the cathedral city's first and foremost contemporary art and craft gallery.

Now in its sixth year, the Gallery exhibits an exciting and diverse collection in light, airy surroundings, on two floors; with some of the region's finest established artists alongside talented newcomers.

Downstairs, an exceptional display of the very best craft jewellery features work from Cornwall and all parts of the British Isles. Throughout the Gallery there is an amazing collection of ceramics, smoke-fired, raku, porcelain, Cornish studio pottery, interspersed with

fine sculptures. Glass House Gallery holds several exhibitions every year and is enthusiastically received by both public and artists alike.

Potters include:
John Bedding, Hugh West, Sam Hall, Eleanor Newell, Christine Gittins, Roelof Uys, Dan Chapple, Simon Rich and Linda Styles.

Jewellers include:
Robert Morris, Jack Trowbridge, Frances and Stephen Park, Margot Hartley, Janet Slack, Sophie Harley, Cornelius Van Dop, Pamela Burrows, Joanne Porter, Anna de Ville and Amanda Ray.
Mirrors by: Emma Edelston.
Printmakers include:
Ian Laurie, Trevor Price, Michele Wright, Rachel Kantaris, Margrit Clegg, Sheila Oliner, Debby Mason and Judi Strega.
Ceramic Sculptors: Shirley Foote, Kathy Luntley and Leah Martin.
Artists include: David Beer, Colin Orchard, Sasha Harding, Sophie Harding, Michael Praed, John Piper, Mary Wastie, Noel Betowski, Biddy Picard, Judy Symons, Lee Woods, Eric Ward and Brenda King.
Sculptors: Stephen Clutterbuck, William Cramer and Rick Borrie.

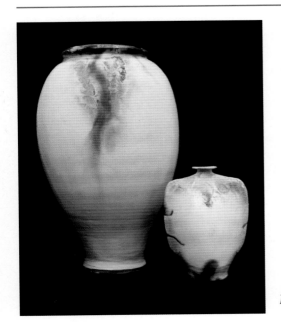

Left: John Bedding

Right: Hugh West
Both photos Mary-Clare Reeve

Glass House Gallery

35

Jack Trowbridge

Jack Trowbridge makes jewellery in gold and silver, mixing the precious metals and their textures and creating forms which reflect his early experience as a sculptor and letter-carver. Jack works in a peaceful wooded valley below the granite moors of West Penwith. He has a particular feel for cutting letters in slate and stone. Wind vanes in copper and aluminium are inspired by the weather, the fish and the birds which are so much part of his environment.

Jack has exhibited widely, including Loot and the Goldsmiths' Fair. He has lettering at County Hall, Truro and in St. Paul's Cathedral, memorials in churchyards (e.g. to Duncan Grant at Firle) and plaques such as those to Edward Johnston and Eric Gill at Ditchling. He is a Freeman of the Worshipful Company of Goldsmiths, and a member of Letter Exchange and Cornwall Crafts Association.

Mike Newman

Frances and Stephen Park

Frances and Stephen live and work from their home on the edge of Dartmoor. They collaborate in the designing and making of every piece of their jewellery, and have done so since 1992. They both trained in fine art at leading London colleges (St Martins and Goldsmiths respectively), which may paradoxically explain their satisfaction in strong, unpretentious and wearable design. The prominent theme in the work is clarity of form and a lasting pleasure in the natural qualities of the materials. They enjoy the fact that their jewellery seems somewhat aloof to the vagaries of fashion, and make no special effort to produce coherent "collections" unless this coincides with their ideas or evolves in the process of making. They certainly welcome the challenge of designing to commission, as this has encouraged new directions in the past.

Robert Morris

Robert has been working for twenty years in silver and gold, and producing his own designs since 1989. He is almost entirely self-taught, his paramount aim being to achieve the highest degree of technical proficiency. He is fascinated and excited by the physical changes that take place in the metals as he works them, and he often finds this an inspiration for new designs, which come from instinct, rather than from any formal training.

The aesthetics (realised mainly in retrospect) of most of his early pieces are based upon the sculptural qualities of the female physique - flowing lines and sweeping curves progressing, sometimes, into flatter planes. His later pieces are largely more contemporary in design, some of which express his own sense of humour and whimsy.

Helen Z. Morris

Dan Chapple

I studied at Plymouth College of Art and Design for four years, finishing in 1996 with a Higher National Diploma in Ceramics and Glass. Since then I have shared a workshop on the Devon and Cornwall border, and have returned to the college as a Ceramics Technician part time.

The work that I produce is made on the wheel and is Raku fired. I first became aware of this technique as a student. The lustrous metallic glazes which first attracted me to Raku no longer hold the same appeal. However, I still admire the effect of a crackle glaze on my work, which I believe produces a more subtle result. A simple but precise form best shows how a particular type of glaze will react with it.

Cornelis Jakob Van Dop

.... and so Everywhere Spirit embraced First Human and smiled: "This small weak one shall be first among you." Hearing this the other Gods replied: "Then let us accompany our brother and share his journey." So saying, one threw himself into the sky and became the stars and Moon, rainbows and Northern Lights so that man need never feel alone........ Another changed into everything that runs and flies, the geese.... and the caribou to feed and clothe his children........ and another smiled and turned into all the plants.... and forests to be a home and shelter and source of wisdom........ So you see, my son, not only is the world eternally alive and knowing, but is really your loving family....

- from 'Old Cree Tales' recollected by Man-in-the-Moon (1896)

Steve Tanner

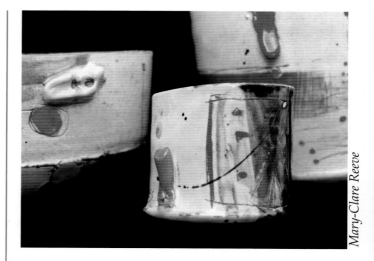

Mary-Clare Reeve

Linda Styles

My reality is less to do with representation, be it 'tile panels' or 'pots'. I am interested in interior realities and emotions, for instance, the way colour is 'read' and the way it is associated with certain feelings. I suppose that I want it to refer to something more than just itself. Colour and shape, or the perception of these two things, are essential to my work, representation versus abstract is not really the issue for me, although my starting point does always come from the 'real world' and the way I perceive reality. My need to blend past and present, memory and experience, perhaps, this is my way of trying to make sense of it all!

Margot Hartley

I remember coveting my mother's collection of jewellery, in particular a brooch made in the form of a bumble bee from tigers eye and diamonds. I have always had a fascination for gems, beads and metals and developed my interest further by formally training in the craft of silversmithing at a local goldsmiths in Truro. In 1986 I embarked as a professional jeweller, creating work with references drawn from the insect world, inspired by a beetle brooch made from tin. Quite by accident, I discovered that heated brass was very attractive, its natural oxide revealing a variety of green, gold and brown hues.

In 1989 I introduced copper, and when combined together, the oxidised brass and copper complemented one another, the warm red copper merging with the gold green of the brass. The use of sterling silver was later introduced as decoration, however, more recently I have used brass on silver, giving rise to a new look; glossy and modern. I have always lived in Cornwall and its influence is inherent. My work is often described as primitive and medieval, I like the term 'primitive', it represents the root feelings I deliver in my work.

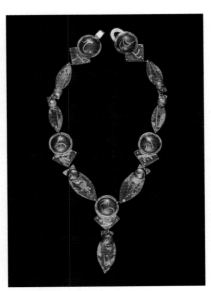

Michele Wright

Printmaking: The drawbacks
It is a messy business. Never start printing in good clothes saying to yourself "I will be careful" because you will get ink on yourself or worse splash some acid. In my eagerness to start a new piece I can still sometimes draw a scene directly onto a plate forgetting that the result will be a mirror image. You just have to start again the opposite way around which can be weird. Then there is editioning - my least favourite task.

Printmaking: The rewards
Lots, as there is always something new to learn. Making a plate is the most interesting. Unlike a normal drawing or painting, until the day you print it you do not truly know what the picture will look like. You hope not to be disappointed with what you have spent hours imagining the end product to look like. So the best moment is when you turn the handle of the press throw back the blankets, slowly lift up the damp paper and all is revealed and it has worked! Then I can go for a walk around St. Ives, the town I love, and be inspired again.

Grove House Studios

64 Newport Road, Barnstaple, North Devon EX32 9BQ. Telephone: 01271 379920
Email: jill@grovehousestudios.co.uk Web: www.grovehousestudios.co.uk
Open Monday - Saturday 10am - 4.30pm

Grove House Studios opened in April 2000 and is already becoming well known as Barnstaple's only showcase for local artists and craftspeople.

The Gallery is situated in Newport, an old and interesting part of Barnstaple, just ten minutes walk from the town centre. It offers a relaxed and friendly atmosphere and a wide and ever-changing selection of quality art and crafts, including paintings, photography, ceramics, woodturning, jewellery and textiles.

We also have an in-house fashion designer and approximately eight themed

Robin Mellor

exhibitions are held in the gallery area each year. New talent is especially encouraged.Browsing is thoroughly approved of and to keep you there a little longer, there is a small tea room offering delicious home-made cakes with a wide range of teas and coffees.

The Guild of Ten

19 Old Bridge Street, Truro, Cornwall TR1 2AH. Telephone: 01872 274681
Open Monday - Saturday 9.30am - 1.30pm, 2 - 5.30pm

The Guild of Ten is a co-operative venture by a group of craftsmen and women living in Cornwall. It opened its present premises in 1979 with the aim of establishing a direct outlet for its members' work.

The shop is staffed by the makers on a rota basis so that customers can discuss their needs with the maker in question. The Guild of Ten has always promoted the highest quality in

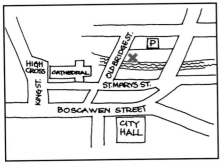

contemporary craft and over the years has counted some of Britain's leading makers amongst its number.

Disciplines currently represented include ceramics, glass, jewellery, textiles, turned wood, automata, leather, and children's clothes.

Mike & Gill Hayduk

Puzzles seen in a new light! These puzzles are not just to play with and then be hidden away in a drawer, they are designed to be displayed as a form of art.
Mike and Gill have been working with wood since 1987. Following a request from his children to make a jigsaw, Michael took his hobby a step further and began producing beautifully intricate puzzles in a variety of woods.

All the puzzles are designed by Mike, most of which combine the two disciplines of woodturning and fretwork. In his designs he tries to emphasise the natural colour and beauty of the wood. Over forty varieties of wood are used, which mostly come from waste or sustainable sources. All the puzzles are oiled and polished by hand and in the finished items they hope to have something that is amusing and decorative. Mike and Gill's work is now widely sought after and collected. In 1993 Mike was commissioned to produce a limited edition puzzle by the National Trust.

Jane & Chris Birchley

Jane and Chris Birchley have been making mechanical wooden toys, intended for adult children, since they moved to Cornwall nine years ago.

Jane set up the Opi workshop after graduating in Sculpture form Chelsea School of Art. Here she and Chris have found an ideal way to express their gentle humour and work together amidst the wild, inspiring landscape of West Penwith.

Opi Toys are hand made and painted either as individual pieces or in small batches using local hard and soft woods and a touch of whimsy. The moving element of the pieces, although important, is always secondary to the decorative. Being surrounded by the sea has greatly influenced much of the work. Recurring themes have been seaside, and food recently expanding to include allotments and village flower shows.
Recently Opi have produced a range of clocks and mirrors designed to complement the automata.

Jennifer Yates

After gaining an Honours Degree in Art and Design at Bristol Art College, Jenny taught Art and Pottery for several years in secondary schools in London. A move to Cornwall in 1988 created the opportunity for her to pursue a career as a jeweller. Since then she has enjoyed building up a successful jewellery business in the vibrant artistic community of the South West.

Jenny works mainly in silver with detail applied in yellow or rose gold, and the effect is often emphasised by oxidation. Texture and surface decoration are combined with innovative shapes to create unusual but wearable jewellery.

Jenny's work is exhibited in other galleries in Cornwall and London.

Les Freke

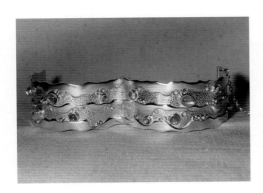

Les Freke originally trained as a furniture designer but chose to study silver and jewellery at Loughborough College of Art and Design. For two years he worked as a designer for a leading silversmith company in London, but missing the pleasure of making his own designs he moved to North Cornwall in 1971, to set up his own workshop.

He enjoys working with silver and semi-precious stones but also likes the richness of gold so that many of his individual pieces combine the two metals.

As well as producing a wide range of jewellery including exclusive 18ct gold wedding and engagement ring sets, he also makes small silver items from spoons and boxes to salvers and goblets. He enjoys working to commission and can be contacted through 'The Guild.'

Sharon Verry

Sharon trained at St. Martin's School of Art, London, gaining a BA in Fashion and Textiles in 1976. Since then, she has been exploring and developing her own unique style of handpainting directly on to natural fabrics, mostly silks, cottons and velvets.

"I love colour, and would like to bring a splash of it to everyone's life with my scarves, bags and jackets. The luminosity of silk and velvet enhances the vibrant colours I see in the petals of the flowers I paint, as well as abstract designs and Cornish scenes.

Cornwall is a very beautiful place in which to live: the wild beauty of the coast and the countryside, hidden valleys, subtropical gardens, and the wonderful National Trust properties are all sources of inspiration. Working with children in collaboration with the National Trust has produced many glorious banners for local schools and exhibitions."

Top: Sarah Bond *Centre:* John Davidson
Above: Robin Snelson

The Guild of Ten

*Marshall Arts Gallery

3 Warland, Totnes, Devon TQ9 5EL. Telephone: 01803 863533
Open Monday - Saturday 10am - 1pm, 2 - 5pm other times by appointment

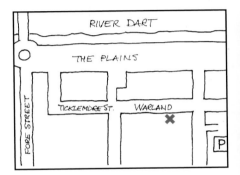

Marshall Arts Gallery opened in 1986 and its new owners are continuing the established tradition of presenting fine crafts in a tranquil setting.

The three spacious rooms, offering glimpses of the peaceful courtyard, give the feeling of a quiet oasis, a retreat from the bustle of the main street.

Ceramics feature strongly in the display and are complemented by wood, textiles, jewellery, glass, original prints and paintings. Items cover a broad price range and feature the beautifully functional, the quirky, the whimsical and the elegantly decorative. The display changes regularly and exhibitions are held at least four times a year.

Mike Wilson

Mike lives and works on the southern edge of Dartmoor, and uses locally grown timber to create his bowls, guided by a deep love of his materials. He harvests the timber from trees that have fallen victim to the strong winter winds or have died, necessitating felling.

The bowls he makes range from tiny, thin-walled vessels in woods such as holly, cherry, walnut, damson, and robinia, to large, rotund pieces which may be over 24" in diameter. Increasingly he makes use of coloured dyes to accentuate the strong patterns of open-grained woods such as ash and oak, or uses sand-blasting or scorching to create variations in surface tone and texture. He also uses carving techniques to create bowls with a strong sculptural element to them.

Lorraine Ditchburn

Lorraine believes that for both craft and industrial design, nature holds many of the answers. Leonardo da Vinci wrote "In her (Nature's) inventions nothing is lacking and nothing is superfluous" and she tries to approach her work with this in mind.

She designs through making and experimentation with materials and the driving force behind her work is the creation of surface texture, which she achieves by slip-casting porcelain in textured moulds. Porcelain is the perfect medium for her work, having the ability to highlight every nuance and minute detail of the delicate surfaces.

Lorraine's current work has been greatly inspired by the linen-wrapped mummies found in ancient Egyptian tombs. Most of her pieces are unglazed, reflecting her somewhat non-traditional approach to ceramics.

0% *# Mid-Cornwall Galleries ♿

St. Blazey Gate, Par, Cornwall PL24 2EG. Telephone: 01726 812131 Fax: 01726 814943
Email: info@mid-cornwall-galleries.co.uk Website: www.mid-cornwall-galleries.co.uk
Open Monday - Saturday 10am - 5pm

Mid Cornwall Galleries is located on the A390 three miles east of St. Austell, just two miles from the Eden Project. Housed in a former Victorian School, the space has proved perfect for our nine annual Exhibitions. Ten years ago it was chosen to be included on the Craft Council Selected Gallery List for the quality of work on display, there are only four such galleries in Cornwall. Even after all this time (we opened in 1980) we never cease to be amazed and delighted at the shows resulting from the work of people involved in the field of contemporary arts and crafts.

At regular intervals, throughout the year, we gather together new collections of paintings, etchings, ceramics (many by Fellows of the Craft Potters Association), blown and formed glass, silks, jewellery, figures in clay, wood and bronze,

paper sculptures, turned wood, clocks and mirrors, textiles, collages and many other wonderfully made pieces to create our next display. All of the work comes from artists and makers living in the UK, except for the occasional exhibition from overseas.

We are open throughout the year and would like to think that those of you who have not visited us will do so before long.

Regular contributors include:
Ceramics: Jon Middlemiss, Andrew Hague, Tony Laverick, John Pollex, Andrew Hill, Laurence McGowan,

Colin Kellam, Richard Wilson, Lucienne de Mauny, Jane Hamlyn, Phillip Wood, James Campbell, Paul Jackson, John Bedding, Tim Andrews, Walter Keeler, Anna Lambert, Delan Cookson.

Ceramic sculptures: Anthony Theakston, Elizabeth Haslam, Ann Legg, Andrew Bull, Jennie Hale, Guy Holder, Sally McDonnell.

Jewellery: Mary Prosperi, Jane Parker, Amanda Ray, Cornelis Van Dop, Margot Andrew, Farah Qureshi, Julie Stockley, Jocelyn Hartridge.

Woodturning: Mike Wilson, Jack Vage.

Wood sculpture: Lynn Muir, John Mainwaring, Jo Perry, Laurence Henry.

Paper sculptures: Jill Booth.

Collages: Zara Devereux, Penny Black.

Silks: Rachel & Mary Sumner, Caroline Hall.

Glass: Lara Aldridge, Stewart Hearn, Sarah Broadhead-Riall, John Dunn.

Etchings: Mark Spain, Mary George, Sonia Rollo, Lee Stevenson, Valerie Christmas, Jenny Devereux.

Print making: Trevor Price.

Silk screen prints: Richard Tuff.

Commissions are accepted. ART CRED GALLERY.

Karen Hamnett

Three things fascinate me - colour, language and texture. Being a singer words have always been important as a means of expression, enriching and illustrating the music. Also, the shape and pattern of words interest me - nearly every piece of work contains words in some form. I am constantly trying to create texture, even in a single layer, through the choice of fabrics, and adding embroidery, layers, resists and masks.

I want people to enjoy the sensation of wearing beautiful fabrics and colours, but I also have to make the piece as a complete work. Finally, colour fills my life - being a synaesthete, colour choice is instinctive and very strong rather than deliberate - I just have to get it out of my system!

Niki Hayward

I have been working as a fine art printmaker and illustrator since graduating from Loughborough in 1989. After taking a step back recently to have our two children, I felt that I needed a new creative direction and I looked around for new methods of working that would bring fresh challenges and inspiration, whilst fitting around life with a toddler and a baby !

After a visit to a local craft shop I found it carried a fantastic range of highly coloured felts and was sure it offered great potential for picture making. I was naturally drawn to making images that would appeal to children and I have had great fun producing this new range of hand cut and stitched appliqué pictures.

Diana Barraclough

I have always used birds in my work. Wherever I look I'm always seeing them perched on bits of this and that and so I place each of my birds on pieces of driftwood collected from the Cornish or Dorset coast. I assemble the wood first and then sculpt the bird to echo its texture and shape. I normally Raku fire as it gives the work an immediacy that seems to capture something of the bird's spirit.

I also make in stoneware, hand-building mostly, using slabs to give me a two dimensional surface. Forms are a combination of wave curves, fish shapes and boat angles; decoration ranges from naive imagery that tells simple stories to repeating motifs based on natural patterns.

Deborah Poole

I am drawn to feltmaking by the textural qualities of the material - a spontaneous expressive medium. My one-off compositions are made by colour mixing and layering dyed wool fleece which is hand milled to create a fabric with embedded image. This intrigues me as the combination of idea and process takes on a life of its own. I enjoy working in a 'painterly' way with areas of colour and line, reflecting patterns of growth in nature and light on form. My inspiration comes from garden flora or the natural landscape and I sketch designs celebrating the vitality of plant life. My Feltworks are decorative framed wall pieces or unframed hangings - Commissions are welcomed. I am a member of the Cornwall Crafts Association and International Feltmakers Association.

Chris Buck

Born in 1956, the son of a toolmaker, Chris Buck studied at Redruth School of Art. Returning to his industrial roots, he worked in several foundries, which gave him a thorough knowledge of casting techniques, and general metal and woodwork. He has been inspired by the St.Ives abstract artists, predominantly Dame Barbara Hepworth and Dennis Mitchell.

Since 1982 he has lived in Twelveheads with his family, where he works from his studio in a converted byre, overlooking fields and hedgerows, which brings a feeling of harmony with the natural world to his art.

Though producing sculpture in both wood and stone, it is in bronze that he finds greatest satisfaction, combining natural forms and industrial precision to achieve individual pieces.

50   *Mid-Cornwall Galleries*

Barbara Cumberlidge

Having originally trained in 3D Design, Silversmithing and Ceramics, I have recently begun to combine stained glass techniques with these more three dimensional disciplines. I work mainly with the copper foil technique, incorporating leading, wirework, crystals and a variety of materials, to create sculptural forms, decorative mobiles, panels, mirrors and lighting.

Organic and elemental themes, both surface and cellular, are expressed in abstract and figurative motifs. Water, light, reflection and movement also inspire much of the work. Nature is the main subject of exploration, though I draw on a wide variety of sources, including ancient mystical symbolism and decoration such as Celtic knot work.

Sue Schwartz

Each of the cats I make is an individual. They are hand built using a variety of methods involving extruded shapes, rolled coils, and modelling. They vary in size from approximately 6" to a 'big fat cat' *(left)* at about 15". They come in a mixture of colours, ginger, striped, black and white or grey. All are hollow and are Raku fired. I also make occasional other animals, at the moment I am making a series of 'fantasy fish'.

I have been making "Cats" since I discovered Raku at a weekend course in 1986. I've always owned cats (varying in numbers as I sneak a new one past my husband!) and we own three Rhodesian Ridgeback dogs. We live in a remote spot in Devon and both pot.

Giles Leigh-Browne

For many years I worked as a professional zoologist in Africa, living and travelling, in particular, in The Horn, East Africa and Southern Africa as far as the Kalahari. During my travels, I became interested in the crafts of the local people and in their self-adornment. This inspired me to begin creating jewellery when I later returned to Britain.

I admire ethnic jewellery and my interest is to reflect this appreciation in the design and making of my work. In technique, I am entirely self-taught and use mostly sterling silver, copper alloys, hand-cut semi-precious stones and Venetian glass.

Besides necklaces, I make earrings, brooches, bracelets and various silver pendants and crosses. I sell in galleries, at craft fairs and also work to commission.

Veronica Polyblank

Veronica Polyblank makes jewellery using silver and semi-precious stones. Sometimes gold is used to give added depth and colour. The surface of the metal is ususally fused, beaten, stamped, engraved or reticulated (the top surface of the metal is melted).

Recently, Veronica's great love has been for semi-precious beads. They have become as important as the metal in the finished pieces. The colours are so varied that a great deal of time is taken in choosing the right combinations.

Throughout time man has made beads from available materials, not only as decoration, but also in the form of amulets and talismans. Different cultures have attributed different powers to semi-precious stones, some of these are :
Amber - Healing Powers; Coral - Good Luck and Strength; Jade - Concentrated Essence of Love and Turquoise - Health and Happiness.

Sara Drake

Having lived and travelled abroad from an early age, I have grown up fascinated by maps. Not surprisingly, these early influences and ensuing wanderlust also dominate my work. I love to go on real and imagined journies, using my own incredibly detailed three-dimensional maps and globes as a vehicle.

The maps are made from papier mache and other found, filched or recycled materials. They are painted in acrylic and include a huge array of handmade, often humorous details, these range from geographical features to a menagerie of weird and wonderful animals. They also feature different forms of transport and major architectural features.

Each map or globe is individually designed to the customer's requirements, with features being added or altered to suit the individuals own travels, background or view of the world.

Richard Godfrey

I live and work in an idyllic setting on the South Devon coast, with a studio overlooking the sea. The surrounding countryside and coastline are the main sources of inspiration for my work. I have a large collection of found objects gleaned from the high tide line and I draw and photograph the coast extensively. I am also inspired by patterns of colour and tone in the hedgerows and by smaller details like butterfly and moth wings, insects, shells and wild flowers.

I find the chemistry of glazes and the infinite variations in forming techniques fascinating. I am constantly testing new materials and techniques, driven by need and desire to make new work, which is an expression of the joy and pleasure I get from living and working here in Devon.

June Hicks

What is it about making etchings that is so enthralling? The answer is a hard one to formulate. Something difficult to define happens when a drawing is transferred to a plate and becomes a print. It is this elusive difference which makes me at any rate want to go on – and on – making etchings. In that sense, I am enthralled by the processes involved, any of which can punish carelessness with disaster or produce a surprise bonus effect.

Printmakers these days fight a constant battle against the assumption that their prints are mechanically produced, as though I place an inked plate on the press bed, twirl a dial and hey presto! we have twenty-five etchings. I try to make studio visitors aware that each image has behind it a careful inking, wiping and pressing of the plate. I hope I share some of the magic too.

Pru Green (Gwili Pottery)

Gwili Pottery is a well established open studio and a gallery in rural West Wales. Gwili produces functional, life enhancing ceramics, using updated traditional slipware techniques.

The colourful designs explore a wide range of motifs including traditional florals and abstract, contemporary mark making. The high fired white earthenware ceramics are hand thrown and individually hand painted.

The staff of Gwili Pottery work as a team, with the inspiration for their work being primarily the colours, shapes and patterns of the natural world, but also their interest in twentieth century painting. Gwili Pottery's work is exhibited in several galleries within the U.K. and abroad.

Julia Mills Gallery

Fore Street, Porthleven, Cornwall, TR13 9HH. Telephone: 01326 569340
Email: julia@juliamillsgallery.freeserve.co.uk Website: www.juliamillsgallery.freeserve.co.uk
Open everyday 10am - 5pm

The Julia Mills Gallery can be found near the Post Office in the popular fishing village of Porthleven near Helston. Its south-facing aspect allows sun to pour in all day - one of the reasons Julia and her husband Gary decided to buy the property in December 2000.

The building is divided in two, one half being the workshop where Julia produces her glass pieces and the other side is the gallery showing her own work alongside local as well as national makers.

Dividing the two areas is a lime-green and turquoise counter made by Jonty Henshall from materials reclaimed from the old

lifeboat house at Sennen. The rest of the gallery interior is fitted in bleached-out wood, which is a perfect setting for the sea-inspired work on show. From the figurehead quality of Jessica Shellard's sculptures to Sarah Young's linocuts of mermaids and fish, this gallery is awash with colour and light.

Melissa Hunt

This collection is an amalgamation of precious metals with found pebbles and pieces of sea-worn glass. The threaded tops of each ring enable them to come apart so that the glass or pebbles can be replaced by another one or simply removed. This interchangeability enables the wearer to participate in the design and construction of each piece in the range.

After growing up in South Devon, I then studied at Sir John Cass School of Art. I am now able to use the skills I have learned to investigate the forms and tones of the coastline that I observed as a child, and translate them in to wearable pieces.

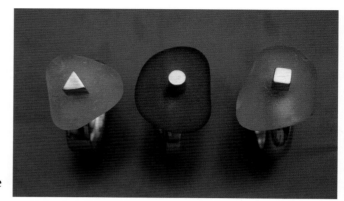

Gillian Stein

Gillian lives and works in Bristol. Her jewellery shows her love of surface textures with simple shapes. Her techniques include reticulation, fusing with fine wire and patterning with the use of a rolling mill. She works in silver with touches of 18ct gold.

A second range of jewellery in copper and brass with touches of silver consists of brooches, earrings and necklaces with a quirky bird or fish theme. Gillian studied painting at Bath Academy of Art and began making jewellery twelve years ago.

Julia Mills

I was brought up in East Anglia and worked for my father, John Fox, who ran a successful woodcarving business.

I worked with him for six years but I felt that wood was not the right medium for me; I found the lack of colour contrasts in wood dissatisfying.

It wasn't until December 1994, when I decided to try working with glass, that I realised I had found my medium. The myriad of colours in hand-made glass is tantalizing and the combinations are endless. Living in Cornwall I have found myself using paler pastel colours which work well with my seascape designs.

The main influences for my work have been Kaffe Fasset, fairytale folklore and Jane Ray.

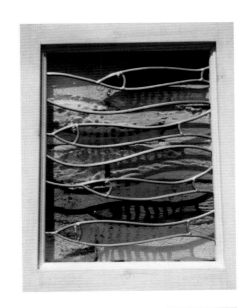

Lucy Clibbon

Lucy is inspired by the world of make-believe, magical childhood experiences and daydreams. She paints and draws people, places and creatures that exist in her imagination and memories. In her pictures she incorporates themes including enchanted gardens and woods, flying ethereal beings and animals. Lucy has a fascination with houses and the wonder of big cities. This contrasts with her love of the wilderness found in the country and coastline. Her paintings are adorned with hearts, flowers, stars, stickers and glitter. She usually works in watercolour and collage, on handmade recycled Indian papers.

Lucy's clients include Café Rouge, Liberty, Osborne & Little, Habitat, Art Angels, Virgin, Gardens Illustrated and the Royal Shakespeare Co.

Kathryn Oaten

Kathryn started making handmade paper collages at Leicester on her textile degree. She makes and dyes her own recycled paper and this gives her work its unique look. The paper is cut and machine sewn onto the backing cloth and the whole piece is then hand sewn to create one off pieces of work. Her collages are inspired by the gardens, plants and countryside around her home in Cornwall.

Her pictures concentrate on wild and windblown blooms of wood and meadows as well as the sub-tropical gardens for which the county is famous. She exhibits throughout the country, and is a member of the Cornwall Crafts Association.

Alison Engelfield

Sarah Young

Caroline Kelly-Foreman

Julia Mills Gallery

The Round House and Capstan Gallery

Sennen Cove, Penzance, near Lands End, Cornwall TR19 7DF.   Telephone: 01736 871859
Website: www.round-house.co.uk

Open Daily 10am - 6pm (10 am - 8pm July & August) and through to early New Year.

The Round House is poised above the tiny fishing harbour of Sennen Cove at the South end of the long sweep of Whitesands Bay. It is a fine setting for the work of some of Cornwall's finest artists and crafts people.

The building itself, completely circular, is a grade II listed building and an integral part of Sennen's history, housing as it does the massive Capstan that used to haul the boats from the water and up the beach. Twenty years ago the net loft was converted into a craft centre and gallery and in 1997 the Capstan Room opened as a unique gallery in its own right.

On show is a selection of ceramics and pottery by, amongst others: Delan Cookson, Barry Huggett, Paul Jackson, Peter O'Neil, Eleanor Newell, Hugh West and a wide range of prints by Ingrid Allen, Richard Lee Stevenson, Michelle Wright, June Hicks, Francois de Mauny, Chris Maunder, Ian Cooke and Jenny Tapping, Roelof Uys, photos by Ander Gunn, Mike Newman and Alastair Common and a display of paintings by local artists. In addition there are hats by Rrappers, Claire Francis coats, reversibles by Sarah Vivian, children's clothes by Feeline, and jewellery by Tony Bird, Case van Dop and Rob Morrison.

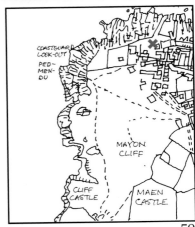

To find us follow the A30 for Lands End, turn right for Sennen Cove and follow the road to the very end, past the lifeboat station, to the car park for the coastal footpath, together with superb views to Cape Cornwall and the cliffs.

The Round House & Capstan Gallery

St. Ives Ceramics

1 Lower Fish Street, St. Ives, Cornwall TR26 1LT. Telephone: 01736 794930
Email: jbedding@st-ives-ceramic.co.uk Website: www.st-ives-ceramic.co.uk
Open daily 10am - 5pm

St Ives Ceramics has gone from strength to strength since it was first opened in 1991 by the potter John Bedding. Over the years has built up a reputation for showing some of the best Studio Pottery in the country.

The gallery is committed to showing a broad selection of contemporary work. There are at present over fifty potters represented including Richard Batterham, Clive Bowen, Svend Bayer, Mike Dodd, Jack Doherty, Sam Hall, Jane Hamlyn and Antonia Salmon. We also display a large range of domestic ware and have a good selection of books for sale.

The range of work on show is constantly changing and there are usually two large exhibitions a year. The gallery is also home to a permanent collection of twentieth century 'master potters'. At any

one time, visitors can expect to see work by Bernard Leach, Lucie Rie, Hans Coper, and Michael Cardew, along with the Japanese potters Hamada, Kawai, Tomimoto and Shimaoka.

Managing the gallery is Rebecca Farrington: "We try to provide the customer with as much information as possible about the work displayed, and are always happy to give out the names and addresses of the potters."

St Ives Ceramics is open daily throughout the year and has a constantly changing display of work. For details of current work please contact Rebecca (see above).

Current exhibitors

Pots

Tim Andrews
Duncan Ayscough
Richard Batterham
John Bedding
Svend Bayer
Clive Bowen
Seth Cardew
Ara Cardew
Willie Carter
Nic Collins
John Davidson
Jane Day

Mike Dodd
Bridget Drakeford
Derek Emms
Ray Finch
Tom Fisher
Christine Gittins
Sam Hall
Jane Hamlyn
Nic Harrison
Joanna Howells
Barry Huggett
Hazel Johnston

John Leach
Walter Keeler
Colin Kellam
David Leach
Andrew Marshall
William Marshall
Eleanor Newell
Wendy Page
Colin Pearson
Katrina Pechal
Jane Perryman
Nic Rees

Simon Rich
Phil Rogers
Ruthanne Tudball
Hugh West
John Wheeldon

Stained Glass Mirrors

Emma Edelston

Raku Ceramic Jewellery

Rebecca Farrington

Christine Gittins

All my pots are thrown, turned and burnished. Forms are based on classical shapes - the round shape, almost entirely a spherical form, being my favourite. In making I deliberately try to push limits to extremes. This subtly changes my work from purely classical to more contemporary in style.

At present I use a white earthenware clay and a method of "fuming" the surface during the firing to leave a wonderful spectrum of subtle colours and random patterns on the smooth surface. This is achieved through the use of salt, copper and sawdust in a saggar in the kiln.

My work is low-fired to keep the clay surface slightly porous to be able to absorb the effects of the treatment during the final firing. A layer of wax polish is applied to seal and shine the finished piece.

As with most potters using smoke-firing, the constant element of surprise is my biggest inspiration.

Eleanor Newell

I work with Raku for its immediacy, risk and the inexhaustible variety of colours and effects it offers. I find the alchemy of glaze chemistry fascinating and love to test and experiment. I am also excited by the direct influence I can exert during the post-firing reduction stage of raku firing.

I enjoy throwing elegant and classical simple vessel forms, as a canvas for my glazes, which are often applied in many layers. I also create more ornate pieces such as jewellery boxes and sgraffito decorated forms. Influences on these include art nouveau, wrought iron and Islamic design.

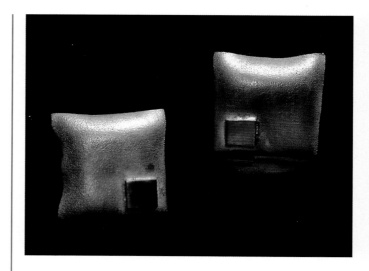

Rebecca Farrington

Rebecca has been producing jewellery since 1995, first working in raku fired clay before moving on to work with gold and silver.

"My work is heavily inspired by the geology of Cornwall, a landscape that has many contrasts. I aim to use these contrasts in my work, producing pieces that have areas of highly polished silver, separated from heavily textured areas by a single line of red or yellow gold." The abstract surface decoration gives the jewellery a very contemporary look, and is simple yet sophisticated.

The range includes a selection of earrings, bracelets, neckpieces, rings and cufflinks. Rebecca has a workshop at St. Ives Ceramics and can be contacted through the gallery.

Peter Swanson

As Cornwall and its recent ceramic history continues to interest, I explore shape and colour combinations using naturally found wood ashes, stone dusts and local clays. These materials are sympathetic to my aims, of having pots large or small emerge from the kiln with a good character, and a timeless quality. This is my indicator of success and reaffirms my part in the making process.

I have been potting in Cornwall for twenty-six years, before this in Hampshire. My work is in many private collections both at home and abroad.

Sam Hall

Sam Hall studied at the Harrogate College and Loughborough College of Art in Ceramics where he qualified in 1990. Since 1990 he worked first in Yorkshire where he was born and more recently in St.Ives, Cornwall.

His work incorporates many of the processes embodied in tradition of which the intrinsic quality of repetition and the use of simplicity of form are the strongest factors. From this starting point the additional use of slips, scored lines and random marks help to create a tension where drawing and form combine.

Nancy Main

My attraction to working with clay comes mainly through its wonderful sensual and tactile properties. I am constantly amazed by the skills, feelings, memories and emotions that the human hand can capture in stillness from such a fluid and free material.

I aspire to instill my work with the engaging qualities of touch, beauty and energy reflected in strong clear forms with their own sense of stillness.

The work is made from a porcelain clay using both oxidisation and reduction firings, often with small details of colour, carving or precious metals.

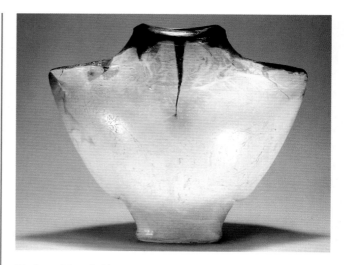

John Bedding

"The choice I made that was to have the biggest influence on my life, was, when I chose to move from London to St Ives in the late Sixties." In 1969, John was taken on by Bernard Leach, first as a student apprentice, and later, after a year in France, as a member of staff.

In 1978 he was to be only the second potter sent by Leach to Japan, where he worked at the Ichino Pottery in Tamba. After a successful solo exhibition in Osaka, he returned to England to start his own workshop.

In the Autumn of 2000 he returned to Japan, after being invited to work for two months as a short stay artist at the Shigeraki Ceramic Cultural Park.

Steam Pottery & Gallery ♿

Pendeen, Cornwall, TR19 7DN. Telephone: 01736 788070
Email: babuska@btinternet.com
Website: www.steampottery.com & beyond-st-ives.com
Open every day 10am - 5.30pm throughout the year. January by appointment.

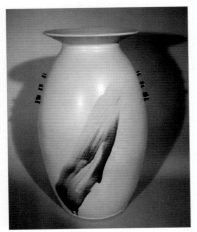

Situated along the dramatic B3306 coastal route between St. Ives and Lands End, the pottery/gallery has now been open for three years and is steadily acquiring an increasing reputation for innovative ceramics of quality. Designed and crafted by the two potters, Patrick Lester (bottom) and Jonathan Hancock (top), the work is varied and imaginative and ranges from domestic and garden ware to a diverse selection of individual pieces of varying techniques using complementary clays. The gallery also features frequent exhibitions by reputed local artists in a congenial atmosphere.

Yew Tree Gallery

Keigwin Farmhouse, Nr Morvah, Penzance, Cornwall TR19 7TS. Telephone: 01736 786425
Open during exhibitions : Tuesday - Saturday 10.30am - 5.30pm   (Other times by appointment)

Yew Tree Gallery re-opens at the end of 2001 after a leap from Gloucestershire to Cornwall. Facing the vast Atlantic, with wild moorland behind, the gallery is now housed in a new barn-like granite building on the site of old stables adjoining Gilly's farmhouse home. Exhibitions are held every few months.

Each new venue for Yew Tree Gallery, since its inauguration in 1971, has stimulated a fresh

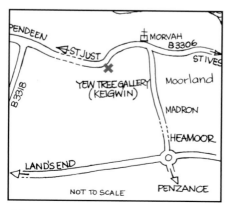

approach to showing fine and applied art by some of Britain's most accomplished and original contemporary artists.

The enticing setting offers gardens for displaying sculpture and furniture, a large organic potager to enjoy (and perhaps to buy a few herbs or saladings!) and a glasshouse where exhibits mingle with tender plants.

Despite the vast numbers of artists working in Cornwall, Gilly will continue to select painters and craftsmen from all over Britain.

Yew Tree Gallery

Between times, the gallery premises is available for renting as a studio, with B & B provided optionally at Keigwin Farmhouse.

Portheras Cove is a mere step away (see main picture) and the Penwith peninsula abounds with beautiful coastal paths and beaches, ancient sites and a variety of hostelries and galleries - not least the Tate St. Ives a few miles along the coast road (B3306).

Environmental projects will still be supported through the exhibitions - once Gilly is in pocket again!

Contact G. Wyatt Smith for further details or to be on the mailing list.

Catriona Macleod

Below: Work in progress May 2001

Magie Hollingworth

I create a variety of papier maché work constantly inspired by the discovery of discarded material, and my ever deepening involvement with surface quality. Found forms are used as moulds and newspaper is the basis of my pulp mix. Although the wall panels may incorporate fabric, paint and plant fragments my vessels are becoming increasingly 'raw', as I prefer now to use only simple forms of decoration.

Using a narrow palette of colour, subtle bands of oil paint are baked into the paper or stones meticulously inlaid into bowl rims. The pulp body is celebrated, not disguised. Full appreciation of the material only comes through handling the pieces.

Edwina Bridgeman

I have always collected fragments, pieces of china, scraps of metal and wood from the beach. I embarked on my current work as a result of wanting to put things together and bring new life to the discarded.

My background as a scene painter in the theatre has been an influence on my themes, performance and voyage. The majority of the pieces are narrative, setting a scene, beginning a story to be taken further. I am keen to promote a feeling of optimism and joy, a sense of moving forward. The assemblages and construction are all figurative. Faces have a fresco like quality, I paint on to a plaster base which allows for fine detail and expression, a contrast to the less predictable nature of the wood. Working with driftwood is a good excuse for numerous trips to the beach.

Yew Tree Gallery

Dillon Rudge Ceramics

Having lived in Cornwall most of my life, I have always been interested in animals both domestic and wild. Some animals have more defined characteristics than others, which made me realise that just copying an animal from life would not be sufficient to capture the true nature of the animal in question. I realised in most cases that realism is good to a certain degree but if nothing personal is attributed by me the Artist, then people may lose insight as to what my motivation was when making the animal.

At present I am trying to capture specific traits of animals, e.g. movement, fluidity, structural form, which when combined with my imagination, observations and modelling skills determines an original composition. All of my new creations are now specifically Limited editions. Only twenty pieces are hand made a year and each piece has a certificate signed and numbered personally by me.

Each piece made is unique in its own right as the raku effects vary due to outside air temperature, humidity levels and sawdust conditions. As natural elements affect the Raku I believe that one should never try to control this amazing random process. Each firing done never ceases to amaze for this reason and there is always an awe of excitement when taking the sculptures out of the sawdust. Raku is the most rewarding of processes and although my patience has been stretched to the absolute limit on occasions, the final outcome makes it all worthwhile.

I hope people gain as much pleasure from my Raku Ceramics as I have creating them.

Trade enquiries ONLY:
Email:
dillon.rudge@btinternet.com
Tel: 01566 781624
Check the makers' index to see which galleries already stock Dillon's work.

Some other Galleries in the South West

Simon Drew Gallery

13 Foss Street

Dartmouth

Devon

TQ6 9DR

Tel & Fax: 01803 832832

Email: simon@simondrew.co.uk

www.simondrew.co.uk

Open: Mon - Sat 9am-5pm

Juliet Gould Gallery

1 Church Street

Mevagissey

St. Austell

Cornwall

PL26 6SP

Tel: 01726 844844

Open: Mon - Sat 10am-5pm

Printmakers Gallery

8 Tregenna Hill

St. Ives

Cornwall

TR26 1SE

Tel: 01736 796654

Open: Summer - every day 10am-5pm

Winter closed Sundays

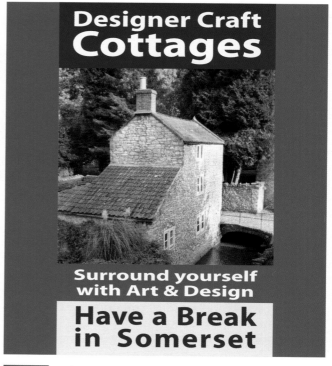

Wessex

98 ● BRISTOL

31.

112.   17.

16,102.

53 ● SALISBURY

13.

● TAUNTON

113.

116.

127.

50.

124.

46.

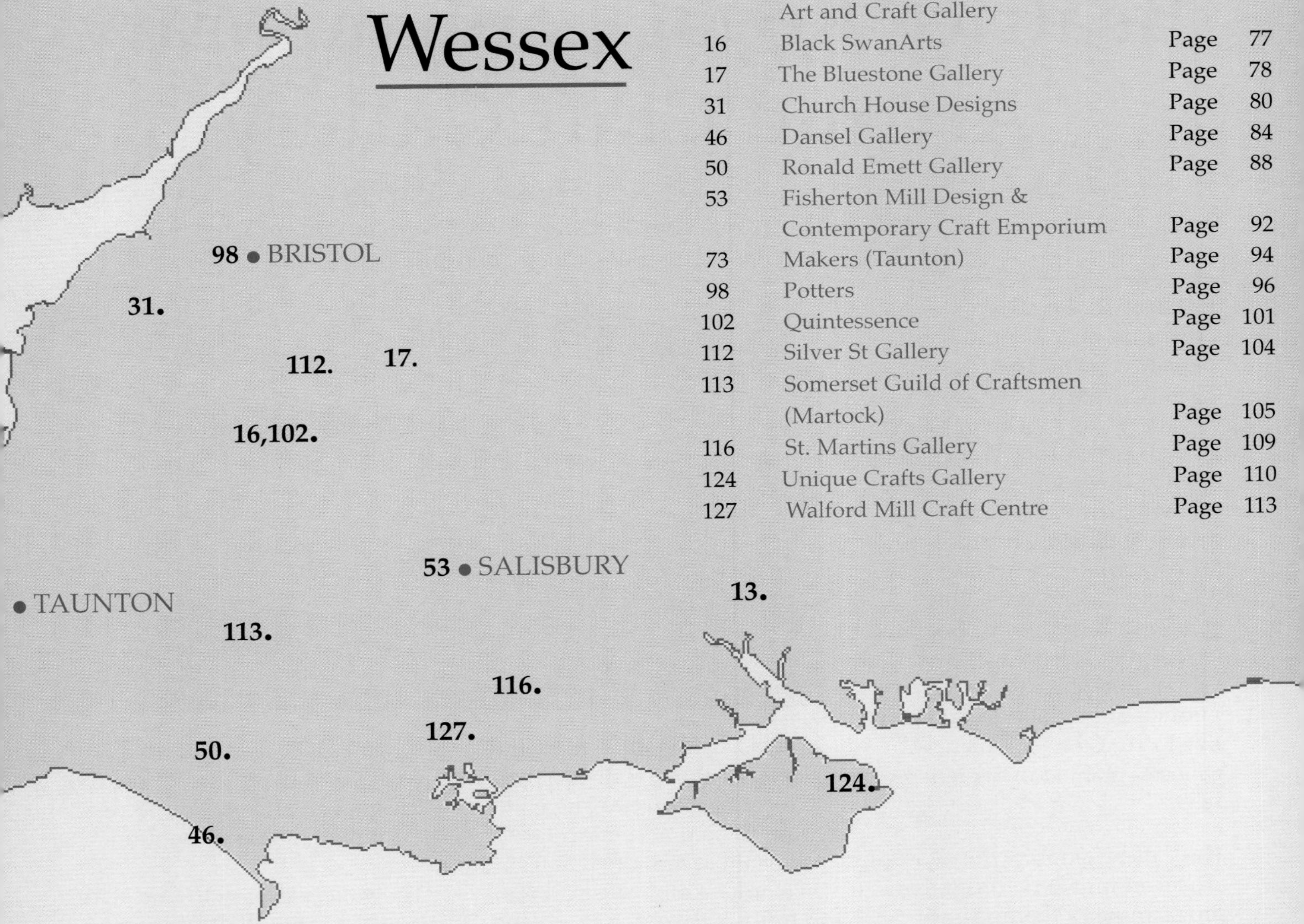

Beatrice Royal Contemporary Art and Craft Gallery

0%

Nightingale Avenue, Eastleigh, Hampshire SO50 9JJ. Telephone: 023 8061 0592 Fax: 023 8065 0566
Email: e:info@beatriceroyal.com Website: www.beatriceroyal.com
Open every day 11am - 5pm and by appointment

The Beatrice Royal Contemporary Art and Craft Gallery is owned by the Tramman Trust, a registered charity set up by David Quayle after the sale of the B & Q chain of DIY stores. Opened in 1994, following David Quayle's dream of creating a superstore for contemporary art and craft, it is now the largest selling gallery in the South of England. In 1997 the gallery was awarded £1m of lottery cash by the Arts Council of England to double its size to 10,000 sq.ft. The new galleries opened in September 1999.

The gallery exhibits the work of artists and makers through a programme of themed and mixed exhibitions in eighteen gallery spaces. The work is

Joe Low

selected nationally and includes pieces from the well established to recent graduates. The gallery has a relaxed and informal atmosphere and offers a friendly welcome to all visitors. It aims to make it easy to buy art and craft by offering several initiatives: an interest free credit scheme, 10% discount off all works if you become a Friend of the gallery, and at the end of an exhibition, a sale promotion.

The gallery is easy to find with brown tourist signs from either M27 junction 5 or M3 junction 13; and has on site parking.

Faith Tavender

Faith Tavender designs and makes modern silver jewellery in her Clerkenwell studio, taking inspiration from the old and new world. Ideas are drawn from her childhood spent by the wild but beautiful Tasmanian coast and the vibrant colours and textures of her travels in North Africa, all influencing the form and colours used in the helix collection of jewellery. Thus pendants, earrings and rings use delicate semi-precious beads and freshwater pearls contrasting with chunky bracelets and cufflinks. Using an oxidized finish to blacken the metal or a shiny silver surface each piece is handcrafted. Garnets, rainbow Moonstones and pearls in grey, pink and champagne colours are highlights of the collection.

Jeremy Heber

Jeremy Heber has been making things from as far back as he can remember. His early exploits in civil engineering were a wonder to behold but as he couldn't afford Meccano set eight (the one with the motor) his talent never flowered.

He was later forcibly ejected from the local art class for reproducing an impression of the milky way on the host's ceiling with a well loaded paint brush and so, once again, his artistic career languished.

Later, at University he began filing away at bits of silver in his bed-sit in order to stave off the insanity of hard study.

Now, ten years on, he produces a successful range of gold embellished silver jewellery in a striking but classic style. He is preoccupied with the notion that jewellery should be something not just to look at but to fiddle with and so he designs pieces that articulate or inter-link in cunning ways.

Mary & Rachel Sumner

Mary and Rachel Sumner are sisters who originally trained as painters, who enjoy hand painting and decorating materials - mainly silk. The intense colours produced by steam-fixed dyes attracted them to silk painting along with the spontaneity of drawing straight on to the material with gutta.

Hand dying, printing and machine embroidery are also employed in embellishing the silk which is sold as scarves, framed pictures, wallhangings and ties. Recently they have launched a series of cards and posterwrap based on their designs.

Mary and Rachel work from separate studios but have a workshop where they collaborate on joint ventures such as public commissions and print projects.

Inspiration comes from many sources, mainly the natural world, resulting in compositions with a sense of humour and well observed detail.

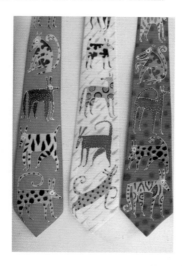

Terence Donovan

Matthew Burt

Matthew found inspiration in the timeless, no nonsense solutions of early English country furniture, and as a designer - maker the ability to both conceive and manifest an idea is the engine of his creativity. After 22 years he is still constantly surprised and delighted with his chosen material of wood.

We provide a design and make service for domestic and corporate clients, most recent being Russell-Cotes Art Gallery & Museum and Stanton Guild House Trust. Matthew also designs and makes speculative pieces, which are put into low volume production.

Our work is shown nationally at selected exhibitions and on the Crafts Council Index of Selected Makers. Matthew is a Fellow of the Royal Society of Arts and in 2001 won the Master's Gold Award from the Worshipful Company of Furniture Makers.

Liz Gale

Liz specialises in stoneware reduction, domestic and decorative - a mixture of wax resist, latex and sponging, her glazes creating a sense of depth. An experienced repeat thrower she produces domestic ware of great consistency - teapots, cups, saucers, bowls, jugs and side plates. She accepts commissions for dinner services, teasets and coffee sets. She also makes individual pieces. Liz makes her own clay body. She uses an electric kiln for bisque firing then a 30 cubic ft propane gas kiln, which she constructed herself, firing to 1280°. She recently fired her new salt glaze kiln which will produce a new series of designs and effects. The Leach tradition has been a powerful influence on her development as a potter and her attitudes towards ceramics as a combination of aesthetics and functionality.

Nigel Rigden

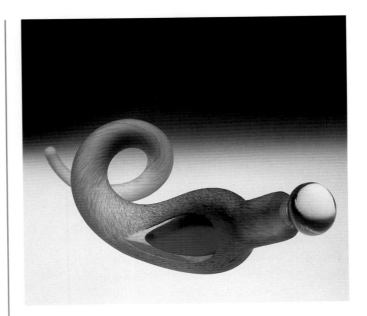

Stuart Akroyd

I don't like to make normal glass, normal glass is symmetrical, round, and regular. I enjoy forms that are unusual, the twist of a shape or the way a spiral can balance so perfectly without falling - these are things I enjoy making.

I have recently started experimenting with some very heavy glass vessel forms which are lightly blown. Carving quite intricate shapes out of the solid mass of crystal, then polishing large sweeping facets to show off the sheer expanse of clear glass, these pieces take less than fifteen minutes to blow in the hot process, but over a day to carve and polish when in the cold shop. This means they are expensive, but stunning to look at and touch.

Jo Mitchell - Hotmetal

Hotmetal offers six contemporary ranges including three new handmade silver collections:-

'Flowers' incorporates double layered, swivelling flower earrings and delicate necklaces with tiny flowers dropping from silver chains.

'Hearts' includes small dotty earrings and necklaces, trimmed with 9ct gold.

'Leaves' (below), featured in Vogue - includes larger necklaces, a beautiful 7-link bracelet and a number of earrings. Some have a 'crinkly' reticulated finish, achieved by melting the surface of each leaf to a shiny liquid state before removing the flame.

'Organics' and 'Geometrics' - two richly coloured ranges in brass, copper and silver, offer many brooches, earrings, necklaces and cufflinks.

'Geometrics' (bottom right)

'Fiesta' is a modern collection of anodised aluminium jewellery in sizzling colours such as violet, turquoise, green, luscious limey yellow and hot orange, all trimmed with silver and gold.

Beatrice Royal Courtyard

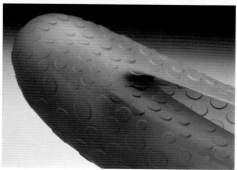

Right:
Glass detail
Stuart Akroyd

Hotmetal

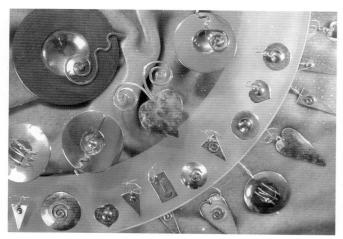

0%

Black Swan Arts

2 Bridge Street, Frome, Somerset BA11 1BB. Telephone: 01373 473980 Fax: 01373 451733
Email: ann@blackswan.org.uk
Open Monday - Saturday 10am - 5pm. Admission is free

Black Swan Arts is a venue for contemporary arts and crafts, with two galleries dedicated to an ambitious programme of changing exhibitions showing high quality, innovative work.

A wide range of contemporary crafts by highly regarded makers of glass, ceramics, jewellery, textiles, wood and metal is available from the nationally recognised Craft Shop. Three studios offer the opportunity to buy direct from the makers or to watch them at work.

The relaxing Arts Café, serves excellent vegetarian food, and offers a full programme of exhibitions. The centre has recently been refurbished, providing improved facilities including a larger café and shop, and better access for people with disabilities, including a lift to Gallery 1. Black Swan Arts is supported by South West Arts, local and regional councils.

David Gilliland

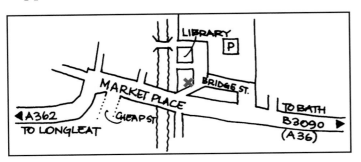

Top:
Matthew Burt

Right:
Marcio Mattos

The Bluestone Gallery

8 Old Swan Yard, Devizes, Wiltshire SN10 1AT. Telephone: 01380 729589 Fax: 01672 539202
Email: guy@avebury-arts.co.uk Website: www.avebury-arts.co.uk
Open Monday - Saturday 10am -5pm

The Bluestone Gallery was opened in May 2000 by Guy and Janice Perkins. Situated in a listed building, the gallery lies in the middle of an attractive group of independent shops in the heart of Devizes. The old market town of Devizes offers many architectural gems, the longest flight of canal locks in Britain and is close to both Stonehenge and Avebury. Guy has been a full time professional studio potter since 1977, for the last twenty years living and working in the middle of Avebury Stone Circle. He specialises in highly decorated stoneware, and his work has been successfully exhibited in many galleries in England and abroad.

The Bluestones form the inner circle of stones at Stonehenge. They were brought from the Preseli Mountains in Wales, and represent an astonishing achievement of vision, determination and creativity. In less spectacular ways those qualities are found in the lives and wares of craftsmen today. The objects they make enrich our lives, and the aim of the gallery is to give expression to the wealth of contemporary British crafts.

Plate by Guy Perkins

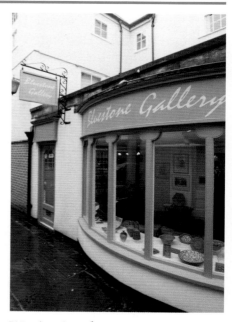

We display the work of over a hundred potters, jewellers, glass makers, wood turners, painters and printmakers. With two floors of work, a peaceful and friendly atmosphere and a very comfy sofa, you will be made welcome!

The Bluestone Gallery

Left:
Phil Rogers

Right:
Margaret
Roberts
Textiles

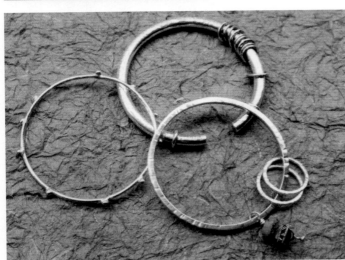

Left:
Fiona Mehra

Right:
Anne Farag

Church House Designs

Broad Street, Congresbury, near Bristol BS49 5DG. Telephone & Fax: 01934 833660
Email: info@churchhousedesigns.co.uk Website: www.churchousedesigns.co.uk
Open 10am - 1pm and 2.15 - 5.30pm (Closed Wednesday and Sunday)

Church House Designs was opened in 1986 by Robert and Lorraine Coles to sell initially Robert's furniture, but over the years it has become a fully established craft gallery with a growing reputation for quality and imaginative work, with particular emphasis on ceramics, glassware, jewellery, wood and textiles.

The gallery is selected for quality by the Crafts Council and is a member of the Independent Craft Galleries Association.

We organise a lively and varied exhibition programme and there is always a cross-section of artists represented on display.

The gallery also runs a Preview Mailing List to allow customers to keep up to date with the introduction of new artists.

The friendly and stimulating atmosphere of the gallery has contributed much to the lively Mendip village of Congresbury, which is situated just off the main A370 from Bristol to Weston-Super-Mare and within a few miles of Junction 21 of the M5.

Holly Belsher

Originally I was inspired by what I found in museums. Artefacts from long lost civilisations, and so called 'primitive' cultures.

Now I am recognising my own culture.

I draw inspiration from the British countryside and what it has produced. From plants and trees, textures in the landscape, to the pebbles, shells and feathers that fill my pockets after a walk on the beach. Now I realise that these things are treasure too.

I am using natural, but very carefully chosen pebbles as 'precious' stones. I hope to show that their intrinsic qualities are as beautiful as those that we usually call 'gem' stones.

Lucinda Bell

Lucinda Bell studied woven textiles at Farnham's Surrey Institute of Art & Design, where she graduated in 1991 with a First Class BA Honours Degree, together with numerous awards resulting in exposure for her collections both at home and abroad.

Daughter of an artist, Lucinda grew up in Hampshire with a vision of producing the finest quality silk scarves and accessories, building her career working alongside top fashion house Louis Feraud and then as Design Manager for Whitchurch Silk Mill. By 1994 Lucinda's own work was being sought after by established names such as the V&A Museum and Barneys New York, who appreciated the dedication in producing such innovative designs.

Using highly textured weave structures, each silk fashion collection is hand finished and created entirely within the UK.

Jane Charles

My interest lies in texture, light and form. Glass is the ideal medium. Each piece is free blown in 24% lead glass and once cooled is hand finished. The pieces are cut, ground, sandblasted, polished and engraved. Each process adds another texture and dimension.

Inspiration comes from working with molten glass together with shapes, colours and moods in the natural world.

Colin Cuthbert

Jeremy James

"Hares as animals and as subject matter for sculpture have long fascinated me. They can be humorous, mysterious, endearing and wild, often simultaneously. To a sculptor they offer a rich range of potential images waiting to be interpreted."

Church House Designs

May Ling Beadsmoore

The characteristic 'soda glaze' is created during a dramatic firing process. Confronting the intense yellow heat, I spray a sodium bicarbonate solution into the kiln. Immediately, the soda vapourises and is carried along by flames dancing around the pots, glazing at random. The results of this type of firing can be as exciting as the process itself - surfaces with varying richness of colour and texture. No two pieces are alike.

Most of my pots are made with the presentation of food in mind. Cheese platters, seafood 'boats' and flower vases are designed to add visual appeal to table-settings while mugs and beakers bear dimples and other tactile impressions which make them a joy to hold.

Janice Gilmore

Janice Gilmore studied Fine Craft Design at the University of Ulster, specialising in Creative Embroidery. In 1989 she graduated and set up her studio producing a range of embroidered jewellery and framed designs.

Janice creates her jewellery using a sewing machine to build up interwoven layers of stitch, forming the designs on a fabric called vanishing muslin. The muslin disintegrates when burnt with an iron and flakes away from the piece. A wide variety of beads are then hand stitched on, creating a rich and decorative finish.

Janice is inspired by a variety of influences including Islamic architecture, Heraldry, Persian kilims, mediaeval tiles and Elizabethan costume. The arts and crafts of various cultures have also inspired her while travelling in countries such as India, Morocco and Turkey.

*Dansel Gallery

Rodden Row, Abbotsbury, Weymouth, Dorset DT3 4JL. Telephone: 01305 871515
Fax: 01305 871518 Email: dansel@wdi.co.uk   Website: danselgallery.co.uk
*Open 10am - 5pm (November - March), 10am - 5.30pm (April - September & October)
and 9.30am - 6pm (July & August)*

Set in a delightful thatched converted stable block near the centre of Abbotsbury village, Dansel Gallery is Britain's leading showcase for contemporary craftwork in wood and one of the Crafts Councils Selected Shops. The Gallery, which is truly a mecca for woodworkers, houses a superb collection of high quality handmade items from the cream of British designer craftsmen. Everything on display is carefully selected for its good design and quality of finish.

In 1979 Danielle and Selwyn Holmes set up a workshop and showroom, initially dedicated to their own work, but soon welcoming other artists in wood. Now more than 200 British woodworkers are represented, probably the largest concentration of its kind in the country. The range is also impressive, running from individually designed pieces of furniture, to elegant jewellery boxes to toys, puzzles and three-dimensional jigsaws to one-off decorative pieces that highlight the inventiveness and versatility of the woodworker.

Jeff Soan

I try to express the essential nature of the animals, birds and fish I create; sometimes by simplification, sometimes by attention to detail and very often by the sinuous movement achieved with the technique of articulation. A large part of my work in recent years has been investigating the possibilities of articulation which is created by cutting the wood into narrow sections and securing it to canvas.

I utilise the woods' natural forms and features; its grain, colour and bark to suggest the creatures' shape, markings and texture. Reclaimed wood is used extensively and it is this found wood that often informs and shapes the work. The constantly varying source of timber helps keep the work fresh and alive.

Robert Parker

Robert lives and works in the Blackdown Hills. His interest in wood came as a result of making wooden toys for his children, which led to woodturning to make various parts of the toys (and the discovery that there were other woods apart from pine!).

From this awakening to English hardwoods, a passion for collecting and hoarding began with an interest in green timber and seasoning of wood.

He now has a wide interest in woodturning, free form carving, furniture, restoration work and garden sculpture.

David Gamm

Dansel Gallery

85

Laurence Henry

Before joining the BBC, I worked freelance illustrating books and magazines and designing cards and textiles.

My last years at the BBC were spent in darkened cubbyholes gazing at TV screens, so I now get enormous pleasure strolling the coast looking for driftwood, varieties of sand, stones, metal, copper and anything else which catches my eye.

The sea washing on pebbles, rusting metals washed up on the shore and patinas on copper are all contributing images to the work I produce, and a recent jewellery course has given me additional skills which have enriched and influenced my work as well as providing a more exacting and precise framework for what I create.

I like to think that the objects I make have a quality of being found on the beach themselves, rusting and weathered by the elements.

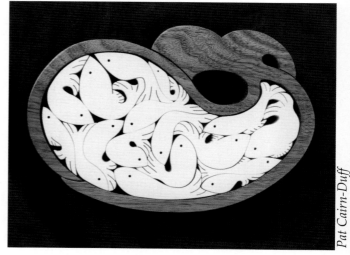

Pat Cairn-Duff

Will Witham

Will is a self-taught woodworker based in South Devon, from where he produces an ever increasing range of original woodworks from a variety of mainly home-grown hardwoods. Will came to his craft relatively late in life "more or less by accident" and his delight in his work is apparent in the range of items, both practical and whimsical, which appear from his tiny rural workshop - whether traditional shelves or art nouveau style mirrors, witty bookends or exquisite, tiny puzzles - all are made by hand with the emphasis on originality of design and quality of finish.

Although probably best known for his intricate puzzles, he doesn't "specialise" as such, preferring to play with new ideas as they arise, and has recently been following an interest in wooden automata.

David Bradford

A graduate of Fine Art at Goldsmiths College in 1970, I now work from a studio in Ditchling, Sussex, where the landscape and wildlife are the inspiration for me both as a sculptor and natural history photographer.

Recurrent themes include: carved relief panels that endeavour to interpret our diverse seashore and downland, free standing sculptures that are the result of my interest in our maritime heritage and the inherent beauty of working boats, particularly sailing craft. I use native hardwoods, natural pigments and beeswax, in a manner that enhances the pieces without diminishing the nature of the material.

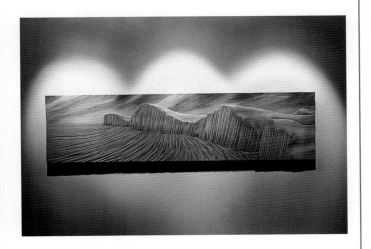

Bob Neill

In the early 60's I was a student at Cardiff College of Art when the 'basic design' philosophy was the new thinking in art education. I have used this as my foundation for my own work and my teaching since then.

I set up my own craft business in the early 80's - having 'escaped' from teaching. It was at this stage that I was able to concentrate on my wood burning - pyrography. At first I used the grain as the main part of the design. Over the last few years I have used a variety of decorative techniques with colour being the main feature. I use acrylic and spirit based dyes for strong geometrical patterns. The work extends from small bowls and dishes to large plates and platters.

Ronald Emett Gallery

2 The Square, Beaminster, Dorset DT8 3AS. Telephone: 01308 863000
Email: ronald.emett@ukonline.co.uk
Open Monday - Saturday 10.am - 5.30pm

In the centre of Beaminster (pronounced Bemminster!) a late eighteenth century town house is the home of Ronald Emett's furniture workshop. The adjoining gallery displays not only some of the fruits of his labours, but also the work of the many artists and craftspeople living and working in West Dorset.

Beaminster Square is full of attractive and interesting shops. This town of mellow hamstone buildings boasts a magnificent fifteenth century church and an abundance of picturesque narrow streets and lanes leading out to the surrounding hills.

Here may be seen fine handcrafted furniture

alongside intriguing locally made ceramics, etchings, original paintings, wood-turning, silver jewellery and silk scarves. All are carefully chosen by 'one pair of eyes' to create a harmonious interior.

The gallery and workshop were established in 1993. The first floor gallery (opened 2000) hosts six exhibitions a year, displaying work mainly by local artists and craftspeople. In 2002 a sculpture court will open in the walled garden.

Ronald Emett

As a furniture maker I aim to capture the essence of Englishness, which is a love of the natural beauty of native hardwoods, clean uncluttered lines and a restrained use of decoration.

I have been making individual pieces of furniture for private collectors, musicians and churches since I graduated from Parnham College in 1992. During that time I have been fortunate enough to receive a number of Guild Marks from the Worshipful Company of Furniture Makers. I work mainly to commission, so each piece is designed with a particular client's needs in mind. My work has strong links with the past, but speaks of the present.

Of course, some things never change - the smell of wood as you open the workshop door at the start of a new day; the whisper of a well-tuned plane across silk-smooth sycamore; the absolute pleasure of seeing a tightly fitted joint go perfectly together. A good life.

Jason Breach

My passion for wood started at an early age. Since then, over half of my life has been devoted to working with this material. I attended college in High Wycombe, where I studied furniture design and management, graduating in 1993.

Turning is a way of making small items relatively quickly, compared to an item of furniture. Therefore more of my time is spent turning or teaching and advising others. Materials are selected from a wide variety of native and exotic timber, paying attention to natural colours and grain patterns like ripples and burrs. By turning, I expose the natural colour and grain, all the beauty that is wood.

The items I create range from the funcitonal, such as fruit bowls and light pulls, to the purely decorative, like fine bowls and boxes.

Liz Clay

Liz Clay makes handmade felt. She uses raw fibres from both animal and plant origins and endeavours to create designs that make use of the natural qualities of these materials in a sensitive but innovative way. She likes to create original pieces that are both decorative and functional; making scarves, cushion covers, blankets, jewellery and garments from bodices to jackets. She is happy to consider commissions. Liz often dyes the wool and silks herself and uses various techniques of printing and resist work such as Shibori and machine embriodery to create interesting surface patterns and textures. She constantly experiments with new ideas and materials. She is always concerned with the entire making process from concept to the finished product and likes to have complete control over it.

Sculptures by
Michael Storey

Ronald Emett Gallery

Mary George

Holly Webb

Barbara Green

Katherine Lloyd

Anne-Marie Marshall

Fisherton Mill Design & Contemporary Craft Emporium

0%

108 Fisherton Street, Salisbury, Wiltshire SP2 7QY. Telephone & Fax: 01722 415121
Email: fishmill@fsbdial.co.uk
Open Monday - Saturday 9.30am - 5.30pm

Built in 1880, Fisherton Mill, a former grain mill, has now been converted to create the perfect ambient setting for the exhibition and sale of contemporary craft, art and design.

Comprising three floors and a converted hay loft, Fisherton Mill presents an exciting programme of exhibitions and special events throughout the year. This includes the showcasing of both new and established talent, through mixed themed exhibitions, solo shows and through Fisherton Mill's extensive lifestyle shopping area.

After experiencing the diverse array of works from over four hundred talented artists, why not indulge yourself with fine teas and coffee, a selection of cakes and pastries, lunches and afternoon teas from the gallery café?

Facilities include free car parking and partial wheelchair access.

Fisherton Mill Design & Contemporary Craft Emporium

Belinda Ferretter

Jeremy James

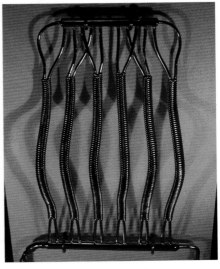

David Booth

Althea Wynne

Caroline Curtis

*Makers

6 Bath Place, Taunton, Somerset TA1 4ER. Telephone: 01823 251121
Open Monday - Saturday 9am - 5pm

Between the Quantock Hills and the Blackdown Hills, lies the Somerset County Town of Taunton. Makers, a thriving craft co-operative, is ideally located in historic Bath Place, a picturesque seventeenth century passageway and Taunton's oldest shopping street.

Since its founding in 1984, Makers has gained a reputation for having one of the West Country's finest selections of contemporary crafts.

Work includes baskets by Sarah Pank; furniture by Rex Helston; knitwear by Buffy Fletcher; jewellery by Bernard Berthon, Pippa Berthon, Holly Webb and Solange; painted silks by Mary and Rachel Sumner; painted silks and velvets by Kate Noble; pottery by Clio Graham, John Harlow and Mary Kembery; prints and paintings by Mary George and Julia Manning, and wood turning by Robert Parker.

Mary George

Makers is owned and managed by the makers themselves and displays a varied collection of their work. A maker is always on duty in the shop to assist you or to discuss commissions. Exhibitions by guest artists and craftsmen regularly take place in the gallery upstairs.

Rex Helston

Makers

Kate Noble

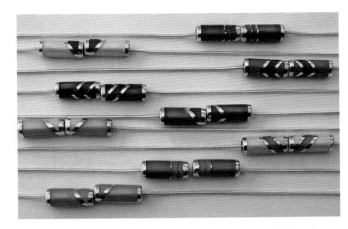

Bernard Berthon

John Harlow

Mary & Rachel Sumner

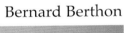

Sarah Park

Potters

Clifton Down Shopping Centre, Whiteladies Road, Clifton, Bristol BS8 2NN
Telephone: 0117 9737380. Website: www.pottersbristol.com
Open Monday - Saturday 10am - 6pm (also Sunday 11am - 5pm in November and December)

Potters, established in 1996, is unique in the UK. We exhibit and sell an exceptionally wide range of studio ceramics, both decorative and functional, made by regional potters, ceramic artists and sculptors. As a marketing co-operative of fifty members who take turns serving customers, we sell our work at very competitive prices and can provide professional advice.

We frequently change our diverse displays of ceramics which appeal to almost every taste: garden pots and ornaments, water features, vases, urns, sculptures, clocks, mirrors, wall decorations, lamps, personal ornaments and tableware in many styles.

We arrange instalment purchases and wedding lists, arrange for orders of work on commission.

Potters is located one mile west of the centre of Bristol on the high street of fashionable Clifton near the entrance to Clifton Down Station (multi-storey car park at rear). Visitors will find a wealth of coffee and wine bars, restaurants and shops nearby.

Ned Heywood

Ned Heywood graduated from art college in 1969 in Industrial Design with the realisation that it was the directness of creation in clay, rather than construction on the drawing board, that provided him with the greatest satisfaction. Teaching Art and Design and later ceramics, gave him the opportunity and incentive to develop techniques and glazes. In 1978 he left full time teaching and in 1983 established the Workshop Gallery in Chepstow. He is absorbed by the challenge and variation of work involved in developing several apparently different but strongly related strands of hand-formed ceramic products: strong, simple, thrown jugs, dishes and bowls with his own versions of classic reduction fired stoneware glazes such as copper reds, celadon greens, wood ash and chun. He also makes stoneware sculpture on the themes of buildings and landscape and large scale, finely modelled, terracotta and stoneware figures. He has recently completed very large tile panel commissions for Tesco and the Celtic Manor Hotel. He sells much of his work directly from the Workshop Gallery

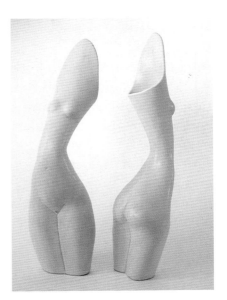

Robin Wade

Robin Wade is a creator of unique hand made ceramic tiles, panels and mirror frames featuring low relief, impressed and wax resist decoration. Using a stoneware/porcelain clay, Robin also uses the textured and patterned slabs to hand form a range of individually designed vessels and platters which she paints with a range of rich lively colours which she has developed over the years.

Robin's work is influenced by Persian ceramic tiles, landscape and still life images. Much of her work is commissioned. She likes to work with the individual clients and interior designers to create work for specific sites both interior and exterior.

Her work can be found enhancing kitchens, conservatories, bathrooms and gardens world - wide as well as in her regular display of individual pieces at Potters.

Julia Land

Julia Land has a studio in the Workshop Gallery where she produces her range of thrown earthenware. She particularly enjoys the figurative properties of jugs, teapots and jars. She throws each item in sections and rejoins at an angle to accentuate their posture so creating quirky and humourous, yet functional pots. Coloured slips, poured freely and often overlapping, are used to decorate and enhance the forms. Finally, the work is glazed with rich blue earthenware glaze which enhances the tonal range of the slips beneath.

Liz Riley

98

Katie Murton

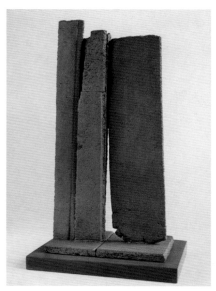

Peter Bridgens

Potters

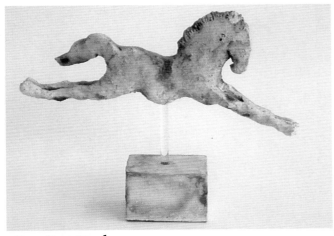

Caroline Roche

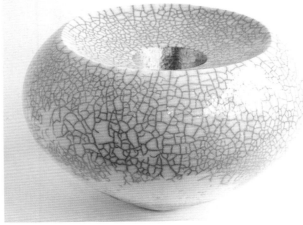

Jenny Ueber

Above: Donald Yule
Left: Huw Powell Roberts
Right: David Brown

Potters

Les & Sally Sharpe   *Right:* Maggie White

Above: Bill Moore

Left: Rupert Blamire

Right: Sophia Hughes

Quintessence

21 Paul Street, Catherine Hill, Frome, Somerset BA11 1DT. Telephone & Fax: 01373 461352
Email: quintessence.uk@lineone.net
Open Monday -Saturday 10am - 5pm, closed Thursday

Quintessence is situated in the heart of Frome's conservation area and was established in 1997 by woodcarver Ian Waller. The aim is to provide a showcase for top quality artists and craftsmen, where people can buy something special for the home, the individual or that unusual gift.

There are several thematic exhibitions during the year as well as work from regular exhibitors throughout, in a wide variety of mediums: some traditional and some in a more innovative style.

Prices range from just over £1 to over £2000. So there is something for everyone and whatever the cost, the essence of quality is maintained.

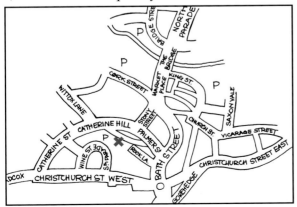

Watercolour by Ann March

Siobhan Jones

Following her graduation in 1996, Siobhan set up a workshop/showroom which has continued to flourish, with work exhibited in established galleries nationwide and abroad.

Inspired by light and the part it can play in bringing life to an object, Siobhan creates unique 'one off' signed pieces. Working exclusively with a high quality translucent glass that is tested for colour compatibility Siobhan hand cuts and arranges the glass and fuses it in the kiln with occasional copper inclusions. Most pieces are then returned to the kiln to slump in a mould to form vessels.

Siobhan's work can be used for many applications; with commissions ranging from decorative room partitions to tables. Housing some of Siobhan's commissions are venues such as cruise liners, libraries and bars.

Steve Climpson

Elaine Peto

After graduating from Exeter College of Art in 1985, I set up my studio in Hampshire.

Animals have been a constant source of inspiration for me. I strive to capture the character and energy of each creature, regarding each piece as having its own unique qualities.

Texture is an integral part of the work, with clay being so receptive. It holds texture and shape, allowing the piece to evolve. It never ceases to amaze me how this basic material takes on such a life of its own.

Subject matter includes agricultural animals, hares, exotic wild animals and most recently dogs.

Phillip Wilkie

My inspiration as a sculptor comes from an interest in natural history and the study of animal behaviour. In my work I hope to capture the true form, movement and character of a subject and create a 3D sketch of a moment in time.

I enjoy working with wire because it gives me the ability to achieve the

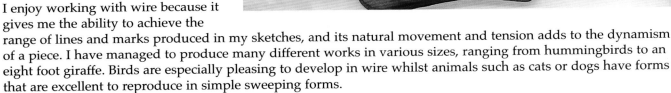

range of lines and marks produced in my sketches, and its natural movement and tension adds to the dynamism of a piece. I have managed to produce many different works in various sizes, ranging from hummingbirds to an eight foot giraffe. Birds are especially pleasing to develop in wire whilst animals such as cats or dogs have forms that are excellent to reproduce in simple sweeping forms.

Sue Smith

Silk is one of the most luxurious of materials. The fabric itself has a feel, drape, sheen and glow unlike any other fibre, and when combined with original hand painted designs, the result is a unique piece of work every time.

I use a combination of silk painting techniques, weights, and weaves of silk to ensure a variety of textures and individuality. On most items a resist method is used where outlines are drawn with gutta, which stops the colour spreading. Liquid dyes are then applied directly to the silk with a fine brush. The finished paintings are professionally steam fixed and can be washed by hand.

I produce a range of items including brooches, ties, cushions, scarves, room screens, pictures and wall hangings. I also welcome commissions.

Silver Street Gallery

12 Silver Street, Bradford on Avon, Wiltshire BA15 1JY. Telephone: 01225 863532
Open Monday - Saturday 10am - 5pm (For Sunday opening please ring to check)

The gallery which was previously ARTWORKS is located in the historic town of Bradford on Avon, we moved to a much better location with room for jewellery workshops on the premises.

The gallery specialises in the exhibition of contemporary crafts, exhibitions of British artists work run for two months at a time. All disciplines are represented: jewellery in precious and other materials, metal-work, ceramics (both functional and sculptural) wood, textiles and glass. Work is selected for its quality, innovation and design.

Victoria Martin runs the gallery and makes her jewellery in the workshop where she has a constant display of work.

We regularly show work by Laurel Keeley, Simon Rich, Eryka Isaak, Samantha Buckley, Joanna Butler, Cathy Tutt, Claire Gregory, Rozie Keogh, Doug Wilson, Beata Höst and many more.

The gallery is bright, friendly, relaxed and worth a visit - everyone is welcome.

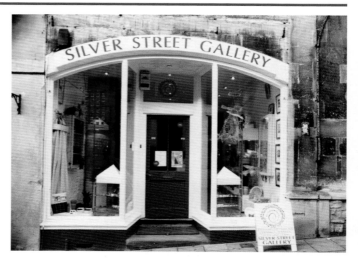

Silver jewellery with moving parts
by Victoria Martin

The Somerset Guild of Craftsmen Home Gallery

Hurst, Martock, Somerset TA12 6JU. Telephone: 01935 825891
Website: www.somerset-guild.co.uk
Open Monday - Saturday 9.30am - 5pm, Sundays (April - December) and Bank Holidays 10am - 4pm

The Somerset Guild of Craftsmen brings together crafts people from Somerset and neighbouring counties. Craft members are selected for the quality of design and craftsmanship in their work which spans contemporary and traditional pieces in a variety of media.

There is a programme of special exhibitions, demonstrations and other events, details of which are available from the Gallery. Introductions can be made to individual craftsmen who are willing to accept commissions.

A coffee shop adjoins the Gallery and there is ample, free parking.

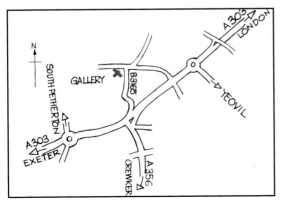

Caroline Lytton

Caroline designs and makes individual items of tableware and jewellery, both decorative and functional.

Simple bowls, beakers and dishes are decorated with chasing; the silver formed and textured with hand-made steel punches to reveal abstract, fossil or plant designs.

Caroline's 'Wave' cutlery is displayed in Sheffield, part of the Lottery-funded Millennium Canteen commissioned by Sheffield City Council and made by the Association of British Designer Silversmiths.

Silver jewellery explores contrasting plain and decorative finishes. Smooth bangles, textured earrings, brooches and neck-pieces with gold accents, oxidation and semi-precious stones.

Chevron bowl

John Lock

Since training under Christopher Faulkner at Dartington, I have been working full time as a furniture maker for over ten years. Commissions include dressers, tables, chests of drawers, dining chairs, children's chairs, desks and benches. I have also exhibited in Devon, London and Somerset.

I use traditional techniques and confine the use of machinery to the preparation and rough sizing of timber. I like to work with English or European hardwoods and finish with natural oils and waxes. By using these methods, I hope my furniture will stand the test of time and provide much pleasure and use for several generations. I like simple designs that will blend with other styles. Often, there is an element of the client's own design ideas.

Mithra Richardson

Mithra paints the Somerset Levels on silk. Her work is drawn directly from nature. This atmospheric work captures the sweeps of the levels. These pieces include Somerset landscapes, handpainted silk cards, scarves, wall hangings and screens. Her work may also be seen at her workshop at Moorlynch Vineyard, Moorlynch, Bridgwater.

Martin Pettinger

My love affair with slip decorated pottery started in 1969. As a professional potter I have found that it has helped people to understand the process of design and how hand making is an integral part of the finished pot - not just a quaint way of doing it. The stoneware pots have taken slip decorating, before firing, into the concept of a pen-and-ink water colour painting.

Initial raw slip coats are the background washes and each subsequent firing adds richer washes. The pen and ink detail is added in the final firing.

Frank Wilson

Frank Wilson is a direct metal sculptor. He was a G.P. and part-time orthopaedic surgeon before retiring.

The mechanics of surgery and his love of steel led him to learn to weld and so what was once a dream turned into a passion and his own particular style evolved. His main interest lies in creating minimalist human relating pairs and larger groups of figures.

Each piece is individually made so there are never two exactly alike. What really fascinates him is the way in which as hard a material as steel can take on a soft organic quality which allows the relationship between figures to show through.

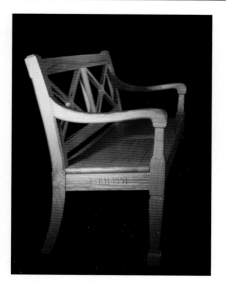

David Applegate

Nancy Wells

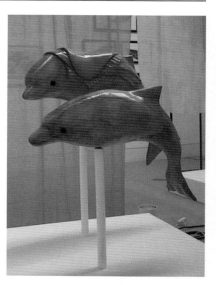

Liz Mangles

St. Martins Gallery

♿

The Old Church, Mockbeggar Lane, Ibsley, Hants BH24 3PP
Telephone: 01425 4809090 Fax: 01202 885282
Open Thursday - Sunday 11am - 5.30pm plus Bank Holidays

Built in 1654, the old church has now become a well established art venue. The carefully restored building offers a perfect setting to view a wide and continually changing exhibition of original paintings and limited edition prints by international and local artists. Also displayed are ceramics, pottery, glassware, craftworks and faux flowers making a delightfully colourful and exciting impact.

Situated on the edge of the New Forest between Ringwood and Salisbury on the A338. Car parking provided in a quiet layby next to The Old Beams, a famous local inn, there is access for all.

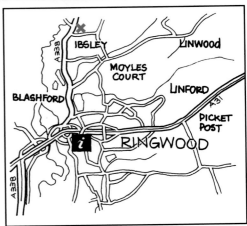

St. Martins Gallery

109

Unique Crafts Gallery

♿

5 Foreland Road, Bembridge, Isle of Wight PO35 5XN. Telephone: 01983 874173/872969
Open Tuesday - Saturday 10am - 1pm & 2.30pm -5pm (Thursday am only)

Unique Crafts Gallery was opened by Marian Kuhns in May 1987. A wide range of handmade one-off crafts are featured: ceramics, textiles, studio glass, papier-maché, jewellery, silk painting and prints.

Many of the exhibitors are members of the Quay Craftsmen, a group formed on the Island in 1986 which meets regularly to share ideas and give mutual support. Other makers who live and work on the Island and makers from mainland Britain exhibit here as well.

Steve Thearle

The Gallery aims to provide an elegant show-case for the display of their work, and to stimulate and encourage the wider community to value and use original hand-made craftworks in everyday living. Year after year clients return, because they appreciate the gallery's high standards of design and craftsmanship and the exciting and innovative work they know that they will

Marian Kuhns

I live on the Isle of Wight and am inspired by the beauty of the sea in all its changing moods. Interesting textures and colours appeal to me. Sometimes I give silver an organic, crinkly looking surface by heating it to a high temperature until it starts to melt. For colour I use enamels, resins and semi-precious stones.

I admire clean lines and elegant shapes and strive to make jewellery that is bold and modern. I like to experiment and increasingly feel free to expand my horizons and my sense of possibilities, for example to combine silver with materials such as acrylic and glass.

I believe that discovering new ways to express one's creativity through one's chosen craft is a joyful and life affirming activity.

Molly Attrill

I trained with Michael Leach in North Devon and with Henry Hammond at West Surrey College of Art and Design. For several years I worked in studios in Canada and France before establishing my own pottery at Mersley Farm on the Isle of Wight in 1982.

I am interested in the timeless appeal of pottery. My work in majolica and slip makes reference to European traditions of decorated earthenware which I reinterpret with my own distinctive figurative designs.

I make functional pots to be enjoyed in use at the table or in the kitchen. I also make hand-cut majolica tiles and larger tile panels on commission.

Pauline Barnden

I studied sculpture and ceramics at Bath Academy of Art and Hammersmith College of Art, and taught art and design for many years on the Isle of Wight. I now work from home in my studio overlooking Ventnor beach.

My work is mainly sculptural and vessel forms inspired by the sea, swimmers and the beach, using the natural colours and rhythms of the environment..

Using stoneware and porcelain I create work based on traditionally 'earthy' subjects - pebbles, stones, fossil ammonites and shells - decorate them with dramatic blue colours and intricate patterns.

I use a variety of methods of construction including thrown, coiled, slab, press moulded and slip cast, and I develop my own glazes.

Stewart Orr

I live by the sea so this is inevitably one of the major influences on my work.

The magic of the sea is the way the surface of the water is always changing in relationship to the sky, winds and tides. This provides a constant source of new ideas for use of colour, effect and composition with which to experiment in my prints and paintings.

Foreign travel is the other main influence on my work. The many places I have visited have left me with a treasure chest of lasting impressions of exotic scenes, colours, textures, perfumes and designs.

Although my work tends to focus purely on juxtaposition of colour and form I sometimes make it less abstract by incorporating hints of real places or lives or historical events connected to my source.

0% Walford Mill Craft Centre

Stone Lane, Wimborne, Dorset BH21 1NL. Telephone: 01202 841400
*Open Monday - Saturday 10am - 5pm, Sunday 12 -5pm including Bank Holidays
except Christmas Day, Boxing Day and New Year's Day (Closed Mondays, January - March)*

Walford Mill is the place to visit if you are looking for the very best in contemporary craft and design, with time to browse and enjoy the surroundings.

There are about eight different exhibitions throughout the year in the gallery featuring work by local, national and international contemporary makers. The shop has an exciting range of high quality craft work including a wide range of pottery, textiles, jewellery, wood and metalwork, plus books and cards in the shop.
When you meet the resident designers and makers in silk weaving and stained glass, you could be inspired to commission your own special piece of work. Walford Mill opened as a craft centre in 1986 and is selected for quality by the Craft Council. On the northern edge of the market town of Wimborne, the eighteenth century mill is a local landmark set in the gardens by the ancient Walford bridge over the river Allen. It has become a popular attraction, both for local residents and for visitors to Dorset.

Walford Mill Craft Centre

113

The centre is managed by Walford Mill Education Trust, a registered charity. An active programme of courses, workshops and exhibition linked events are run throughout the year.

The Mill has its own car park and licensed restaurant. The gallery, restaurant and grounds are fully wheelchair accessible and there are facilities for disabled visitors.

Top: Debbie Kirby & Liz Farquharson
Centre: Geoffrey Bickley
Bottom: Karina Gill

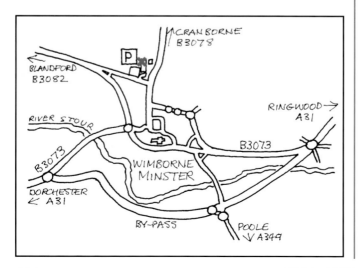

Jonathan Gooding

J.Watton FRPS

Jonathan Gooding

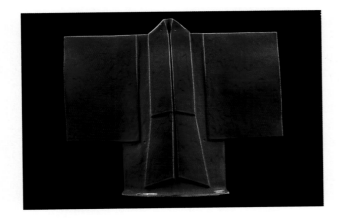

Peter Moss

Peter trained at Bournemouth and Poole College of Art and The Royal College of Art. He is currently vice-chairman of Society of Designer Craftsmen and professional member of the Craft Potters Association, fellow of the Royal Society of Arts and an original member of the Contemporary Crafts Network. He has exhibited widely nationally and internationally including Germany, Finland, Estonia and Russia. His work now follows two distinct lines of enquiry and development:

* High fired sculptural ceramics of medium and
   large scale
* Large and small decorative ceramics concerned
   with the constant search into order, using
   unique methods of multi-fired on glaze enamel
   and precious metal lustre.

He is still as enthusiastic now about the qualities of clay, glaze and decorations as he was when a student.

Debbie Kirby

Debbie has worked as a weaver since 1984, after completing a degree in woven textiles at West Surrey College of Art. She moved into her present workshop at Walford Mill Craft Centre in 1986.

She has a long-standing interest in natural forms and this, combined with her love of colour, provides a starting point for her designs. These are usually simple in structure, allowing the silk to speak for itself. Items produced include scarves, cushions and bags and a range of men's accessories.

"My ideas are formed from many different sources, mostly beginning with studies of light in nature and the environment. Because of the way I dye my silk (dyeing and over-dyeing to build up a freeform design that still has structure and control) each piece is unique."

Chris Twilley

Jonathan Gooding

Kathryn Arbon

I have close links with Walford Mill Craft Centre, where I sell my work, having been the resident jeweller there for three years. I now work from home since starting a family.

I work in a wide range of metals including 9ct and 18ct gold, and silver, specialising in the reactive metals titanium and niobium. Also through my interest in gemmology I like to incorporate unusually cut semi-precious and precious stones.

As well as working on new ranges of jewellery bringing together the contrast between silver and titanium, I continue to remodel old jewellery and I am often commissioned to design and make individual pieces.

Jane Green

Jane has lived in Dorset for most of her life and has always had an interest in crafts. She has been fascinated with stained glass using both the Tiffany technique and the traditional lead to produce a range of individual items in her gatehouse workshop at Walford Mill Craft Centre.

Photographs and the natural environment inspire Jane to breathe life into her work.

From her riverside workshop Jane hand crafts stained glass objects which include mirrors, lamps, terrariums and jewellery. Jane often works to commission producing larger pieces such as windows and door panels. These produce endless challenges for her.

She organises and runs both adult and children's classes in stained glass to encourage public awareness of this very much revived ancient craft.

116

Some other Galleries in Wessex

Alpha House Gallery
South Street
Sherborne
Dorset
DT9 3LU
Tel: 01935 814944
Fax: 01935 8633932
Open Tues - Fri
10am - 4.30pm,
Sat 10am - 5.30pm

Bettles
80 Christchurch Road
Ringwood
Hants
BH24 1DR
Tel & Fax: 01425 470410
Open Tues - Fri 10am - 5pm,
Sat 10am -1pm

Candover Gallery
22 West Street
Alresford
Near Winchester,
Hampshire
SO24 9AE
Tel: 01962 733200
Open Mon- Sat 9.30am -
5.30pm

The Red Gallery
98 Marmion Road
Southsea
Hampshire
PO5 2BB
Tel: 02392 793924
www.theredgallery.co.uk
Open Thurs - Sun
10.30am - 6pm

St. James's Gallery
9B Margarets Buildings
Bath
BA1 2LP
Tel & Fax: 01225 319197
www.
bathshopping.co.uk
Open Mon - Sat 10am -
5.30pm or by appointment

Vena Bunker Gallery
166 Park Road
Stapleton
Bristol
BS16 1DW
Tel: 0117 9586190

Open by appointment
except during exhibitions

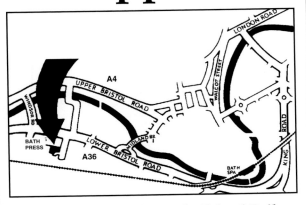

London and South East

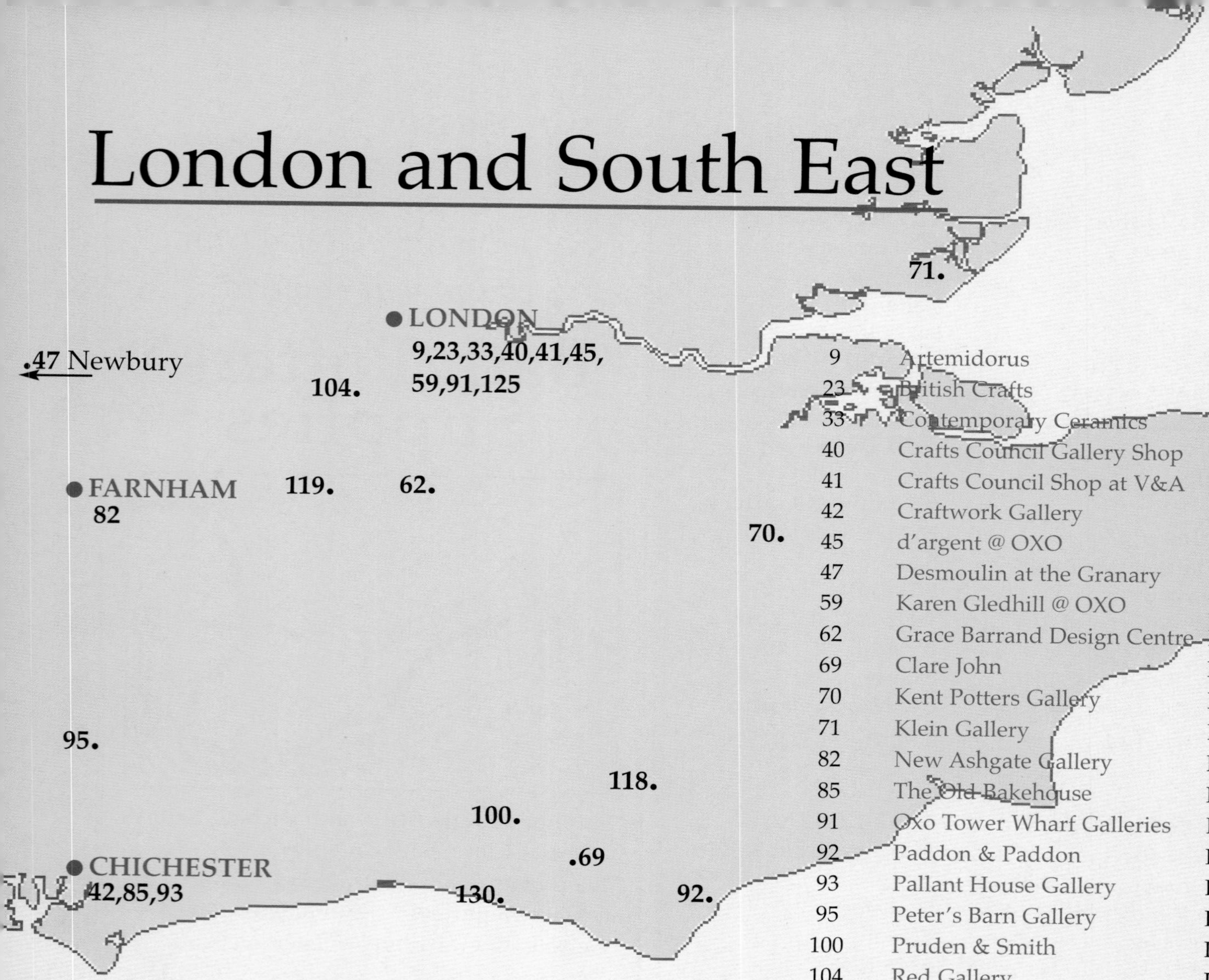

.47 Newbury ←

● LONDON
9,23,33,40,41,45,
59,91,125

104.

● FARNHAM   119.   62.
82

95.

118.

100.

.69

● CHICHESTER
42,85,93   130.   92.

70.

71.

ARTEMIDORUS

27b Half Moon Lane, Herne Hill, London SE24 9JU. Telephone: 020 7737 7747
Open Tuesday - Friday 10.30am - 7pm, Saturday 10.30am - 6pm
December Monday & Sundays 10.30am -7pm, Sundays 11am -4pm

Artemidorus

ARTEMIDORUS

Artemidorus, celebrating its tenth anniversary this year, was created by Amanda Walbank and John Bell. It is a delight to visit and a great source for inspiration.

The range of stock by contemporary British artists and makers is unexpectedly large and comprehensive. A saleable price, quality and Amanda's taste are the factors that determine the contents.

The building is set back slightly, narrow, suggesting perhaps a chapel, its singularity catching the eye, appears Victorian, but was built in 1989. Though one never forgets the slimness of the rooms, which is part of their appeal, there is a sense of lightness and space - allowing Amanda the opportunity to exercise her instinct for decorative artefacts. You enter a space filled with colour. Deeply coloured glass and textiles, richly glazed ceramics, wooden vessels and toys, reflective metalwork and exciting jewellery; all amidst cool white walls. It is clearly a place that people like to enter and absorb.

The original pieces are complemented by blue bottles of essential oils, which capture and reflect the light, and an exceptional choice of cards and wrap that you find only occasionally even in central London. Upstairs, run to complement the shop, is The Gallery for exhibitions of work by British artists. Artemidorus flourishes deservedly. It is a vindication of the fecundity and the delightfulness of contemporary British

craftsmanship - an excellent reason to visit Herne Hill and Dulwich Village with their parks, village like character and one of the finest and earliest picture galleries in Britain.

'Artemidorus', by the way, was a Greek philosopher and soothsayer who offered 'the interpretation of dreams' - the name is not inappropriate.

A Crafts Council Selected Gallery

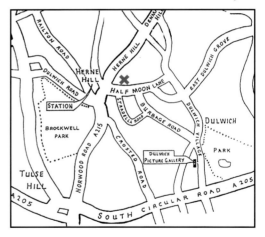

Travel Links By Train:
to Herne Hill from Victoria (10mins), Blackfriars & Thameslink (12mins)
By Bus to Herne Hill routes:
3; 37; 68; 68a; 322;N3 & S13
By Road or walking:
Herne Hill is 4 miles south of the City of London. Trafalgar Square is 4 miles, Westminster 3 miles and Dulwich Picture Gallery, park & village are less than 1 mile east.

Christine Savage

Christine's jewellery is based on natural organic themes such as rock strata, animal skin, leaf patterns, moulds and fungi. Different metals and oxidised surfaces form layers and textures creating relief and depth.

Her stunning work is contemporary yet classic. Using sterling silver, 18ct gold and semi-precious stones the pieces are fabricated rather than cast; their precision and scale appeals to the eye.

They are designed to be worn. She produces jewellery for men and women - cufflink designs echo earrings, brooches and rings. Her necklaces compose themselves on the wearer following the body's natural curves.

Christine trained in London as a graphic designer and jeweller. She is a member of the Surrey Guild of Craftsmen.

Commissions via Artemidorus include a cross of St Brendan in silver and gold worn (safely!) on the BT Global Challenge yacht race.

Michael Ruh

Born in Minnesota, England is now his home. He has been a restless traveller on an artistic journey. Pausing, he studied sculpture at Drake University Iowa, before continuing his travels. Eventually in Belgium, Michael was introduced to glassmaking at the Instituut voor Kunstambachten.*

He was instantly fascinated by glass for its reflection of light and its subtlety of movement, as well as the contradictions of its nature - "cool and tactile when annealed, violent and dangerous when molten".

Ruh approaches his glassmaking with a minimum of simple tools utilising the nature of glass itself often resulting in archetypal pieces of near sacred simplicity. These pieces carry a record of their journey from molten glass to finished piece. They are alive with light and shadow. He is inspired by "the transient nature yet structured intent of cocoons and wasp nests and the dream-like light which reflects and courses through their layered constructions".

Michael exhibits in England, Germany and the United States.

*The Institute for Artisan Trades.

Maurice Long

Maurice studied under an acknowledged master blacksmith, Ivan Smith before graduating from Camberwell in 1981 with his degree in Silversmithing and Metalwork.

By 1986 he had taken over a disused forge in central London from whence he migrated to Oxfordshire.

"Through the discipline of silversmithing and the unrestrained techniques of blacksmithing I have developed a style that bridges both crafts by way of refinement in design and spontaneity in craftsmanship".

His work, predominantly in steel, has naturally reflected organic and flowing forms which in turn reflect the spontaneity of the forging process.

Past commissions include church screens, installation pieces for major buildings, substantial gates and domestic furniture.

Due to the demand for his skills his work is only displayed by a few established galleries. Commissions will be undertaken.

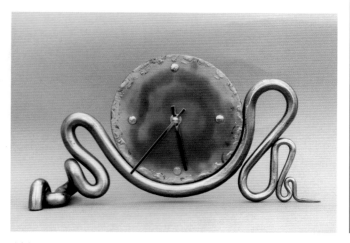

Jane Cox

Jane, an internationally acclaimed ceramicist, trained at Camberwell College of Art and The Royal College of Art, and currently works from her studio in S E London.

The speciality and uniqueness of her work is its style and precise eye for detail. Using a combination of techniques such as throwing, press moulding, casting etc., she creates clean graceful forms given life and energy by her vibrant and translucent colours.

Water, nature, reflections and translucence are inspirational in her work. She uses the pot as canvas. Some are left plain and others decorated either with calligraphic patterns or free flowing abstract brushed designs.

She has established a palette and style which, although the pieces are things of beauty in themselves, intermix effectively for maximum visual impact and enjoyment.

Her work has featured extensively in a variety of publications including the Craft Council's Ceramics Guide. Individual pieces or collections may be commissioned and appreciated for their aesthetic value and function.

BRITISH CRAFTS

4 Riverview Grove, London W4 3QJ. Telephone: 020 8742 1697
Email: britishcrafts@lineone.net
www.britishcrafts.co.uk
*For a preview or to order catalogues visit the website, email
or write to the above*

Launched in September 1999 - British Crafts mail order catalogues enable you to 'browse' through a 'gallery on the page' and return to it time and time again without having to get into your car.

The catalogues feature stunning and unusual jewellery, ceramics, glass, textiles, silver, wood and papier maché - much of the work designed especially for British Crafts. As well as well-established designer makers you will also find a selection of 'newcomers' offering an opportunity to acquire early offerings from burgeoning talent. An innovation in issue three is a regional section featuring work from several talented makers living and working on the beautiful Orkney archipelago. The photographs featured here illustrate only a very small selection of the work available from British Crafts.

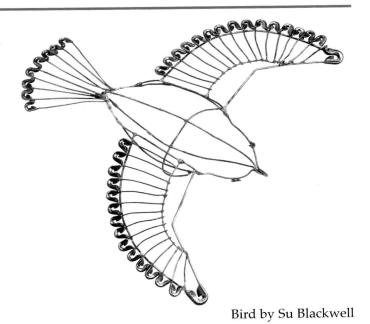

Bird by Su Blackwell

British Crafts Mail Order Catalogue

Clockwise from top left:

Gemma Stacey

Alex Bernard

Julia Ogborne

Glynn Sheppard

James C. Cochrane

British Crafts Exhibitions

As well as the catalogues British Crafts organises exhibitions showing work from some of the finest makers from all over the UK.

These exhibitions showcase everything from all the British Crafts mail order catalogues as well as offering a unique opportunity to buy direct from many fine crafts men and women not featured in the catalogues. Many customers commented that the shows were 'better than Chelsea'.

Avocets by Mike Lythgoe

For more details and dates for 2002 please visit the Exhibition page on the website:
www.britishcrafts.co.uk

Contemporary Ceramics ♿

7 Marshall Street, London WIF 7EH. Telephone: 020 7437 7605
Email: contemporary.ceramics@virgin.net
Open Monday - Saturday 10.30am -6pm (except Thursday 10.30am - 7pm)

Contemporary Ceramics is the retail outlet for members of the cooperative Craft Potters Association and has been selling the work of the finest potters and ceramicists in Britain since it first opened in 1960.

The CPA was formed in 1958 to sell the work of potter members and to increase general awareness of studio pottery through its gallery in London's Marshall Street, which has recently been refurbished and greatly improved as a result of a successful application for a lottery grant.

The Association promotes exhibitions, potters' camps, lectures, workshops and travel, and is always looking for ways to bring awareness to the ever changing and creative craft. As well as maintaining a wide range of pots on display from accessible domestic ware to rare collectors' items, Contemporary Ceramics mounts regular exhibitions of new

work and our 'In the Window' space offers members a further opportunity to display new work, attracting the attention of passers by. In the gallery we have a permanent selection of functional tableware, including Winchcombe, A & J Young and Muchelney pottery, with Dartington ranges adding a splash of colour. Other

work is as diverse as our membership. Handbuilt pieces in all their guises contrast with the wheel thrown work of many different potters. The ceramics on show include work by Svend Bayer, Peter Beard, Clive Bowen, Sandy Brown, Ian Byers, John Calver, Daphne Carnegy, Bennett Cooper,

Jane Hamlyn, John Higgins, Walter Keeler, Anna Lambert, Nigel Lambert, John Maltby, Jane Perryman, John Pollex, Mary Rich, Phil Rogers, Duncan Ross, Antonia Salmon, Micki Schloessingk, Josie Walter, John Ward, David White and many others.

Our stock of books on ceramics is one of the largest in the country, from classic texts such as Bernard Leach's 'A Potter's Book' to carefully selected books on all aspects of history, aesthetics and techniques. Inspiration can also be found amongst the selection of magazines. We stock many titles from around the world along with our own 'Ceramic Review' and the newsletter 'CPA News.' A range of potters' tools completes our selection of ceramic supplies. As the public face of the CPA the gallery aims to provide a stimulating showcase of British pottery.

Please contact Marta Donaghey for more details.

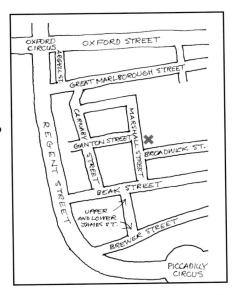

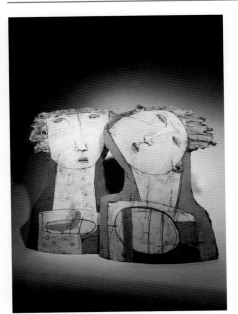

Christy Keeney

"My work is an investigation of the human figure. Form is stretched to the point where sculpture and drawing overlap. Both minimal and direct, the surface moves through a palette of soft washes that lifts the narrative and expresses not only the nature of the image but also the expressive quality of the materials".

The clay is a raku-crank body which is coated with a white earthenware slip. Coloured stains are painted freely onto the dry clay. After the biscuit firing, oxides are rubbed into the piece and washed off to reveal the drawing marks on the surface and finally fixed at a temperature of 1120°C.

Mike Dodd

Form, quality of surface, sensitivity of touch, appropriateness of clay and firing incidentals all contribute to a visual and tactile language, more visceral than conceptual, which deepens through continual acquaintance and use. To help develop this language I use naturally occurring rocks, clays and wood-ashes in formulating glazes. The search for strong form and for glazes, which can enhance and elucidate this formal language requires commitment and continual choice.

Finally, the work is surrendered to the fire. Although disasters occur, they are more than compensated for by 'gifts from the kiln' - those pots that are better than you could have hoped for. These provide the spur to deeper understanding - an understanding, it is hoped, that quietly communicates itself at times of use and contemplation.

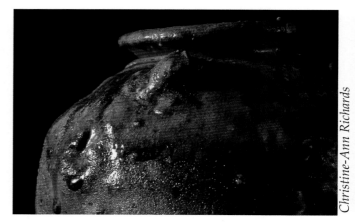

Nic Collins

Nic Collins taught himself to throw pots before going on to get his HND in Studio Ceramics at Derby in 1985-86. He widened his experience by working as a thrower in potteries in Italy and Germany and eventually set up his own workshop in a remote part of Dartmoor.

Here he built his own Anagama-type tunnel kilns, fired by wood, each firing involving four long days of heat, flames and smoke. The pots which finally emerge from this dramatic and exciting process glow warmly with the patina of deposited ash and need no further decoration. It is generally accepted that the 'flame pattern' of wood fired pots is almost uncontrollable - indeed it is the uniqueness of each pot that is one of the attractions of the process - but Nic had found by experiment that he can achieve a degree of control over the final effect by carefully considered packing of the kiln and regulation of the firing.

Nic is a Fellow Member of the Craft Potters Association (CPA). He became a member of The Devon Guild of Craftsmen last year. He is always pleased to consider commissions for his domestic ware as well as for his occasional one-off pots.

Anne Kari Ramberg Marshall

I was born in Norway in 1971 and studied ceramics at Harrow.

I make white and black porcelain tableware.

The rhythms of throwing with soft clay inspire me. The challenge is to freeze this freshness and vitality in the finished work. The capturing of that brief moment when the clay is moving through my hands, and preserving it for eternity in the fired piece. I feel a responsibility towards those who will own and use my work for the true beauty of functional ware appears when the user interacts with it. My work needs not only to please the eye and look inviting, but also be good to touch and satisfying to use.

Joy Bosworth

The ability of clay to mimic other materials interests me and its use historically to make cheaper copies of objects made in more valuable materials like pewter, bronze and silver.

Informed by observation of the found detritus of an industrial society, I make non-functional vessel forms which use the source material as a starting point. Often precisely made, these discarded objects become distorted and altered by their misuse. Some pieces are raku fired and others are saggar fired with sawdust inside a gas kiln. Their "value" is enhanced by the use of gold and painted silver leaf.

The Crafts Council Gallery Shop

44a Pentonville Road, Islington, London N1 9BY. Telephone: 020 7806 2559 Fax: 020 7837 6891
Email: trading@craftscouncil.org.uk Website: www.craftscouncil.org.uk
Open Tuesday - Saturday 11am - 5.45pm Sunday 2 - 5.45 pm   Reg. Charity Number: 280956

The Crafts Council Gallery Shop has been situated at the Crafts Council headquarters in Islington since 1991.

The Crafts Council Shops provide a showcase and retail outlet for the best contemporary designers and crafts people from across the craft disciplines. The shops have a selection criteria, which is available upon request.

The Gallery Shop has six Exhibition Showcases a year. For the most recent listing of the Gallery Shop Showcase Exhibition programme, please view the Crafts Council website.

As well as selling craftwork, the Gallery Shop has an extensive range of craft related books, Crafts Council publications, specialist magazines, postcards and handmade cards. We provide a mail order service and will send a free booklist on request. The booklist is also available to download from our website.

During Chelsea Crafts Fair the Gallery Shop runs a highly successful bookshop.

A commissioning service is available with access to Photostore, a visual database containing over 40,000 slides of contemporarycraftwork. Trained staff with specialist craft knowledge are able to assist and advise.

Photo: Tony May

Crafts Council Shop at the V&A

Victoria and Albert Museum, South Kensington, London SW7 2RL. Telephone: 020 7589 5070
Fax: 020 7581 2128 Email: trading@craftscouncil.org.uk
Website: www.craftscouncil.org.uk Reg. Charity Number 280956
Open Tuesday - Sunday 10am - 5.30pm, Monday 12 - 5.30pm

Tony May

The Crafts Council Shop at the V&A opened in 1974, as a result of a dialogue with the then Director of the Crafts Advisory Committee, Victor Margrie and Sir Roy Strong following the landmark exhibition 'The Craftsman's Art'. The shop provides a showcase and retail outlet for the best of contemporary designers and crafts people selected by the Crafts Council. A wide range of work across all media including ceramics, glass, jewellery, metalwork, textiles and wood is shown from both well established and new, up and coming makers.

The shop has established an annual programme of seven showcase exhibitions to promote the work of one or more makers. One of the most successful shows is 'New Faces'.

Held each June, it features work by four or five recent recipients of a Crafts Council Setting Up Grant. This is an opportunity to purchase crafts from new innovative makers.

A commissioning service for customers is available. This ranges from replacing a beloved lost earring to large one-off pieces. Repairs and valuations can also be arranged for jewellery purchased in the shop. In addition a postage and packing service is offered. Staff are highly trained to handle enquiries and offer specialist knowledge in crafts.

*Craftwork Gallery

18 Sadlers Walk, East Street, Chichester, West Sussex PO19 1HQ. Telephone: 01243 532588
Open Monday - Saturday 10am -5pm (Closed Sunday & Bank Holidays)

Michael Pryke was drawn into the world of crafts and craftsmen many years ago through his wife's pottery, and subsequently by his involvement with the Sussex Guild, of which he is a Vice President. His business background, coupled with his appreciation of good craftsmanship and deep concern for standards in design, proved a good combination when he set up Craftwork in Sussex, originally in Lewes and now in Chichester.

The gallery, now well established, shows a wide range of British made work which embraces ceramics, glass, and an attractive selection of wooden items. Including intricate fretwork tree sculptures by Richard Maw, Nigel Lucraft's unique book covers and the carved ducks of Ian Short as well as a multitude of smaller wooden items. The three dimensional work is complimented by a fine selection of local Sussex watercolours and prints, etchings by Robert Greenhalf, embroidered pictures by Wendy Dolan and wall hangings by Fay Hankins. There is also a wide range of batik cards by Buffy Robinson, Jill James, Jane Hickman and Rosi Robinson.

132

Jill Pryke

Jill Pryke studied at Wimbledon School of Art (NDD in Pottery) and went on to gain her Art Teacher's Certificate at London University Institute of Education. However, most of what is relevant to her work now was learned during her years teaching both children and adults. Jill set up her workshop in Ditchling in 1975, throwing pots in red earthenware. She has developed a range of pots for daily use and for decoration, including a variety of candleholders: light seen through pierced work and cut away openings always seems doubly attractive.

Her work is characterised by soft green, blue and grey glazes. She often decorates her pots with designs based on natural patterns and textures, using the sgraffito technique of scratching through one layer of glaze to reveal the colour underneath. She also accepts commissions for commemorative plates and bowls with inscriptions. Jill has been a member of The Sussex Guild almost from its beginning and has exhibited with the Guild all over Sussex.

Clare McFarlane

Clare started a two year Higher BATEC Diploma Course in Ceramics at Croydon College, after completing a one year foundation course at Hastings College. In 1984 she left college and rented a work-shop near Uckfield, in Sussex. To start with, she had a part- time job, but after three years she began work-ing fulltime for herself. She concentrates on modelling the more popular animals such as cats, frogs, chickens, pigs and sheep.

Her work is slipcast in semi-porcelain, bisque fired, then handpainted and fired again to stoneware and porcelain temperature. Many glazes have been discovered by accident, and many are difficult to reproduce exactly as on previous pieces. Many designs are modelled from life, most cat designs are from her own pets. Photographs and drawings are also used as reference material. Clare sells to many retail outlets and exhibits in some local galleries. She is a member of The Sussex Guild and shows her work at some of their craft exhibitions.

Desmoulin at the Granary

The Wharf, Newbury, Berkshire RG14 5AS. Tel: 01635 35001 Fax: 01635 37001
Email: snail@desmoulin.co.uk
Open Daily 10am -5pm. Sunday by appointment

Desmoulin is housed in the granary on the Wharf, in one of the town's finest old buildings. Established in 1999, this new contemporary art gallery is showing an ever changing collection of quality art and artefacts - paintings, photographs, furniture, fine jewellery in silver and gold, glassware and ceramics - created by our best artists and makers, many of whom are local.

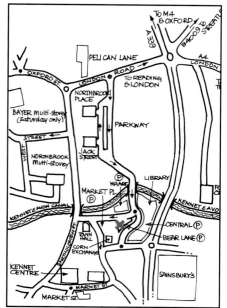

The gallery is host to a variety of different exhibitions throughout the year and is always an exciting place to visit. Its café serves 'the best coffee in town' and does tasty light lunches and excellent soups, with vegetarians well catered for.

Jo Andreae

Desmoulin also runs its own programme of evening chamber concerts featuring internationally renowned performers.

0% The Grace Barrand Design Centre ♿

19 High Street, Nutfield, Surrey RH1 4HH. Telephone: 01737 822865 Fax: 01737 822617
Email: info@gbdc.co.uk   Website: www.gbdc.co.uk
Open Tuesday - Saturday 10am - 5pm

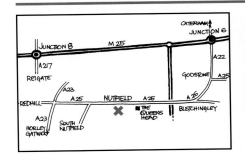

The Grace Barrand Design Centre was established in 1996, and has rapidly developed a reputation for showing and selling the very best in contemporary craft and design.

Set up by textile designer Rosemary Hufton and her husband David, the centre is committed to promoting the work of some of the very best new and established designers, while retaining a relaxed and welcoming atmosphere. The concept of the centre was inspired by Rosemary's own involvement in textiles and her wish to provide contemporary designers with a space to exhibit their work. The gallery, which is housed in a converted post office and general store, is set in beautiful courtyard gardens full of specially commissioned work by the artist Terence Clark, furniture by Gaze Burvill and Wales & Wales, subtle water features and a mews studio where short courses are held. These courses are in a wide range of subjectsand are taught by leading designers and crafts people, including Lorna Moffat, Lois Walpole, Janet Bolton and Teresa Searle. Since its foundation, the gallery has evolved into an exhibition area and shop selling a diverse range of gifts, homeware, furniture, textiles, ceramics and glass at competitive prices as well as offering a flexible interior and garden design service. Car park.

The Grace Barrand Design Centre

135

Rosemary Hufton

Rosemary is a mixed media artist, specialising in work using hand dyed and painted fabrics embellished with stitch. She often incorporates materials such as dyed aluminium, textured rubber fabric, handmade paper and felt, fused glass, beads and sequins - to give texture and intrigue to her designs. She loves to experiment with new techniques and ideas, and also enjoys the challenge of incorporating as many recycled materials as possible into her work.

Past commissions have ranged from large wall hangings for an oil company, which were required to look boldly industrial; to a triptych for the Millennium Dome made from rubber wet-suit material, hand embroidered and dye-painted. Bright colours, strong patterns and graphic quality characterise Rosemary's work, as does her creative use of stitch.

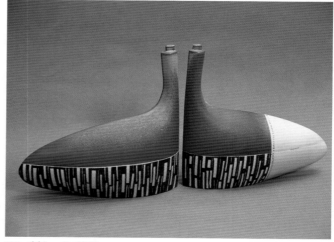

Kellie Miller

Kellie's ceramic vessels and wallpieces have a constant repetitiveness. This theme is reflected in the visual content as well as in her main making process of combining hand building techniques with slip casting. Thus creating limited edition designed forms, which are unique in surface decoration.

Concepts behind the work are concerned with notions of hybridity and relationships. The communication between each form is emphasised by space, decoration, coupling and grouping, creating an interdependency between the objects. Equally important to the finished pieced is her use of glaze and colour.

Influences are attributed to the work of William Scott, Antoni Tapies and Brian Rice. Together with her years of training at Wimbledon School of Art, Camberwell School of Art, Brighton University; and her MA in Arts Criticism at City University London.

Ray Key

Ray has been working with wood for most of his life and turning it for over forty years. Seven in industry, eight as a hobby and the past twenty-eight as a full-time career. Ray is known internationally for the purity of his work and through seminars, workshops, books, videos and tools. His work is in a number of museum collections around the world and most notable private collections in the USA. He was selected to the Craft Council Makers Index in 1977. Strong aesthetic design of elegant simplicity dominates his working philosophy. He specialises in making boxes, bowls, platters, dishes and vessels. At this time he is drawn to making more sculptural objects. He was the founding Chairman of the Association of Woodturners of Great Britain and is now President. He was made a Life Member for his services in 1997.

In 2001 he was made a Life Member of the Association of American Woodturners *(the first overseas turner to receive this honour)* in recognition of his contribution to the field.

Amanda Brisbane

The technique and process used in most of the work is that of sandcasting hot glass.

It is a process that is spontaneous and organic in that it uses the sand as a manipulable moulding compound to make detailed, delicate forms with textures.

The hot glass replicates these images with its own unique quality, with further manipulation post casting the pieces can adopt different dimensions.

All the colour used in the glass sculptures and cast objects is made to my own recipe, I work with different oxides to achieve unusual colours.

I am passionate about glass and all its possibilities, I challenge myself to create magnificent abstract forms that appear frozen in space.

Janet Bolton

Janet Bolton creates textile pictures using the simplest of techniques. Working directly with the fabric she combines colour and imagery until the composition is complete. 'Drawing' is done by cutting the shapes and turning in the edge of the fabric with the needle. Originally working with paint, she now prefers the medium of fabric, both for the qualities of the fabric itself and the spontaneity and freedom it allows. Inspiration comes from all areas of life; direct observation, memory and imagination. Janet is on the Crafts Council Selected Index of Makers, has exhibited worldwide and has published books for both adults and children. Her work is also in the British Council collection, the Crafts Council collection and the Embroiderers Guild Museum collection. During her career, Janet has taught all ages, from infant to post graduate level at the Royal College of Art, as well as being a visiting lecturer at the Victoria and Albert Museum.

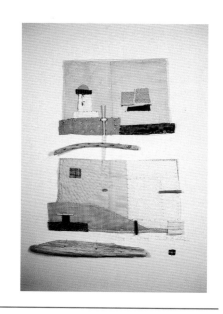

Diane Flint

My current work includes pewter dishes, bowls, goblets and tumblers and a range of chunky cast silver jewellery. I trained in jewellery at Middlesex University, where I worked in mild steel.

I then discovered sheet pewter, and with mixed media, started making one-off objects. After a time experimenting with different materials, I found cast pewter was perfect, and I developed a range of candlesticks. I like the colour and texture of pewter, and do little to alter the surface. I cast into silicon rubber, making the original from either wax or plasticine.

I draw inspiration from travel and architecture, I store information without being conscious of it, then later I recognise aspects emerging in my work which remind me of a place or feeling a place has evoked in me.

Emma Johnstone

I made my first pot at nine years old haven't really stopped since then. I worked in several different fields before taking a degree in Ceramics at the University of Westminster at 26. As part of my degree, I spent six months studying in Jerusalem. I had come across Raku before, but it was whilst in Israel that I became really inspired by the technique. My approach to ceramics markedly changed there, and the beginnings of my present work began.

I make a range of hollow thrown raku-fired bowls and vessels. The controlled forms contrast with the firing method I use, and I enjoy the tension between these two stages. The gilded centre of each piece is the final layer. I am very lucky - I love my job!

Sandra Eastwood

Sandra studied ceramics at The Royal College of Art after finding a deep fascination for clay during her Sculpture Degree at Gloucester College of Art and Design.

She has had a ceramics workshop in Teddington since 1976 making and selling original work. Her current work and techniques have evolved from experimenting with new ideas and materials to create highly fired and coloured hand built forms, which are concerned with strong sculptural forms and rhythmic patterns.

She uses T-material and a range of customised, coloured porcelain engobes, glazes and lustres.

Sandra shows regularly at The Grace Barrand Design Centre and will have a major exhibition there in 2002. She is a Professional Member of The Craftsmen Potters Association and has work in private collections worldwide.

Abbott + Ellwood

Living and working on the edge of dramatic moorland outside St. Ives, the influence of light and colour that envelopes their garden studio and surrounding ocean landscape can clearly be seen in Abbott and Ellwood's work.

Graduating from the Royal College of Art and Middlesex University, they set up a studio in 1990.

Their recent collection of jewellery and clocks continues their interest with painted and printed metal and the simple concepts of old tin toys.

The success of this colourful range, together with their one-off exhibition pieces and work to commission, their fresh, creative outlook, unique designs and attention to detail, have built them a considerable reputation.

Their work is held in many public and private collections and is widely exhibited in the UK, Europe and the USA.

Lucinda Bell

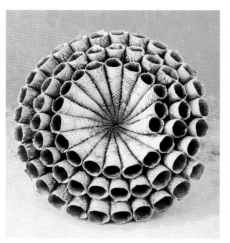

Lisa Ellul (*Ceramics*)

Kate Schuricht

The Grace Barrand Design Centre

Clare John

18a High Street, Lewes, East Sussex BN7 2LN. Telephone: 01273 486988
Email: c.john@silver93.freeserve.co.uk Website: www.lewesartisans.com / Clare John
Open Monday - Saturday 9.30pm -12pm and 12.30 -5.30pm (Closed Wednesday afternoon)

The shop is really a jewellery gallery with a workshop at the back. Clare John trained at Middlesex Polytechnic and she makes some of the work on display. But one of the best parts of her job is hunting out new jewellery from all over the country and finding great designs in all sorts of materials and price ranges.

In stock there are over thirty makers including Jane Adam, Teresa Samson, Katie Weiner, Hot Metal, Sim, Linda Jolly, Connell and Hart, Gill Forsbrook and Caroline Reynolds. Clare works in silver, gold, semi-precious stones and resin and has a catalogue of her collection for mail orders.

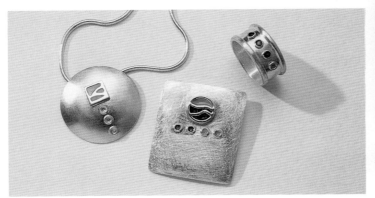

Jewellery by Clare John

Caroline Reynolds

I work mainly in gold and silver and aim to make my pieces lively, enchanting and wearable. I often contrast colours and textures through a variety of techniques and materials.

I have been a professional jewellery designer and maker since 1991 and my jewellery has won awards from Goldsmiths Hall and appeared in Harpers & Queen magazine and various exhibitions. I also teach jewellery making in Kent and Sussex.

Gill Forsbrook

I make jewellery from plastic. The design of my work develops from my exploration of the materials I choose to use. I am attracted to plastics for their qualities of colour, flexibility, lightness and optical properties.

The bangles illustrated are part of a range of jewellery made from thin sheets of flexible, translucent plastics, layered together and anchored with silver.

142

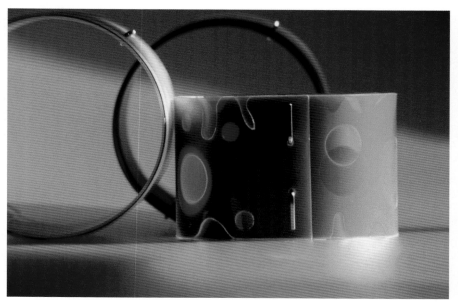

Clare John

Diane Hart & Paul Connell

Diane Hart and Paul Connell have worked with glass for the last thirteen years. They have developed an extensive range of decorative objects, jewellery and clocks, all made using an interpretation of the Pâte de Verre process.

This involves fusing grains and powders of coloured and clear glasses in a kiln to a temperature which allows the glasses to flow, capturing tiny bubbles within the glass, whilst retaining the separation of the different colours and grains. Some pieces are then decorated by applying 22ct gold or white gold leaf.

They live and work in Northumberland, the archaeology and architecture of the area providing a constant inspiration for their work. They supply outlets throughout the UK, Europe and Japan and also work to commission for larger items.

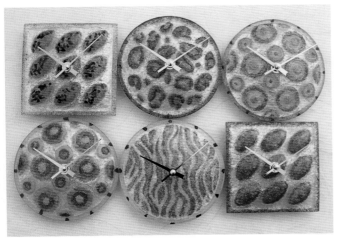

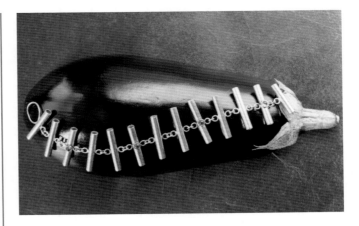

Katie Weiner

Katie graduated from Wolverhampton University with a BA Honours in 3D glass design in 1994. She then trained with a jeweller in London. Since then she has sold her work in various outlets in the UK and through a small chain in Japan.

She enjoys using and manipulating eastern influences and futuristic ideas, incorporating silver, brass and gold along with semi-precious stones in her designs.

In the last six months, along with an illustrator, she has set up a company called 'Nymph' producing silver and semi-precious body pieces. Commissions include a silver ornate bikini for a dancer and most recently headresses for cats on a series due to be aired on the Discovery channel followed by a feature on matching human and feline jewellery for the Daily Mail.

Clare John

Kent Potters Gallery

22 Union Street, Maidstone, Kent ME14 1ED. Telephone: 01622 681962
Open Tuesday - Saturday 10am -5pm

The Kent Potters Gallery, based in Maidstone, Kent, is conveniently located in the conservation area of this historic market town. The Gallery offers a continually changing exhibition of members' work. Originally opened in 1994, the Gallery now resides in ground floor premises, thus enabling easier access for customers. It is also within walking distance of rail and bus services as well as local parking facilities.

The aim of the Gallery is to promote original, exclusive and innovative work. It is the centre of excellence for the Kent Potter's Association. The Gallery is organised and stewarded by active members of a co-operative. They are able to discuss with visitors and customers ceramic issues such as techniques, practical advice, local courses and provide information about displayed work and their makers.

At any one time twenty five potters are represented. A calendar of mini-exhibitions are held to high-light members' work and to encourage that of new makers. Work is for sale and/or commission, offering something new and different for the home or special gift occasion.

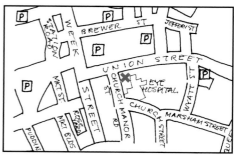

Klein Gallery

793 Southchurch Road, Southchurch, Southend-on-Sea, Essex SS1 2PP. Tel & Fax: 01702 615056
Email: info@kleingallery.co.uk Website: kleingallery.co.uk
Open Monday - Saturday 9.15 am - 5.15 pm (Wednesday closing at 1pm)

Jeweller Jeffrey Klein's dream of making art available to everyone came true in 2001 when he opened the Klein Gallery in Southchurch in the heart of Southend-on-Sea, Essex. It heralded a change in business direction and the total refurbishment of his successful goldsmith shop after declaring: "I have the firm belief that art should be in every home".

The gallery's emphasis is on functional art and Jeffrey is fortunate to have gathered together examples of workmanship from some of the most exciting and revered artists and makers of our time.

The exquisite fruits of Jeffrey's own labours sit alongside a diverse array of works carefully selected to create a stunning, yet harmonious, blend of aesthetic

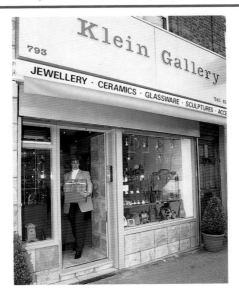

and functional craftsmanship entwined with innovative design. On display and for sale is jewellery made from a variety of metals along with platinum, gold and silver as well as paper. Complimenting the array of jewellery are ceramics and china ware, clocks, fine original illustrations, sculptures,

irregular designed yet fully functional crockery, picture frames, mirrors plus many more accessories and disciplines.

Personal favourites Bert Kitchen, Sue Dyer and David Booker lead a host of celebrated artists such as Sanders & Wallace, Loco, Peter Layton, Tony Theakston, Tony Foard, Jo Mitchell, Liz Riley, Colin Andrews, Kerry Whittle and many more. The Klein Gallery, which is unique for this region of England, also showcases many of the new up-and-coming artists alongside established ones, assuring the gallery's customers a fresh and innovative choice will always be available. Clients will also be pleased to hear that the gallery happily takes commissions on behalf of the artists.

Jeffrey Klein, committed to quality and service says: " I am proud to be able to boast the choicest of fine and original art that can be enjoyed today, in the knowledge they are assured of being prized antiques of the future.

It is a delight to offer these individual, yet affordable, items that each have a life of their own, something that simply cannot be mass produced".

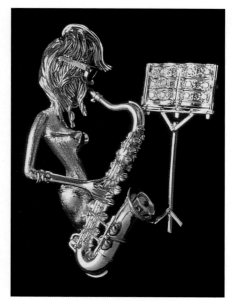

Jewellery by Jeffrey Klein

Trained in London under the renowned jewellery designer Andrew Grima, Jeffrey set up his first showroom in Southchurch in 1976 and soon established a regular clientele who still visit from all over the south of England and beyond. Today, customers can view a host of designs in various mediums all in a comfortable and relaxed atmosphere with Jeffrey, or one of his staff, personally on hand to assist.

The Klein Gallery is just over an hour from London, with excellent road connections via the M25 and then A127 or A13. A choice of two rail services from the capital (London's Fenchurch Street to Southend East or London's Liverpol Street to Southen Victoria) offer a speedy service to Southend-on-Sea.

David Booker

Every David Booker clock, contemporary in their design and concept, is hand made in solid American hardwoods such as Cherry and Maple.

The clocks feature strong shapes and curves, designs that would usually be associated with ceramics, and David adds a quirky humorous element by playing with the balance and symmetry of his creations to give them an animated feel. The feet and plumes are turned on a wood lathe and the cases are shaped using planes and steel scraper. The dials, in either wood veneer or solid brass, draw from architectural details and patterns, contrasting the simplicity of the cases with intricate patterns. On completion, the clocks are individually stamped and numbered.

David Booker, whose customers extend to America and Japan, says: " I am pleased my work is being included at the Klein Gallery".

Sue Dyer

The predominant influence of Sue Dyer's work with porcelain has been Japanese, resulting from her study of Ikebana, the art of Japanese flower arranging which represents asymmetrical design in its most perfect form.

The delicate, decorative vessels created by Sue in white, black and blue porcelain, incorporate curvilnear, subtly coloured inlays in blues, black and grey. An incised line is cut into 'leather hard' porcelain. The grooves are then filled proud with stained porcelain slip and once this has stiffened, the piece is painstakingly scraped and sanded, revealing fine decorative designs. Many colours can be inlaid in successive operations, inlaying one upon another.

Her latest pieces combine elegant austerity with a new lightness of spirit, as winged patterns of flecked colour swoop and dive, animating the immaculate surface with fresh vivacity.

New Ashgate Gallery

Wagon Yard, Farnham, Surrey GU9 7PS. Telephone: 01252 713208 Fax: 01252 737398
Email: gallery@newashgate.co.uk Website: www.newashgategallery.com
Open Monday - Saturday 10am - 5pm

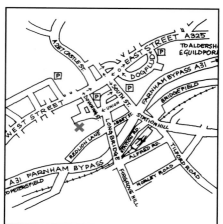

The New Ashgate Gallery has achieved national recognition for the quality of the work that it displays, and is included in the National List of Craft Shops and Galleries.

The New Ashgate Gallery Trust is a registered charity whose aims are to promote new talent and further the visual arts in the area. The Trust runs a lecture programme and offers opportunities for local children and young adults to visit the exhibitions and talk to some of the artists about their work.

The dynamic exhibition programme combines the work of both fine artists and crafts people, some established with international status and some at the outset of their exhibiting career. In addition to the spacious exhibition rooms, there is a comprehensive, well-stocked craft and print shop and jewellery gallery. Upstairs Ruta Brown has her jewellery workshop. All work is for sale and the gallery uses the part-payment scheme supported by South East Arts.

Commissioning Service

The New Ashgate Gallery Commissioning Service provides professional and practical advice, and hopes to promote a greater appreciation in contemporary and applied arts. The gallery has an extensive slide library, specifically aimed at providing detailed information on a wide range of work by selected artists and makers.

Commissioning a unique piece of work is rewarding, and at the same time is also fun, exciting, and doesn't necessarily have to be an expensive venture. There is a definite growing interest in wanting one-off pieces of art, specifically tailored to your own requirements, be this for a corporate gift or for something more personal. Commissions can encompass small scale objects such as a porcelain mug, to bespoke furniture for the home or office, or to larger scale installations such as a wrought iron gate. The possibilities are endless.

Sideboard by Toby Winteringham

Ruta Brown

One of the leading exponents of reticulation, Ruta Brown continues to design and create highly individual jewellery from her workshop at the New Ashgate Gallery.

Inspired by contrasts of texture, form and colour, each piece is individually fabricated in 18ct gold or silver. Directional heat is applied to the forged, folded forms, in exploration of the structural possibilities of the metal. The resulting jewellery represents a variety of unique designs that also incorporate stones and pearls, and include rings, necklaces, tiaras, brooches, earrings and cufflinks.

Ruta Brown, who has received a number of awards in recognition of her work, including the winner of the 'Ounce of Silver' competition by the Worshipful Company of Goldsmiths, has exhibited widely across the UK, and also in Switzerland, Japan, Egypt and the USA.

Julian Belmonte

Julian has for some time been working with white earthenware. Through a process of change and refinement he continues to develop his designs for jugs, bowls and containers. Working towards achieving an overall feeling of purity, which celebrates strength of form, his work remains uncluttered by decoration. His precise forms explore issues of scale and balance, and the relationship between the interior and exterior of each piece.

Julian has recently begun to develop a new strand of work in terracotta brick clay which compliments and echoes the qualities of his white earthenware work. The use of this additional material has allowed him to introduce to his work the warmth and richness of red brick clay and to explore monochromatic glazes.

EM Jewellery

The work of Evangelos Pourgouris and Miranda Falkner is inspired by natural organic forms and textures. Their principle when creating a genuine hand made piece, is to emphasise the simplicity of the design and its finish. With these bases, silver and gold are the choice of the materials for their design products and while co-ordinated with vibrant colour precious gems, the result is simple and yet sophisticated; which reflects our lifestyles and personalities.

Numerous pieces of their work have been shown and exhibited widely in prestigious galleries and shops, and events organised by the Goldsmiths' Company, Craft Council and DTI, which brought along private commissions.

Peter Parkinson

The experience of hot forging metal gives rise to the thought that iron and steel are soft materials which just happen to be frozen hard at room temperature. But you must work quickly and decisively because the metal doesn't stay hot for long. It is an endless challenge to give new life to some unprepossessing piece of material. The finished work may look cool and calm but it is born out of heat, noise and a degree of hazard. Overheat the metal, or strike one blow in the wrong place and it can be ruined.

And all this is just as true if I am making a small box, or a large piece of architectural metalwork or public art.

Nicola Becci

Nicola has been producing her range of jewellery in Glasgow since graduating in 1992. Her work is really an exploration of decoration, incorporating many sources, particularly the symbolism of religion and royalty, confectionery and food, toys and calligraphy. She is also fascinated by secrets and compartments. Often pieces have moveable elements that create a fun, playful feel.

Recently Nicola has produced a collection of larger pieces including boxes, spoons and cruet sets. She works mostly in silver, with brass and gold detailing, utilising etching and oxidisation to create jewellery with a quirky edge to it. Her work is in the collections of Merseyside Art Galleries and actress, Dame Judi Dench.

Duncan Ross

Duncan Ross has work in many important public and private collections including the Victoria and Albert Museum. He is on the Crafts Council Index of Selected Makers and is a Fellow of the Craft Potters Association. His in-depth knowledge has enabled him to refine the ancient use of terra-sigillata slips creating an exuberant and sophisticated result. He has developed a unique process using layers of polished sigillata slips applied to finely thrown forms; the patterns and surface textures are created by resist techniques. His highly controlled use of smoke firing produces a warm orange and deep earth browns and blacks, giving depth and dimension to the surface. Dynamic rhythms of lines, zig-zags and repeating motifs energise the surface and describe the form. Duncan Ross's work achieves an unmistakable balance between decoration and form, the geometric and the organic, the classical and the vibrantly modern.

Neil Bottle

My designs are individually created using a combination of hand painting, stencilling and printing directly onto silk. This allows limitless possibilities for producing one-off images for decorating and embellishing various silks including Silk Satin, Dupion, Silk Georgette and velvet. I use a selection of acid dyes, discharge dyes and pigments which are steamed and heat cured to fix the colour. I work with silk because it has an amazing feel and lustre, yielding extremes in colour from vibrant hot reds to cool greens. An architectural feel is conveyed in the construction of the designs, building up layer upon layer of colour and pattern.

The complex tapestry of eclectic images includes inspiration drawn from life, architecture, botanical drawings, maps, figures, calligraphy and a large vocabulary of painterly marks and textures.

Pauline Zelinski

Pauline Zelinski trained at West Surrey College of
Art & Design, graduating in 1970. She uses white
earthenware clay, to produce large platters, bowls,
jugs and cups etc. More recently, her work has been
applied to interior decorative tiles with colourful
and subtle designs. The platters in particular
provide a large area on which to explore various
designs and colour combinations. Several layers of
underglaze colour are hand-painted onto each
piece to give a richness and depth, which is then
completed by a transparent glaze.

Lara Aldridge & Jon Oakley

Vibrant designs, encompassing subtle resonant colours and hues, kiln
formed glass with metal inclusions. Elegant shallow bowls and free-
standing curves now complement our contemporary range of interior
mounted wall panels, table pieces and tiny jewellery forms.

Having relocated from the Cumbrian countryside to the Sussex coast,
inspiration is taken from the irridescent blue of the lakes and the sea, and
the beautiful contrasts of colour found in the rugged Cumbrian fells and
the ever changing sunlight on the South Downs; intermixed with the
influences of artists such as Gustav Klimt and the more geometric style of
Charles Rennie Mackintosh, an affinity established early on in our
training. Inspirations are translated into the resilient tones that
characterise our work.

The Old Bakehouse

Main Road, Fishbourne, Chichester PO18 8BD. Telephone: 01243 573263
Website: www.oldbakehouse.co.uk
Open Wednesday - Saturday 10am -5pm, Sunday 12-5pm

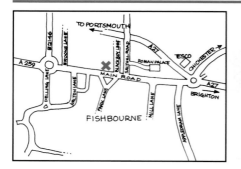

The Old Bakehouse is a fascinating complex of buildings, which over its three hundred and fifty year history has served as both a bakery and general store. Many of the original features can still be seen as visitors browse through the extensive showrooms, courtyard and gallery.

The creative talents of over one hundred of this country's finest craftspeople are brought together in a continually changing display of ceramics, glass, jewellery, wood, paintings etc. While outside the courtyard never fails to amuse with witty sculptures, fountains and original pots.

Craft Council Listed, the Gallery holds five or six exhibitions a year, which are detailed on the Web site, along with an innovative on-line 'Wedding List' service. The owners Ally and Ray Long make sure this unique showcase is never intimidating, always intriguing and has something to suit most pockets. The Old Bakehouse is on the A259 in Fishbourne, a short walk away from the famous Roman Palace, while the historic city of Chichester is just two miles away.

Oxo Tower Wharf Galleries

D'Argent - Unit 1.01, Karen Gledhill - Unit 1.10 & Alan Vallis - Unit 2.09

Oxo Tower Wharf Galleries

D'Argent Gallery @ OXO ♿

Unit 1 .01, OXO Tower Wharf, 111 Bargehouse Street, London SE1 9PH. Tel: 020 7401 8454 & 020 7519 6389

Open Monday - Saturday 10am -6 pm (Oxo open 7 days 11am -6pm)

D'Argent opened in 1996 at the Oxo Tower, and due to great success and demand the company opened their second site at Canary Wharf in August 2000. D'Argent has the simple theory of showcasing young leading designers'

jewellery, which embodies strong contemporary designs and well crafted hand made and bespoke pieces, to captivate the growing one off market that is in the UK today.

D'Argent is proud to boast an eclectic mix of forty leading designers housed at the two sites, with an ever changing appearance of guest designers work. A few of our permanent showcase designers include Paul Finch, Iain Henderson, Andrew Georghegan, Nikki Morris and the proprietor Louise Sherman.

D'Argent also offers a bespoke design service where the customer has first hand involvement in designing their jewellery, to choosing from a range of stones to suit their

design and budget, to the finished piece. We enjoy the interaction and brainstorming with the customer to create the perfect piece for their needs and requirements.

Jewellery by Louise Sherman

D'Argent @ OXO

Karen Gledhill @ OXO ♿

Unit 1.10, Oxo Tower, Barge House Street, London SE1 9PH. Telephone: 020 7401 2401
Open: Monday - Saturday 11am - 6pm

Karen has been developing and refining her indivual style of jewellery for sixteen years. She produces a range of uniquely designed and handcrafted pieces, from stylish every day wear to chunky dress jewellery in silver and gold, incorporating an array of precious stones, including a range of engagement, wedding and eternity rings in 18ct gold and platinum with diamonds.

Commissions also welcome.

Alongside Karen's work, she has two to three guest jewellers exhibiting in her shop with work which is complimentary yet quite different from her own.

Saskia Shutt is one of the jewellers whose work is shown here.

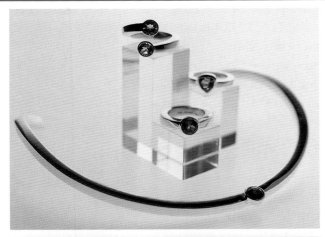

Top: Saskia Shutt *Right:* Karen Gledhill

Karen Gledhill

Alan Vallis @ OXO ♿

209 OXO Tower Wharf, Bargehouse Street, London SE1 9PH.

Telephone: 020 7261 9898 Fax: 020 7359 1803 Email: alanvallis@mistral.co.uk
Open Tuesday - Saturday 11am - 6pm

Alan Vallis @ OXO is situated on the South Bank of the Thames in the Oxo Tower, amongst an eclectic mix of housing, restaurants, Courtyard cafe, flower shop and design workshops. Alan's studio faces south from the second floor balcony overlooking the courtyard and is five minutes walk from the Tate Modern, Shakespeare's Globe and the National Theatre.

Alan exhibits at national shows and prestigious events like Goldsmiths Fair, the Chelsea Crafts Fair and Dazzle, held in Edinburgh, Manchester and London.

He is also a member of the Gloucestershire Guild of

Craftsmen and participates in their annual events. The Workshop / Gallery, established in 1996, provides

a permanent venue to showcase Alan's diverse collection of imaginative jewellery and allows clients the space and opportunity to discuss commissions.

His selections of work include his 'Red Sea Fish' based on forms and textures from the tropical marine environment, together with jewellery inspired by archaeological artefacts and tribal symbols.

His highly popular 'Stacking Rings' are textured, patterned, or gem set bands, designed to be worn together as sets.

Left:
3 stacking rings in 18K gold with Aqua-Marine, Diamonds & Sapphires

AlanVallis @ OXO

Alan Vallis @ OXO

The combination of component and hand made elements which Alan uses in his work has an in-built design flexibility which provides the client with the opportunity to make a personal contribution to the final piece. Alan enjoys working with his clients to develop unique items within

his original design concepts, and welcomes visitors to his South Bank studio where they can also view the work of other invited jewellers.

Please feel free to make an appointment to discuss your project at any other time.

Ear studs *(Clockwise from top left:)*
Garnet Cabochon studs, Sapphire Moonstuds
Diamond cupstuds & Black Pearl studs.
Left: Frances's Diamond Ring
Right: Stacking ring in 9K gold with Amethyst *Below:*
5 spear silver necklace on Grey Fresh Water Pearls

Paddon & Paddon

113 South Street, Eastbourne, East Sussex BN21 4LU. Telephone: 01323 411887
Open Tuesday - Saturday 10am - 5.30pm

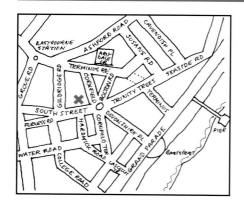

Established in December 1992, Paddon & Paddon Gallery offers a diverse and evolving selection of crafts and paintings by leading contemporary makers and artists from throughout the country, and the Sussex area in particular is well represented.

At any one time, the work of around ninety individuals in a range of media is represented: ceramics, wood, metalwork, glass and jewellery. In addition to the works of individual furniture makers, printmakers and textile artists are also featured.

The Gallery is included in the 'National List of Craft Shops and Galleries' published by the Crafts Council, and participates in the "pARTpayment" scheme administered by South East Arts. The Gallery hosts a minimum of two mixed exhibitions a year.

Visitors are assured of a warm welcome, in a comfortable setting.

Zara Devereux

In 1992 when Zara was working for a fine art framers and restorers in London, she began to collect the scraps of paper that littered the workshop floors. With the addition of plant fibres, seeds and silks she recycled them into handmade papers. These papers, along with others from Thailand, China and India now form the foundation of her work.

Returning home to Cornwall the work took on a more organic nature incorporating pressed leaves, feathers and bark. All these fragile elements are permanently bonded together with PVA glue and embroidery. Recently Zara has begun to include tiny one-off collagraphs in her work, printing onto tissue paper so that the paint beneath glows through. Printmaking is a process she is finding increasingly enjoyable and she is now producing small limited editions.

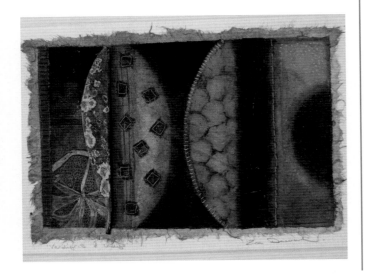

Brian Denyer

I work on a single plate, incorporating all the colours on to the plate by inking 'a la poupee', which I find gives a much softer and more atmospheric effect, than when printing from a separate plate for each colour. Most of my subject matter is based on sketches or paintings done in situ, ranging from architectural and landscape to still life. I try to capture the effects of light and atmosphere, by using a combination of various etching techniques, aquatint, softground and drypoint, all on the same plate. One of the pleasures of etching is the constant discovery of fresh techniques, which I use to develop my work into new areas.

I find this both stimulating and challenging, and I believe it helps to bring freshness to my work. I rely very much on my drawing ability, which is fundamental to producing work of the highest quality.

Linda Jolly

When Linda had completed her 3D Design/Ceramics degree at Leicester Polytechnic in 1983, she moved to London to set up her first workshop. Since then she has specialised in designing and making porcelain jewellery and buttons.

In her experiments with surface decoration she has combined her experience of painting, gilding, sponging and print with ceramic techniques and a love of geometric designs. Flat shapes of porcelain are cut out with hand tools (like pastry), then polished and decorated with glaze, enamels and precious metals. Gradually layers of pattern and colour are built up, each piece enduring at least five firings. The finished pieces are complimented with silver findings.

New designs are introduced each year and add to a wide range of earrings, brooches, neckpieces, cufflinks, buttons and clocks.

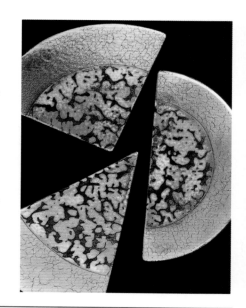

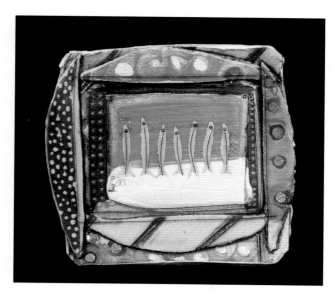

Laurel Keeley

I am a suburban child; my view is domestic. I glimpse worlds through window squares, in gardens and ponds. I long ago saw salmon climbing the weir in the river that runs through the city, and that was the start of it: fish swimming upstream, past streets and gardens, year after year, to spawn.

So, I paint fish in contained water: in ponds, in a river that runs through a pattern of roads and fields. Sometimes I put the fish in the same rows in which we grow plants; the crops make a pattern and so might the fish. There is a mystery within the boundaries: so do I make pots.

Mary Rawlinson

Mary Rawlinson left the security of teaching to study furniture construction in order to concentrate on an unusual but lifelong passion for chair making.

She prefers to use only native timbers and searches these out in all parts of the country; fruitwood from Kent, oak, yew and holly from the New Forest, willow from Somerset, and elm which can still be found in Scotland, all from trees lost to thinning, disease or storm damage.

Trees grown naturally with all their imperfections can only be worked by hand which makes each chair unique. Her designs may be a modern interpretation of an old favourite or an entirely new concept. Seats and cushions are of leather, cotton or pure wool and chosen to complement the colours in the timbers.

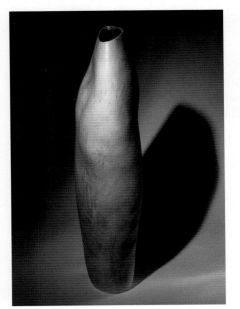

Signe Kolding

I was born and educated in Denmark, where I taught and exhibited for some years before returning to England where I had studied Art in the 70's. I now live in Hastings where the sea and surrounding landscapes are continual sources of inspiration. I am fascinated by the visual and tactile effect of erosion by wind, water and fire.

I like making sculptural vessels, caressing the shapes out of the clay and experimenting with different clays (including paper clay), oxides and engobes to catch textures and images as they appear and disappear - like memories - like archeological objects.

My work has been exhibited in England, Denmark, Holland and New Zealand and is in collections throughout Europe, Japan, New Zealand, South Africa and the United States.

The Garden Gallery at Pallant House

9 North Pallant, Chichester, West Sussex PO19 1TJ. Telephone: 01243 774557 Fax: 01243 536038
Email: pallant@pallant.co.uk Website: www.pallanthousegallery.com
Open Tuesday - Saturday 10am - 5pm Sunday 12.30 -5pm Admission free to Gallery Shop and Café

Pallant House Gallery is a restored Queen Anne town house situated in the heart of Chichester. It is home to an important collection of twentieth century paintings, drawings and sculpture and hosts several major exhibitions every year.

The commercial side of the Gallery shows changing displays of fine art, ceramics, sculpture, unique glass and jewellery. Our aim is to provide a showcase for the work of some of Britain's most talented, dedicated and sometimes unusual artists and craftspeople. There is always something interesting to see, from the work of graduates to that of long established makers. We also

stock a select range of greeting cards and postcards based on our art collection, art books and periodicals.

Pallant House Gallery is easily reached by motorway. There is ample parking nearby. Train and bus stations are a few minutes walk.

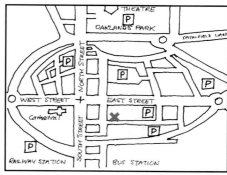

164

Peter's Barn Gallery

South Ambersham, Nr Midhurst, West Sussex GU29 0BX.
Telephone: 01798 861388 Fax: 861581 Email: peters.barn@ic24.net
Website: www.petersbarngallery.co.uk
Open Tuesday - Friday 2 -6pm, weekends and holidays 11am - 6pm April -December

Norman Hollands

Garrick Palmer

Widely acknowledged as one of the most enchanting 'Garden Galleries' in the South. Peter's Barn shows work by known, established and up and coming artists. Set in a wild wooded water garden, this little gallery makes full use of the beautiful garden space giving artists the opportunity to exhibit their work in an outside environment.

The varied exhibitions change monthly.

Directions: From the A272, 3 miles east of Midhurst and 3 miles west of Petworth, take the road opposite the halfway Bridge Inn and follow the brown gallery signs.

Mo Jupp

"...Jupp is an Artist; not simply definable as a sculptor or ceramicist but like Giacometti, an artist who makes art, whether two dimensional reliefs, sculptures or drawings. a consummate professional and compassionate worker, he is not afraid to acknowledge his debt to those he admires ."

Piers Ottey

Norman Holland

Nicholas Homoky

Line and form are my chief concerns. I am interested in painting sculpture and the world of ceramics as well as folk art and design. My work attempts to close the gap between the innocence of Alfred Wallis and the purity of Ben Nicholson. I am still on the look out for their true equivalents in clay.

Norman Holland

Colin Pearson

"Colin Pearson is widely credited for the lead he has given to studio ceramics in Europe in both his work and his teaching. He is a potter who has shown where an informed and sustained meditation on form can lead to: a body of work that converses across cultures and across time"

Edmund de Waal

Annabel Munn

Using eclectic reference from the zoomorphic to the engineered, Annabel Munn combines the ideas or images to create pieces with a strength of form and line that play with extremes of scale and balance.

Jacqui Ramrayka

Jacqui trained at Harrow College, University of Westminster, gaining a BA(Hons) in Ceramics. Before embarking on this course, she travelled extensively around the Caribbean and Asia. She currently works from her studio, a converted railway arch in the East End of London. From here she produces a range of high fired, thrown porcelain and stoneware vessels, working in series and making one-off pieces. Her work is multi-glazed and multi-fired. By building up layers of oxides and glazes she can achieve a richly textured and vibrantly coloured surface. The pieces are sometimes fired up to three times, each time; layering more oxides or glazes, to attain the desired effect. Jacqui's work has appeared in a number of publications, including Marie Claire and Inspirations for Your Home. She is a professional member of CPA.

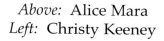

Above: Alice Mara
Left: Christy Keeney

Walter Keeler

Pruden & Smith

Silversmiths & Goldsmiths, 2 South Street, Ditchling, East Sussex BN6 8UQ. Tel: 01273 846338
Fax: 01273 846684 Email: info@silversmiths.co.uk Website: www.silversmiths.co.uk
Open Tuesday - Saturday 10am - 5pm

Anton Pruden (above) and Rebecca Smith (right) set up their silversmithing workshop in Ditchling in 1989. Lying in the heart of Sussex, this picturesque village is famous for its crafts. Anton's grandfather Dunstan Pruden was the silversmith in the Guild of St. Joseph and St. Dominic founded by Eric Gill.

Using sound Arts and Crafts values as their starting point , Pruden and Smith quickly established a name for high quality, handmade contemporary silverware. Their full range of silverware and silver and gold jewellery is on show in their new gallery on Ditchling crossroads. This is complemented by the work of six guest jewellers and silversmiths, black and white works on paper and sculpture. Catalogue available.

The Red Gallery

17a Spittal Street, Marlow, Buckinghamshire SL7 3HJ. Telephone & Fax: 01628 483169
Email: micky@redgallery.co.uk Website: www.redgallery.co.uk

Open Monday & Saturday 10am - 6pm, Tuesday - Friday 10am - 5.30pm, Sundays or late by request
Closed for lunch 2 - 3pm

The Red Gallery is located in the pretty Buckinghamshire market town of Marlow on the River Thames. Since opening in 1998, we have had a warm welcome from our local community as well as visitors from further afield.

We are committed to an ongoing, ever-changing exhibition programme, which endeavours to charm, excite, humour and stimulate every visitor! There is a continual display of new work by our popular gallery artists, as well as inspiring newcomers and respected makers who are chosen for their dexterity, innovation and our passion for unexpected and whimsical characteristics.

With a wide range of media including bronze, ceramics, prints, glass, wood, textiles, paper mache and mirrors, the gallery also houses a broad array of refreshing contemporary jewellery from jewellers all over the UK.

Specialising in makers from the West Country, we display an eclectic range of craft and paintings from celebrated and collectable artists such as Paul Jackson, Norman Stewart Clarke, Tobias Trenwith, Judy Symons, Ponckle Clarke, Eleanor Newell and the Rudge family.

Accepting all major credit cards and offering an interest free instalment plan, we hope to make it as simple as it is appealing for our visitors to purchase a beautiful piece of art.

A visit to The Red Gallery in Marlow is a rare treat indeed! Or log on and take a peek at www.redgallery.co.uk

Also we have our new sister gallery in Oxfordshire: 54 North Street, Thame OX9 3BH

Donald Smith

Rachel Ricketts

Born and educated in Warwickshire, Rachel began her studies at Bourneville School of Art, Birmingham, before going on to take a degree at Norwich School of Art.

Since 1990 however, her studio and home has been in Dorset, where she produces sculpture which is largely inspired by animals. Horses and dogs are prominent subjects, though her full range extends from a long eared bat to a mountain gorilla!

Her work is either cast in small limited editions, in bronze or resin/bronze, or else one-off ceramic sculptures usually in stoneware.

Raku animals by Lawson Rudge Senior

Charlotte Hardy

My work is a celebration of familiar things, creating through small details. 'Less important' things matter most, seeming most real and inspiring the greatest affection. I draw collections of unassuming objects grouped together, developing the idea of lists and ingredients.

I am concerned with form, colour, line, pattern and space. I am driven by colour, by its emotional effect and the relationships between colours. I want the colour to feel so intense that you become absorbed in it.

It is a world of the imagination, where I enjoy playing with perspective and scale. I strive to capture a child's sheer wonder and delight with objects that appear ordinary and insignificant. I paint what is intimately rooted in our lives, with an urge to discover a simple, yet authentic world.

Debbie George

Debbie's work as a painter is primarily concerned with still life. The paintings are simple observations which explore the relationship between objects such as vessels, plants and flowers, and the space that they occupy.

These themes are explored through mixed media. Building up layers, this creates a richly textured surface from which elements of the original images emerge.

There is a history evident in the way they are made, layer upon layer, unearthing signs of how they came to be, like peeling back layers of wallpaper through the ages.

The Red Gallery

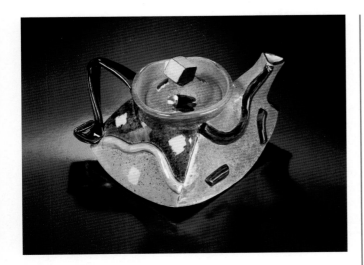

Paul Jackson

The slow evolution of my work, around a number of themes, is based on revisiting ideas and on experimentation. Energy, vitality, humour are all guides but not the whole. Passions for water colour, life drawing and sculpture all play their part.

Although my work is initiated on the potter's wheel, the pieces travel through a long journey with many alterations. Some pieces gain great size; up to 4'.

To set form against decoration requires many painful decisions if that combination is to compliment both. It is an endless quest, a compelling challenge.

Latham & Neve

Design duo Anna Latham & Helen Neve studied jewellery together over ten years ago at Kent Institute of Art and Design.

"Our jewellery is bold and sculptural, drawing inspiration from shapes, form and textures found in the natural world which are reworked in contemporary forms. We believe that this approach together with an adherence to high standards of craftsmanship produces quality British jewellery with a unique appeal. We focus on small production runs using hand-made wax models which are then cast predominantly in silver and finished by hand. Working in this manner enables us to achieve form and texture that is not always possible in flat sheet metal. We often work to commission in either silver or gold."

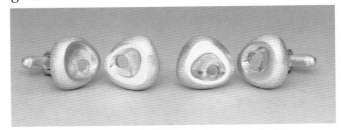

Julie Bharucha

My work is mostly figurative and reflects the complex and contradictory aspects of human emotion, which exist within our diverse human forms.

The tall-elongated figures that I am making have their roots in the two years that I spent as a V.S.O. in Africa with unforgettable echoes of the Fulani people of South Mali.

These figures have developed now to hold a rich tapestry of decoration. These worlds within worlds fuse together allowing their dream-like quality to draw the viewer into patterns and scenes as they wind around the work returning to the stance and expression of the figure.

There are all sorts of games at work here, multi-layered colours, textures, scales and cultures. There is never just one story.

Stanley Dove

I love the touch and feel and the permanence of bronze. It was only after I had witnessed the pouring of molten bronze at the foundry that I fully appreciated the power and drama involved. There is the blasting roar of the furnace using massive amounts of energy to melt the bronze at 1,200 °C. The delicate care with which the silver clad founders move the heavy crucible of glowing white hot metal and the pouring of the molten bronze into waiting moulds through funnel shaped apertures that connect to runners and finally glow into the often complex shape determined by the artist. I believe this to be a serious act of creation that seems to add a spiritual quality to that form created by the sculptor.

Angela Cork

The Red Gallery

Linda Macdonald

Linda Macdonald graduated from the Glasgow School of Art in 1996 and started her business of making handmade, designer, silver and gold jewellery a year later. Her aim of making quality, contemporary jewellery at competitive prices helped achieve her goal of supplying a growing number of galleries and shops including a large department store chain throughout Britain.

Linda uses simplistic lines and contrasting metals when designing her jewellery, which ranges from stud earrings to tiaras. The 'Crown' range featured is one of eight styles made by LMDJ, she also has a 'Heart', 'Flower', 'Daisy', 'Square', 'Dot', 'Millennium' and 'Swirl' range.

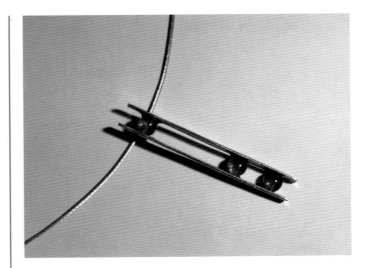

Christine Stainer

I have been fascinated and excited by jewellery ever since I can remember and after completing my degree in Leicester, I decided to specialise in gem-set jewellery. I am interested in developing new ways of setting stones. Settings are important because they help to present the beauty of the stone, they show the way that the stone has been cut and the colour and the transparency of the stone.

I like to use contrast in the colour and the texture of metal, and incorporate brightly coloured stones. I hope I am creating small pieces of art that are personal and are enjoyed by the wearer.

Catherine Williams

Catherine graduated in 1997 from the University of the West of England, where she received the Rebecca Smith Award for Printmaking.

The inspiration for Catherine's work comes from the textural qualities of landscape, particularly the rugged Cornish coastline and the effect that the sea has on the landscape. Colour and light also play an important part in achieving a sense of place.

The prints are usually made by using the etching or carborundum processes - both of these processes lend themselves well to the subject matter.

Carborundum, which is an intaglio process like etching, except instead of eating into the surface of the plate, the plate is built upon using a mixture of acrylic paste and carborundum grit thus making a very hard surface, giving a very strong embossed quality.

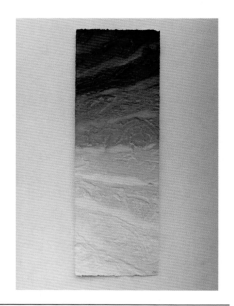

Annie Appleyard

With a degree in Fine Art (painting) Annie has explored various media. She has most recently become captivated by the magical art of enamelling - fusing glass to metal in a kiln.

Through working intuitively, Annie finds her personal experience and development is reflected in, and is indeed part of her work. Themes explored in the pieces encompass the ideas of balance, change, contrasts and opposites.

Whilst working, she allows the materials and processes themselves to suggest the next stage for an item of jewellery. Recent pieces combine the use of cloisonne and champleve techniques with gold foils and textured metal beneath the enamel.

As a contrast to this meticulous art, Annie enjoys the immediacy of stringing bead necklaces, as well as the freedom of working on larger enamel wall panels.

The Red Gallery

Gabriella Corbani

Inspired by mathematical laws, I attempt to find balance and rhythm in metal, constantly seeking the perfect proportions for each piece. I articulate my ideas through geometric shapes and decorative detail through simple design.

I predominately work in wires of different sections and thickness. Pierced lines cut into the metal and oxidised black achieve the decoration in silver pieces. I work in gold and platinum to commission, as well as small scale silverware. Spoons and cutlery are particular favourites of mine.

I very rarely sketch as a precursor to design, preferring to work directly with the wire or models in creating new ideas and jewellery collections.

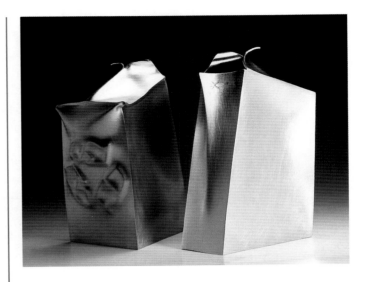

Peter Musson

Born in 1977, Peter completed his BA (Hons) Three Dimensional Design Degree at Manchester Metropolitan University in 1999.

"Within my design I use the language of mass production but at the same time I aim to give my objects a more human quality through imparting individual touches upon them. I use industrial methods of production yet distort the perfect form to give each object an individuality. I achieve this by using craftsmanship ideals which I believe create an emotional connection to the user through the object."

Peter is currently undertaking an MA Degree in Goldsmithing, Silversmithing and Metalwork and Jewellery at The Royal College of Art, London where he is now based.

The Sussex Guild Shop ♿

Bentley Wildfowl and Motor Museum, Halland, Near Lewes, East Sussex BN8 5AF.
Telephone: 01825 840573 Fax: 01825 841322 Email: info@thesussexguild.co.uk
Website: www.thesussexguild.co.uk

Open daily from mid-March - end October 10.30am - 4.30pm,
Weekends only in November, February and March 10.30am - 4pm

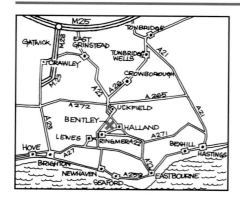

'Mary Fraser' St. Leonards

The Sussex Guild shop is housed in the entrance building to the Museum which is owned and run by East Sussex County Council. The twenty three acre parkland setting with formal gardens and woodland trails provides a good background for the work of some twenty craftspeople, all of whom are members of the Sussex Guild.

Although the shop is staffed by Bentley, policy and display decisions are made by the Guild committee working with the Estate manager. Visitors will find a fascinating variety of craftwork on sale including, animal sculptures, ceramics, jewellery, metalwork, framed etchings, batiks and embroidery, quilts, cushions and wearable textiles.
Exhibitors details, alongside photographs of work not on show are supplied in a visitor information book, enabling and encouraging direct contact between potential clients and makers considering a commission.
Entry to the shop is free.

The Sussex Guild Shop

Frances Westwood

Goddesses and Maidens,
Jesters and Fools,
Angels and Daemons,
Villains and Loons;

Peacocks and Turkeys,
Gods and Poltroons,
Harpists and Fiddlers
And Knives, Forks and Spoons.

I love to sew and free-machine embroidery is my favourite technique. Using rich fabrics and a wide range of exciting threads, sometimes incorporating beads, bibelots and metal foils, I make garments, hangings and accessories for people with imagination and élan.

Wendy Dolan

My stitched textile designs are created by building up richly textured surfaces. Fabrics are pieced and patched in layers and colour is applied by painting and printing, using light fast pigment dyes. Surface texture is then built up and developed by applying more fabrics and yarns and embellishing with machine and hand stitchery. Landscapes and natural forms, inspired by the Sussex Downs, are a regular source of inspiration and I have developed themes based on fish, ancient relics and Mediterranean environments.

Commissioned works include two embroidered stage curtains for two Royal Caribbean cruise liners - Legend of the Seas and Grandeur of the Seas, each measuring 13 x 4.5metres and 'Aspiring Arches', a large stitched Millennium wallhanging for Ashridge in Hertfordshire, measuring 8.2 metres x 3.4 metres.

Matthew Bayman

I became interested in pottery twenty years ago and it's been my occupation for the last fifteen years. As well as making pots I also teach and my students soon find out what a difficult material clay is and what demands it places on the user!

Pottery is a very technical craft. Most of my time as a self-taught potter has been spent trying to understand the materials and processes involved: How to design and make clays and glazes; how to build and fire kilns; and how, amid a wealth of possibilities, to make the pots themselves.

Now I feel that I've started making pots in a more personal and creative way, with less emphasis on 'how' and much more focus on the spirit of the work itself.

Above: Caroline & Stephen Atkinson-Jones

Left: Louise Bell

Right: Brian Denyer

The Sussex Guild Shop

Temptations

4 - 7 Old Kings Head, Dorking, Surrey RH4 1AR. Telephone: 01306 889355
Open 9.30am - 5.30pm (Closed Sundays)

'Temptations' is set in one of Surrey's prettiest courtyards, with other galleries, where people can enjoy home made refreshments, eating outside in the summer. Old Kings Head Court is next to Dorking's West Street with its wealth of Antique Shops. Ample parking nearby.

Visitors to the galleries find that we stock a wide variety of colourful British ceramics, wood, original paintings, jewellery, glass and some of the best hand made cards available. Everything is personally chosen from selected craftsmen, by the owner, Pauline Watson, echoing the maxim 'only the best is good enough'. Our speciality is definitely

studio glass, with the largest selection to be seen in Southern England, including over thirty established glass blowers, while still encouraging the most talented of new designers.

We hold exhibitions throughout the year culminating in the 'Christmas Exhibition', which always includes a fine display of crafts, fresh to the gallery.

0%

White Gallery

86/87 Western Road, Hove, Brighton BN3 1JB. Telephone: 01273 774870 Fax: 01273 748475
Email: artists@whitegallery.co.uk Website: www.whitegallery.co.uk
Open Tuesday - Saturday 10am - 6pm , Sunday & Bank Holidays 11am - 4pm

Launched by two brothers in early 1999, The White Gallery is the largest contemporary gallery in the area. Situated in the historic Brunswick Town area, the listed building was originally a Victorian haberdashers. Its large period rooms, with original details but otherwise entirely white, are a stunning setting for the art and craft that they display.

On three floors you can see jewellery, ceramics, glass, photographs, prints and paintings. We have solo and group shows as well as a constant supply of makers, combining international names with less established but outstanding young artists and designers.

The display is constantly changing so that even regular visitors find something new and for those who come to the gallery from as far away as London, the experience of discovering a Cork Street space by the seaside is a treat. In the short time that it has opened it has attracted a loyal following who have long been waiting for a gallery of this style in an otherwise culturally rich town.

The White Gallery is on the Western Road which is the main Brighton and Hove route, the Gallery can be found just east of Palmeira Square.

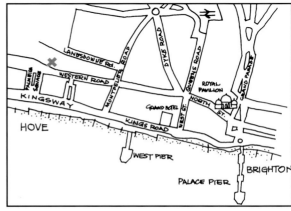

White Gallery

Disa Allsopp

Jane Muir

Chris Keenan

Belle Walker

Mikala Djorup

Some other Galleries in London and the South East

The Bank Gallery
73 High Street
Chobham
Surrey
GU24 8AF
Tel: 01276 857369
Email:
bankgallery@aol.com
Open
Tues - Sat 10am- 5pm

Lesley Craze Gallery, Craze Two & C2+
33 - 35a
Clerkenwell Green
London
EC1R ODU
Tel: 0207 608 0393
Fax: 0207 251 5655
Email: gallery@
lesleycraze.demon.co.uk
www.lesleycrazegallery.co
.uk
Open
Mon - Sat 10am -5.30pm

Rye Art Gallery
Easton Rooms
107, High Street, Rye
East Sussex TN31 7JE
Tel: 01797 223218/222433
Fax: 01797 225376
Open
Mon - Sun 10.30am - 5pm

Turning Heads
52 Meeting House Lane
Brighton
E.Sussex BN1 1HB
Tel: 01273 772645
Fax: 01273 777197
Email: enquiries
@turning-heads.net
www.turning-heads.net
Open
Mon - Sat 10am -5pm

The Workshop
164 High Street,
Lewes
E.Sussex BN7 1XU
Tel: 01273 474207
Open
Mon - Sat 9.30am -5pm

Eastern England

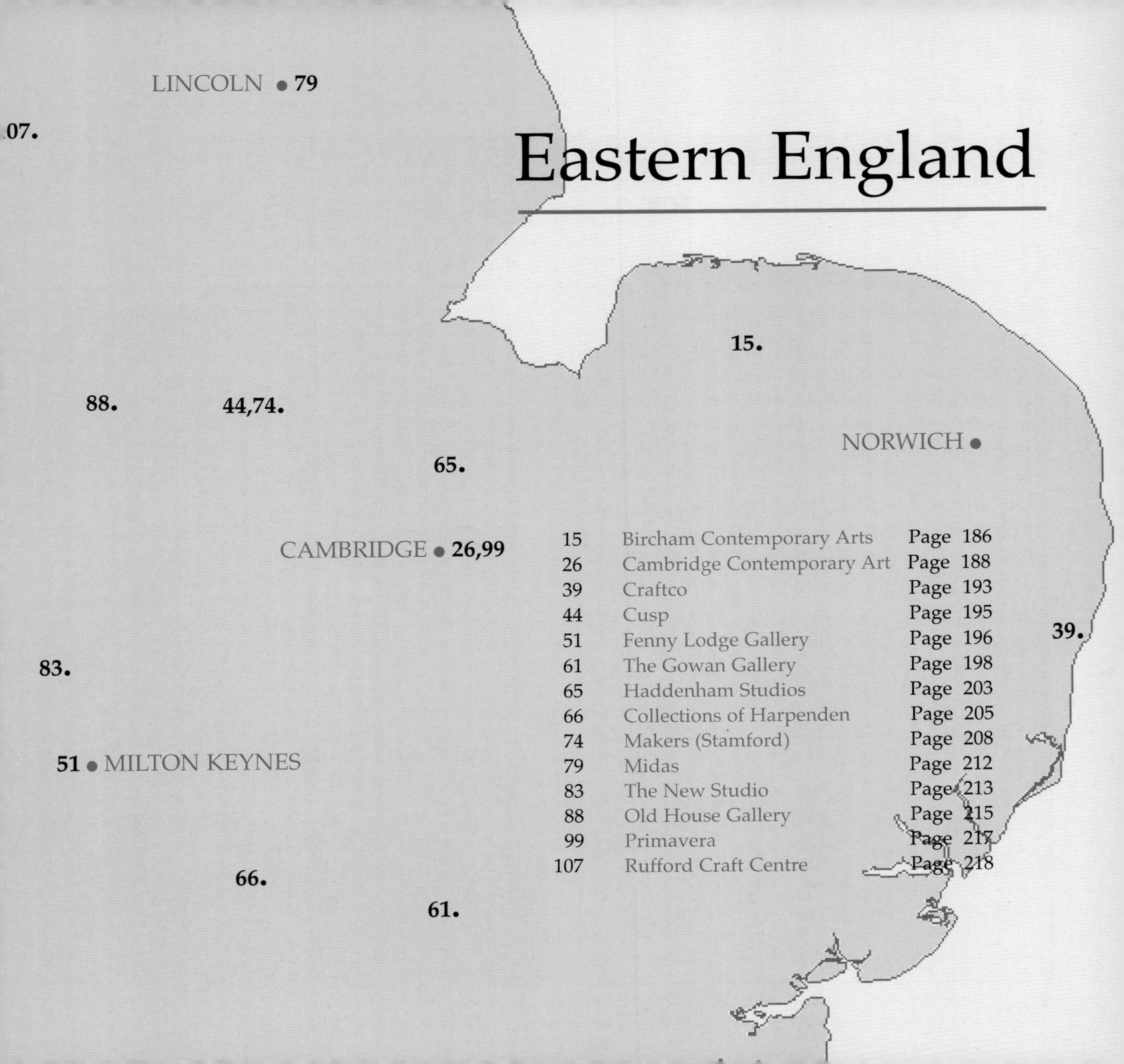

LINCOLN ● 79

07.

15.

88.   44,74.

65.

NORWICH ●

CAMBRIDGE ● 26,99

83.

51 ● MILTON KEYNES

66.

61.

39.

0% Bircham Contemporary Arts

14 Market Place, Holt, Norfolk NR25 6BW. Telephone: 01263 713312
Email: birchamgal@aol.com Website: www.bircham-arts.co.uk
Open Monday - Saturday 10am - 4pm

Having been established for over ten years, Bircham Contemporary Arts has developed a reputation as a leading independent gallery for contemporary fine art and craft, exhibiting the finest artists and crafts people from East Anglia and beyond.

The gallery is housed in a fine pink Georgian building in the historic town of Holt, being just four miles away from the north Norfolk coast, and combines both an exhibition area and shop in an open, spacious, airy and well lit space. The gallery presents a full annual programme of exhibitions, covering a wide range of contemporary art forms.

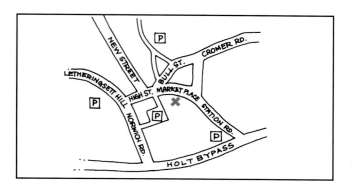

Bircham Contemporary Arts

Above: Vanessa Pooley

Top left: Lara Aldridge
Centre: Elaine Cox
Below left: Tony Foster

Below: Lucy Butterwick

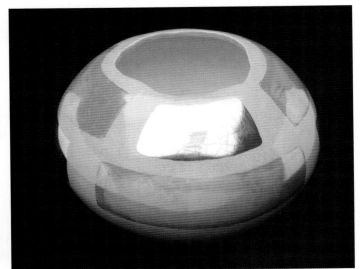

Cambridge Contemporary Art

6 Trinity Street, Cambridge CB2 1SU. Telephone: 01223 324222 Fax: 01223 315606
Email: cam.cont.art@dial.pipex.com Website: www.artcambridge.co.uk
Open Monday - Saturday 9am -5.30pm

0%

Cambridge Contemporary Art has an unrivalled reputation for the quality of its artists, the innovation of its shows and the range of its services to collectors - locally and internationally.

Our constantly changing exhibitions highlight paintings, sculpture, limited edition hand made prints, textiles, crafts and furniture, with work by acknowledged masters, established artists and exciting young talent yet to be discovered. Many of our exhibitions and artists have received favourable reviews in the national art press and interiors magazines.

The Gallery has assembled the most exciting breadth of work for sale to be found under one roof in East Anglia. Whether your interest is in figurative or abstract work, watercolour or

mixed media, ceramic or bronze, etching or screenprint and whatever your price range, we have something that will inspire you. We offer a wide range of services - including our Collecting Art Scheme, Corporate Art, Framing and Conservation, Gift Vouchers, Interest Free Credit - so make us your first port of call for any art enquiry. If you would like a

copy of our exhibition programme with information on the Gallery, please do not hesitate to contact us. Cambridge Contemporary Art is a Crafts Council Listed Gallery. *"Thank you for providing an excellent gallery - the imagination and sheer hard work that you obviously contribute is remarkable. Our favourite place in Cambridge".* (Customer comment)

188

Cambridge Contemporary Art

Alice Palser

Alice Palser was born in Kenya 1938 and came to England to study art at Hornsey College of Art and The Slade. She taught herself ceramics whilst teaching in Hertfordshire and set up her first workshop there in 1974, moving to Suffolk in 1983, where she now lives and works.

Alice's work constantly changes and develops. In recent years she has started having ceramic pieces cast in bronze and copper resin, which she then decorates. Her work is diverse and eclectic and draws on her imagination, which is fuelled by drawing nature, the human figure, doodles and studying the art and mythology of ancient civilisations. The long elongated figures for which she is best known are evoked by memories of the tall nomadic tribes people of East Africa.

Sarah Cox

I graduated from Central Saint Martins College of Art and Design in 1991. Two things had a great influence on me whilst on my degree course, firstly my tutors and then Kew Gardens and its delights. Having grown up in Northamptonshire, we were not exposed to such tropical delights! The plants were astounding, the fish fantastic and curious coral inhabitants were amazing. These influences quickly turned my second year work around from being figurative to what it is today, complete escapism. The pieces are the adventures of my creatures, i.e. Blue Bird on the Moon or Golden Fish Swimming Through the Kelp Beds. My themes range from aardvarks, elephants, blue birds, sea creatures and dogs. My pieces are hand built using coils and slabs, and sprayed with various Barium Glazes.

Jane Hollidge

Although starting out as a painter, Jane soon found her passion was in Ceramic Art. She began studying Ceramics in 1990, in Cambridge, where she has now lived for over thirty years and set up her own workshop in 1992.

Basically self taught, some of her inspirations came from living in the Far East for a while. She has a vivid imagination, and a great determination, which has helped her to overcome the difficulties of not having had technical background in Ceramics.

Her work is diverse, but always immediately recognised for its distinct style. Jane is a Selected Member of the East Anglian Potters Association, and she is exhibiting her work nationally, and also has her work in private collections worldwide.

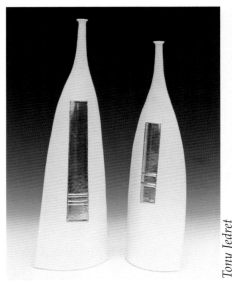

Tony Jedret

Paul Smith

I consider myself very fortunate to be a full-time gallery artist, living and working on the edge of the Peak District. The countryside around my home, and the Highlands of Scotland, provide much of the inspiration for my sculptures on the subject of animals and associated legends.

I prefer to work in a bold semi-abstract style, looking for a purity of form, gesture and colour. My creativity is influenced both by nature and a strong sense of geometry.

After my sculpture degree at Leicester, and several years as a commercial artist, I have found that the most fulfilling medium for my art is ceramics.

My work can be seen at major art fairs, galleries and ceramics festivals across Britain.

Cambridge Contemporary Art

David Carter

It all started as they say, with a poem written to enliven the cover page of my final year project. It ignited something in me the previous years of studying Biology had failed to do. After graduating, I experimented with various arts for a year, before becoming fired by iron in 1986, and setting up my first studio. I have since worked in various types of engineering workshops to support myself, and gain valuable skills and experience in manipulating metals, becoming proficient in everything from blacksmithing to CAD/CAM.

I like the robust nature of the material (handy when you are as clumsy as I am), and the variety of methods available, from ancient techniques to the latest technology. My latest work (not shown) uses laser cutting, producing delicate looking, but strong pieces.

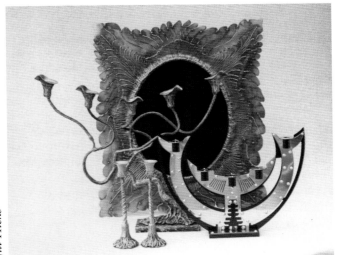

Jill Hicks

Photo: *A.V.Krumins*

Gunta Anita Krumins

Kiln fused glass, for Gunta Anita Krumins, is an exciting medium, capturing a very specific and clear luminescence in her individually crafted work. Her work is a fusion of ancient glass technology, married with modern metals and chemical formulas.

In her glass pieces there is an immediacy - a subtle, contemporary sense of the instant. Yet the work also allows the freedom to return and reflect on the changes within. Her work is characterised by a powerful dialectic: as if the pieces of glass were petrified in a continual state of flux.

Gunta Anita Krumins has developed her work through small scale wall hung framed pieces and craft work, to which she is beginning to add a new body of larger scale architectural work and installations.

Eoghan Bridge

Sculpture has a great history stretching back maybe thirty thousand years from prehistoric man through to the great civilisations of Egypt and Greece to name but two. It is a unique language offering both a visual and tactile experience often not translatable into words. There is something earthy about the process of making sculpture using basic materials like clay, stone, wood and plaster - all of which have been used for thousands of years.

I choose to make sculpture because I find it the most rewarding way of expressing my feelings and thoughts about life; a way of celebrating all that is thrown at us. I strive to create timeless work that's a touch innovative and thought provoking.

My work is available in bronze and ceramic editions and occasionally unique resin pieces.

Rosalind Rosenblatt

Rosalind came to ceramics later in life with a determination to master the technique of throwing on the wheel. She completed a Bachelor of Design degree in her early fifties which introduced her to the craft.

Her original inspiration came from the planets Saturn and Venus with their ringed formations. Her ceramics manage to be beautiful and fragile, yet at the same time keep a very organic feel, reflect the rich, deep colours of the planets.

After the initial wheel throwing, the vessels evolve through the fine tuning process. The coloured top and inside are glazed, while the smooth bodied earthstone clay (whose glazed ingredients are imported from America) is left unglazed to achieve the required finish. Each piece is unique, with its own individuality, shape and form.

Craftco

40A High Street, Southwold, Suffolk IP18 6AE. Telephone: 01502 723211
Open each day 10am - 5pm, Sunday 2 - 4pm (Closed Wednesday)

Ten Suffolk crafts people got together in 1987 as the Great Eastern Craft Co-Operative Shop, a much needed outlet for the fine local contemporary crafts.

Having opened in shared rented premises, selling their own work and that of an ever increasing number of other East Anglian makers, they moved in 1993, turning a run-down end-of-terrace house into a vibrant new gallery/shop. As you enter the charming seaside town of Southwold, look out for us on the left at the beginning of the High Street.

Long running displays are enlivened throughout the year by special mini-exhibitions spotlighting member's and guests' work.

Members include:
Julie Carpenter, Ron and Moss Fuller, Jacky Linney, Mary and Peter Lister, Sophie Milburn, Jenny Nutbeem, Alice Palser and Mark Titchiner.

Craftco

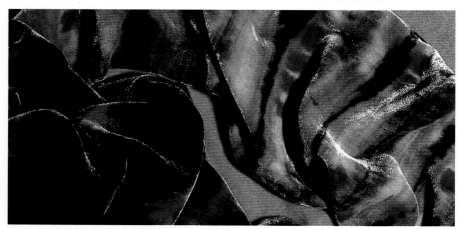

Left Jenny Nutbeem

Bottom left (Painted Tableloth) Jacky Linney

Centre Plate Mark Titchiner

Centre (Figure) Alice Palser

Below Sophie Milburn & Joey Scholfield

Cusp Gallery

Burghley House, Stamford, Lincolnshire PE9 3JY. Telephone: 01780 481040
Open annually from 1st April - 27th October
Wednesday - Sunday and Bank Holiday Mondays 12 - 5pm
Burghley Sculpture Garden is open daily 11am - 4pm
Please contact the gallery for Christmas opening times

The Cusp Gallery is set within the beautiful architecture and gardens of this historic house close to the visitors' entrance, above the gift shop.

The aim of the gallery is to showcase the best contemporary Art and Craft, with work by established and emerging artists and makers. We believe that art should be something that people want to live with and hope to break down some of the barriers between 'fine art' and 'craft' by exploring the cross over between these too often separate categories, whilst at the same time showing the best examples of each genre.

Burghley House is ninety miles north of London, close to the A1, one mile east of Stamford on the B1443 and is clearly signposted from all major routes.

Fenny Lodge Gallery

76 Simpson Road, Fenny Stratford, Bletchley, Milton Keynes, Buckinghamshire MK1 1BA.
Telephone: 01908 639494 Fax: 01908 648431 Email: sophie@fennylodge.demon.co.uk
Website: www.fennylodge.co.uk
*Open Monday -Friday 9am - 5pm, Saturday 9am - 4pm, late night opening
till 7pm on the last Friday of every month*

"Worth a special trip", said Homes & Gardens. We agree. On the banks of the Grand Union Canal, this 18th century cottage provides a contrasting backdrop to a large range of high quality, innovative work from today's best designers.

With major exhibitions in spring and winter, and one-off exhibitions throughout the year, the gallery is a reliable source of work by highly sought-after, well-known designers and up-and-coming artists. It's the perfect place to buy pieces for everyday use or to build up a collection – whatever your style or budget.

Come to us for our imaginative range of paintings, limited edition prints, clocks, mirrors, ceramics, glass and wood objects, and a dazzling array of

jewellery – plus bronze, stone or clay sculptures, garden pots and seats, decorative side tables and carvings.
Commissions can be arranged.

Pots, dishes and bowls can be decorated with words to commemorate a special occasion. Why not make that special trip?

196

Fenny Lodge Gallery

Peter Hayes

After travelling and working in Africa, India, Japan and Korea, Peter arrived back in England in 1982. Since then he has developed his ideas using many of the techniques and methods learnt on his travels.

By building up layers of textured clay combined with burnishing and polishing of surfaces, he tries to achieve opposites of rough and smooth. For the last two years he has been working on large scale ceramic forms which he has placed in the landscape. His main aim is that the work should not compete with nature but evolve within the environment. With this in mind he has introduced other minerals into the 'Raku' surface such as iron and copper. With the element of time and erosion the individual piece takes on its own developing surface.

Tony Laverick Ceramic vase

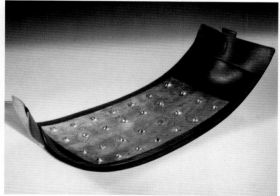

Joy Bosworth
Raku platter

Sheila Holness
9ct gold ring with ruby & diamonds

*The Gowan Gallery ♿

3 Bell Street, Sawbridgeworth, Hertfordshire, CM21 9AR. Telephone: 01279 600004
Fax: 01279 832494 Email: joanne@gowan-gallery.co.uk Website: www.gowan-gallery.co.uk
Open Monday - Saturday 10am - 5pm (Closed Bank Holidays & one week Christmas-New Year)

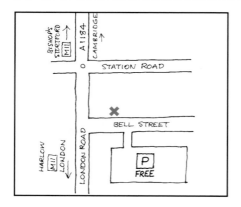

The Gowan Gallery was opened in 1988 by Joanne Gowan, following a decision to combine her jewellery workshop with a retail space and a wish to promote other contemporary craftwork.

The eighteenth century shop, situated in the picturesque town of Sawbridgeworth on the Herts/Essex border, has a long tradition as a jewellers. It was carefully refurbished in 2000 to give a stylish modern interior whilst retaining the old display cabinets and original features.

The Gallery now specialises in contemporary jewellery and glassware by British makers, but also stocks designer pieces in ceramics, wood and metalwork. There is a continually changing display of beautiful and unusual quality pieces, both one-off and limited production items. An artist information card is provided with every sale and commissions with any makers can easily be arranged.

The Gallery is a member of the Independent Craft Galleries Association and is recognised under the National Register of Craft Galleries.

Joanne Gowan

Joanne's jewellery workshop adjoins the Gallery, where she designs and makes fine precious jewellery alongside gallery manager and jeweller Lorraine Burden. Many pieces are one-off designs and individual commissions such as wedding and engagement rings can be designed in consultation with the customer.

18 carat gold and Platinum pieces are made by hand using a variety of techniques including repoussé and forging. Curved, twisted, organic shapes are produced in her own particular style and often incorporate faceted gemstones. A wide range of stones can be obtained on approval to suit each clients' requirements. Joanne also makes a distinctive range of jewellery in silver, with 18 carat yellow gold details.

Joanne started her business in 1986 and exhibits her work at a few selected venues including at the prestigious Goldsmith's Fair.

Diana Porter

Diana Porter's contemporary jewellery is chunky and androgynous and has an intrinsic integrity in both design and finish. Her creative inspiration comes from personal and political belief, often expressed through words which form a major feature of her work. Often, words are split across two or three pieces so that apparently indecipherable marks make sense only when pieces are joined together, giving Diana's work an intriguing additional dimension. She is best known for her acid etched pieces in matt silver with 22ct gold detail but is increasingly working in white and yellow gold and platinum, especially for her unique partnership rings. The most recent additions to her collection contrast textured silver with fine gold moving pieces (see picture).

Diana has a wide range of designs, particularly rings, which are complemented by bangles, brooches or neckpieces. Her career moved from teaching to arts administration, to University in 1993 for a BA Hons in jewellery and silversmithing. Diana also designs and makes one-off pieces to commission and was awarded 'Designer of the Year' 1999, at the UK Jewellery Awards.

Catherine Hills

Catherine Hills is at the forefront of British jewellery design. Having left the Royal College of Art in 1993 with a Masters Degree, she received a setting up grant from the Crafts Council. Her work is designed and made from her central London studio in Clerkenwell workshops.

Her production range, mainly in silver, is for women and men, she also works to commission and makes large one-off pieces in silver and gold. The jewellery is inspired by natural forms and is characterised by the contrasting use of different metal colours, finishes and interchangeable components.

She is the winner of the British Association Jewellery award and is featured in the recently published 'Jewellery Source Book' and 'The Ring'.

Commissions include cufflinks for His Royal Highness the Prince of Wales and cufflinks for No 10 Downing Street, London.

Catherine sells her work in over sixty galleries and shops, in the UK and abroad, including Selfridges, Contemporary Applied Arts, the Crafts Council shop at the V & A Museum, Lesley Craze, Eton Applied Arts, Jon Dibben Jewellery and Design Yard. Buyers include Dawn French, Wayne Sleep, Gillian Anderson and Ned Sherrin.

LoCo Glass

LoCo Glass have a fresh and innovative approach to glassmaking; whether it be one-off commissioned pieces, interior accessories or the production of functional ware. The aim of the partnership, formed by Colin Hawkins and Louise Edwards in 1998, is to produce work that is forward thinking, exciting objects for the modern interior with an emphasis on creative designs and high quality craftsmanship. Each of their original designs is hand blown without the use of moulds and is made in their characteristic style using both modern and traditional techniques.

Lesley Strickland

Lesley is a British jeweller specialising in the use of cellulose acetate combined with sterling silver. Her passion for designing and making jewellery started in 1976 at The City Literary Institute, London. Since then she has continued to develop her personal style.

Lesley's inspiration comes from natural forms although her latest work has been influenced by sculpture of the 1950's. The final finish of her work is vitally important to her, as she wants the wearer to have a very tactile relationship with each piece. The methods used are traditional jewellery techniques with hand thermo-forming.

Her work can be seen in many leading galleries in the UK and abroad. She has exhibited at the Chelsea Crafts fair for the past seven years and will do so again this year.

Iestyn Davies

One of my main styles, revolves around my preoccupation with snipping and cutting gathers of molten glass straight from the furnace onto blown forms :

'drawing' a three dimensional form with a singular material that can only be manipulated for a few seconds before it sets.

The main form is blown and allowed to cool to around 500 ^{0} C .The body is gathered, rolled onto gold and silver leaf, shaped, then cut onto the blown form. The arms and legs are then added in a specific order and shaped with just a knife, wet newspaper, and a pair of shears .

The animal imagary chosen has to be sympathetic to the material. Frogs, octopi and gecko forms all have a natural empathy with the inherant 'sticky' nature of molten glass.

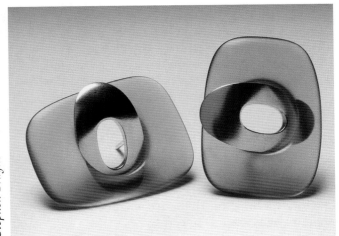

Stephen Brayne

Rachel Gogerly

Rachel Gogerly is a Designer Maker of contemporary silver and enamel jewellery, based in Solihull. Simplicity of design and the clarity of transparent enamel define her work.

Ideas come from a range of sources, often from the natural world. Some pieces are completely handmade others may be cast or stamped. The enamel techniques of champleve and basse taille are used which involve engraving recesses and patterns into the surface of the metal before applying the enamel.

Rachel trained at Middlesex Polytechnic and received a BA (Hons) in Jewellery Design in 1986. Commissions include Libertys of London and the Lord Mayor of York and Rachel has also won several business and craft awards. Her work has been shown in many exhibitions and she is a regular exhibitor at Goldsmiths' Fair, London.

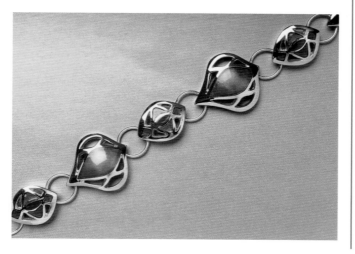

Siddy Langley

Working with molten glass gathered from the furnace and precious metals such as gold, silver and tin, the individual pieces are fashioned by hand. This free blowing ensures that each signed and dated piece is quite unique. The decoration, applied before the glass is blown, grows and evolves with the piece to form delicate and intricate patterns.

I get inspiration from travel. Whether it is a Mexican sunset, Islamic architecture in Marrakech or the Ecuadorian jungle, I can always be sure that a trip abroad will fuel a new design.

The making of glass combines all the elements - earth, wind, fire and water and as such seems a wholly natural process. I sometimes feel I am no more than the catalyst bringing all these elements together for their own mysterious purpose.

Haddenham Studios & Gallery

20 High Street, Haddenham, Ely, Cambridgeshire, CB6 3XA. Telephone: 01353 749188
Fax: 01353 740688

Open Monday - Friday 10am - 5pm, closed 1 - 2, weekends 10am - 5pm during exhibitions

Haddenham Studios and Gallery is an innovative and creative art gallery, with studios for artists and an ethnic gallery.

The gallery runs a programme of changing exhibitions and workshops for children and adults, offering opportunities to work alongside professional artists.

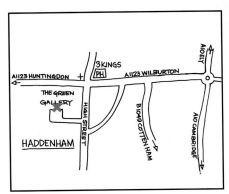

A wide range of contemporary arts and crafts from regionally and nationally known artists and craftspeople is shown. Paintings, prints, textiles, ceramics, sculpture, wood, metal, glass and jewellery are represented in exhibitions during the year. The Gallery particularly encourages work from emerging artists.

Please telephone the gallery for details of exhibitions and workshops.

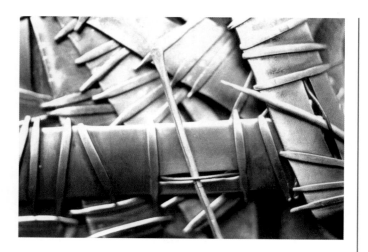

Lisa le Brocq

I use traditional jewellery-making techniques, such as Repousse, rolling, texturing and etching. My jewellery designs are inspired by modern art and architecture and feature strong contrasts between soft, rounded and organic forms and hard rectangular, asymetrical lines.

To create these effects, I use texture and various polishing techniques. I combine different materials such as gold, copper, brass, stainless steel wire and rubber, for contrast and durability. I produce a range of jewellery including earrings, brooches, pendants, bracelets and rings.

I was selected by the Society of Designer Craftsmen as a new licentiate for the Designer Crafts 2001 Exhibition. I was awarded a distinction for my work, which is currently on display in galleries in Brighton, Wales, London and Jersey, as well as at Haddenham.

Naomi Matthews

My work is inspired by my strong belief in respect of the environment and how we either use or abuse it. This has been influenced by my rural upbringing.

Natural shapes and forms have always interested me as well as animal behaviour. Poetry and sayings have also inspired me giving me another perspective through which to view animals. 'Fat cat' referring to wealthy people made me look at cats in a new way and produce cat forms 'rich in fish'.

I try to depict animals that do not display any sentiment, but affect the observer's senses and emotions in various ways. My pieces are slab built around newspaper using various clays including paper clay. I use terra sigallata slip and smoke fire them to achieve the surface colours.

204   *Haddenham Gallery*

0% Collections of Harpenden &

The Leys, 38 High Street, Harpenden, Herts, AL5 2SX. Telephone & Fax: 01582 620015
Email: prcollections@aol.com
Open Tuesday - Saturday 10am - 5pm

Situated in the High Street of this thriving town, and just five miles from historic St Albans, Collections has been open for business since November 1999, and has already been selected for quality by the Crafts Council.

In the short time since its opening, Collections has gained a reputation for high quality, innovative and desirable arts and crafts; something which is totally new but has been greatly welcomed in this part of Hertfordshire. Customer response has been delightful and very positive.

Everything is personally chosen by the owner, who is constantly seeking out new and different work. Her aim is to provide customers with a constantly changing display, whilst always maintaining a very high standard. Ceramics, jewellery and glass form the hub of the Gallery, but metals, wood and textiles are also featured. Work is by both recognised and up-and-coming British artists from all around the country.

Caroline Sibun

Caroline Sibun M.A. (R.C.A.) is a jeweller working in both silver and gold, precious and non-precious stones. Using a combination of techniques including casting, fly pressing and fabrication, Caroline creates a range of handmade jewellery with a very individual flavour, using subtle texture and finishes to give a soft and sensuous surface to the metal. Her work includes a strong reference to the natural world.

Caroline combines limited batch produced jewellery, hand finished to a high quality, with exclusive one off pieces, for example silver brushes, paint boxes, sunglasses and hats. She also works to commission, particularly wedding jewellery, engagement and wedding rings, tiaras and headresses.

Sue Jarman

Sue Jarman uses the landscape in various forms for her inspiration. Her work includes wallhangings, banners, fabric stretched frames, drawings and paintings as well as one off interior and fashion accessories.

The work, predominant in wool and silk, uses muted colours and abstract marks to create mood and essence, and emphasis is placed on line, colour, surface texture, composition and contrasts in scale.

Hand painting, silk screen printing, mono-printing, machine and hand stitching are layered to create richness and depth in the final fabrics.

Sue develops the work from her own initial concept or client brief, through to the finished pieces and their installation where appropriate. The work is both large and small scale, and suitable for private and public spaces.

Angela Farquharson

After initially studying fashion at college, Angela pursued a variety of careers before returning back to art, gaining a first class honours degree in ceramics at Wolverhampton University. Her work revolves around the exploration of the female form and the identity of the ideal woman. Looking at the sensuality and inherent beauty of the female form, drawing influence from the catwalk, classical sculpture and more recently contemporary dance.

Angela uses a variety of ceramic techniques and hand finishes, but specialises in slip casting, using this process to enhance the delicate qualities of the sculptural forms. Smoked surfaces are used as a contrast to the purity of porcelain. Angela has recently introduced new materials to her work including bronze and aluminium.

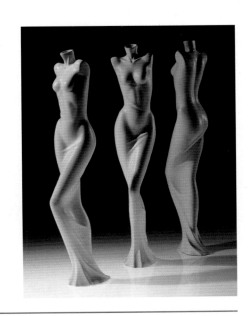

Norman Young

Rob Sollis

Rob Sollis trained as a Production Thrower at Dartington Pottery training workshops in Devon from 1984 - 1988. Prior to establishing his own workshop in Littlehampton, near Totnes, Devon in 1990, Rob worked extensively as a Repetition Thrower in Norway.

Rob's work remains hand thrown, burnished and glazed finished; obtained through the Raku process.

Makers

43 St. Pauls Street, Stamford, Lincolnshire, PE9 2BH. Telephone: 01780 762281
Email: illsley@makers43.freeserve.co.uk
Open Monday - Saturday 10am - 5pm

Situated in the fine stone Georgian town of Stamford the gallery was established in 1987 and moved to its present more central location in 1998. Makers specialises in Contemporary Craft from regional and nationally known craftsmen and women and shows a wide range of studio ceramics, wood, glass, jewellery and hand painted silks.

The owners Will and Chris Illsley both supply the gallery with their own work. Will produces a range of high fired stoneware pottery and Chris hand painted silk scarves. Makers is situated in the town centre just a few yards from the main pedestrian precinct.

Will Illsley

All my current work is reduction fired stoneware, most of it domestic ware - creating something for use has always been important to me. I used to saltglaze but had to give this up with the move to the more urban surroundings of Stamford over ten years ago - however, some recent developments, on the pots illustrated, have seen a return to using the shino and green ash glazes which were originally used for saltglazing. Inspiration comes from a wide range of sources, too numerous to mention, and ultimately the finished product must speak for itself - after all they are only pots - if they can, in their use, impart some of the enjoyment that I have had in their making, then they have gone some way towards fulfilling their purpose.

Chris Illsley

Chris Illsley produces a range of hand painted scarves on a variety of silks. Beautiful swirls of vibrant colour on sheer chiffons and georgettes, shiny pongees, fluid crepe de chines and textured devore silk and viscose. One-off designs for scarves and pictures are produced using the gutta technique. The silk is stretched on frames and painted - often with several layers of dye. When the silk has dried it is steamed to fix the colour and then washed thoroughly to remove any excess dye. Chris trained as a textile designer at Leicester Polytechnic and taught textiles and art for ten years before setting up her own business. She now lives and works in Stamford and shares the running of MAKERS gallery with her husband.

Carlos Versluys

For inspiration I am indebted to the times I have spent in the arid, bleached landscapes of Africa, Aisa and the Mediterranean. Some of the simplicity of that parched beauty has, I hope, trickled into what I make. I approach my work intuitively, and sometimes accidents reveal new creative directions.

I carve directly into the wet clay at the wheel using simple handmade tools. These forms are further manipulated or stretched, until their edges begin to tear. I am interested in texture that is integral to the vessel, and use layers of dry ash glaze to accentuate this. I produce individual, related forms. My work is reduction fired to 1300°C. I have exhibited both in the UK and abroad. I currently have my studio at home on the Lincolnshire/Cambridgeshire border.

Rob Bibby

I produce a range of hand made pottery designed to be useful as well as bright and colourful. I work with a mixture of terracotta and stoneware clays fired to 1100°C producing a durable pottery, when covered with a tin glaze. This is a modern development of traditional Maiolica.

All items are made on the wheel either hand thrown, or as with the plates, on a machine called a jigger and jolley. My pots are decorated with lively colours painted on using brushes and shaped sponges which I make myself.

I try to produce pots which are entertaining and enhancing to their environment but which people can afford to buy to use.

Makers

Rosemarie Cooke

Rosemarie graduated from Reading University in 1966 with a biological degree. She attended various evening and day classes in ceramics and art eventually setting up a workshop at home in Cambridgeshire in 1980. Animals, birds and figures are individually hand built in a variety of stoneware clays. They are biscuit-fired then glazed thinly or finished with various stains and oxides before firing to 1260°C in an electric kiln.

Rosemarie enjoys the challenge of manipulating the clay into the desired form, be it a dodo standing precariously on two legs or a large squat toad firmly resting on its belly. Texture is of great importance in her work. She is a Selected Member of the East Anglian Potters' Association and takes an active part in all their exhibitions.

Kerry Richardson

Kerry's main inspiration comes from the combination of the African landscape of her birthplace and personal symbols which have become unique to her work. The use of different metals and the incorporation of non-precious and natural materials achieve a versatile colour palette.

Alongside a love of working metals, Kerry entertains a fascination with ceramics. This has led to the creation of a lustre and porcelain range of jewellery, the diversity of which epitomises the colour sense, the unique patternation and the versatility of Kerry's work.

As well as promoting her work extensively at craft fairs and exhibitions, Kerry also specialises in private individual commissions.

Joel Degen

Midas

31 Steep Hill, Lincoln LN2 1LU. Telephone: 01522 532299 Website: www.midasarts.co.uk
Open Monday - Friday 10am - 5pm and some Sundays.
Please ring Dee Barnes for details.

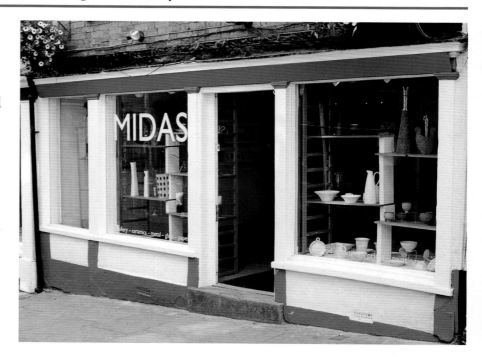

Midas is situated in the historic City of Lincoln, just around the corner from the Cathedral and Castle on the atmospheric and aptly named Steep Hill. Midas has approximately fifty makers' work on display including jewellery, ceramics, glass, metal, textiles and wood.

Alongside regular best selling stock, smaller themed displays are exhibited. Established makers such as Diana Porter, Jane Adam, Nicola Becci, Tessa Wolfe Murray, Vivienne Ross and Anthony Theakston are shown alongside up and coming makers such as Bryony Burn, Kevin Wallhead, Claire Troughton and Mikaela Bartlett.

Having been selected to appear in the Craft Council 'Gallery Guide' Midas prides itself on the high quality and craftsmanship of all the work exhibited.

The gallery aims to reach a wide audience by providing work which is accessible and affordable.

The New Studio

Rose Court, Olney, Buckinghamshire MK46 4BY. Telephone: 01234 711994 Fax: 01234 241405

Open Monday - Saturday 10am - 4.30pm , Sunday 12 - 4.30pm

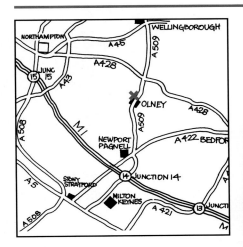

The New Studio opened in October 1997 in the thriving market town of Olney, North Buckinghamshire.

The Studio functions on two floors, each with its own particular mood: downstairs displays are full of colour and energy: upstairs is a calmer more reflective exhibition space. A wide range of media includes ceramics, furniture, sculpture, painting, glass, wood, metalwork, jewellery and textiles.

The New Studio seeks to support and promote the work of contemporary artists and crafts people at individual and group level, including local Craft Guild members. Exhibitions are staged on a monthly basis, with two major exhibitions in June and December.

Situated seven miles north of Junction 14, M1 motorway on the A509. Equal distance from Bedford, Northampton and Milton Keynes.

Nathan Smith

Nathan Smith trained in London in Theatre Design and worked as a scenic artist and prop maker before moving into ceramics. His theatrical background is evident in all of his work: each piece is a mini theatrical event in itself.

Currently Nathan produces imaginative sculptures using unconventional techniques and materials such as collage and acrylic paint. His pieces are inspired by his fascination for machinery, mechanical flight and architecture. Nathan has exhibited in France, Germany and the U.K.

Nathan lives and works near The New Studio where he amuses and delights a wide audience, some of whom return again and again when he is exhibiting.

Kate Wilkinson

My designs are highly decorative, joyous, celebratory and flamboyant. Drawing on an eclectic range of inspirational material including renaissance clothing, Japanese prints, and more recently the paintings of Georgia O'Keefe. I make three dimensional necklaces and chokers which have nostaligic qualities but are strikingly modern and extremely feminine.

The jewels incorporate contradicting ideas of restriction, liberation, seduction and protection, they intrigue both onlooker and wearer alike.

Each piece is carefully crafted, generally employing a series of repeated tin or silver units combined with dyed nylon wire, elegant feathers, sumptuous velvet flowers and sparkling Swarovski crystals that dance around the face.

Seasonal colour changes add spice to a classic collection which offer an ideal solution to dressing up that faithful frock or adding a touch of glamour to t-shirt and jeans.

The New Studio

Old House Gallery

Market Place, Oakham, Rutland LE15 6DT. Tel: 01572 755538
Open Monday - Friday 10am-1pm & 2 -5pm, closed Thursdays, Saturday 9.30am -5pm

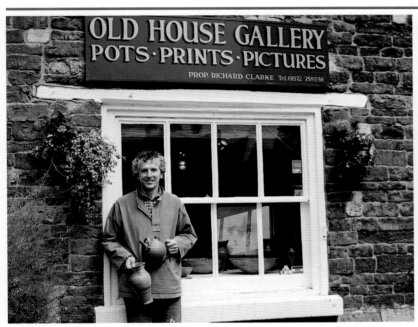

Stoneware

Potter Richard Clarke has run the gallery for twenty one years. It has recently metamorphosized into a rich tactile environment, which features work by individual makers from across the UK and Ireland. Studio ceramics, woodturning, textiles, glass and jewellery all make their mark.

Work by gallery regulars such as potters John Leach and Roger Cockram, furniture designer Steve Handley and Irish woodturner Liam O'Neill are always to be seen and new works by makers such as Clive Bowen, Emmet Kane and Lisa Hammond keep the gallery moving forward. Not to mention Richard's own production of reduction fired stoneware and raku pottery.

Richard Clarke

Richard taught ceramics full time in Staffordshire before establishing a pottery here in Rutland in 1980. Working mainly in stoneware he throws a functional and individual range, which is reduction, fired to 1289 ^{0} C. Using ash glazes combined with samples that he scrapes from the sides of mountains, he produces individual one off effects. Glazes bear names such as 'Bow Fell',

'Stack Polly', and 'Ben Lomond'! Inspiration comes from the simple forms and shapes of nature and the contrasts between glaze and body.

Richard also produces an expressive range of Raku pots. Glazes are applied outside, which 'feels right' as this is where they are fired and smoked. His studio overlooks his organic vegetable garden in one of Rutland's most beautiful villages, Barrowden.

Raku

Steve Handley

Steve Handley, born North Staffordshire, 1948, Dip AD Fine Art Sculpture 1967 -70. Taught mainly in further education until 1988. 1989 - present, travelled in Bohemia, Moravia and Southern Poland. Set up furniture workshop 1994 -full time.

Steve makes unusual furniture from local hardwoods and reclaimed timbers combined with found objects and

fastenings. Much of his work has its source in the debris of the rural past. He is also inspired by things made by the 'unskilled' through resourceful necessity and his recent travels in the countryside of Southern Poland.

He came to furniture making through sculpture and likes the idea of combining sculptural, poetic and decorative elements. His work has a presence beyond its function.

Old House Gallery

Primavera

10 King's Parade, Cambridge, CB2 1SJ. Telephone: 01223 357 708 Fax: 01223 576920
Email: julia@artandcrafts.co.uk Web: www.primaverauk.com
Open Monday - Saturday 9.30am - 5.30pm Sunday 11am - 4.30pm

Situated opposite the entrance to King's College, Cambridge, Primavera brings together a well-researched exploration into some of the finest art and crafts in Britain today.

Exhibitions run alongside displays of jewellery, furniture, ceramics, sculpture, glassware, woodwork, silverware, wrought iron, textiles and hand-made paper.

Founded by Henry Rothschild, Primavera first opened its doors at 149 Sloane Street, London in 1946. In 1967 Primavera (London) moved to 17 Walton Street and remained there until its closure in 1970. In 1960 Primavera (Cambridge) opened at its present site and is the oldest contemporary art and crafts gallery in the country.

0%

Rufford Craft Centre

Near Ollerton, Newark, Nottinghamshire NG22 9DF. Telephone: 01623 822944 ext. 207
Fax: 01623 824702 Email: ruffordceramiccentre@nottscc.gov.uk
Website: www.ruffordceramiccentre.org.uk
Open 10.30am - 5pm (March - December) 11am - 4pm (January - February)

Rufford Craft Centre is set in the beautiful grounds of a fourteenth century abbey close to Sherwood Forest in north Nottinghamshire. The Gallery and Ceramic Centre are situated in a converted sixteenth century stable block, once part of a grand country house. The Gallery has gained a national reputation for its craft exhibitions, which include a varied programme of all craft disciplines; from furniture to jewellery, prints to automata, textiles to ceramics. Exhibitions include the work of European, national and regional makers. Work can be purchased on the 0% interest scheme run by East Midland Arts.

Adjacent to the Gallery is the Ceramic Centre, which houses an exhibition illustrating the

development of British studio pottery. The Centre has a library and a bank of computers containing a large amount of study information and linked to the web. An eventful range of educational activities, including artists talks, workshops, performances and residencies are also available. The Ceramic Centre holds a retail area for the contemporary ceramics, which shows the work of more than thirty makers including; John Leach, Jane Hamlyn, John Maltby and Robin Welch. The grounds at Rufford spread through woodlands, a large wildfowl lake and formal gardens with contemporary sculptures. Rufford also provides a restaurant and café, garden centre, craft shop, outdoor living and souvenir shops.

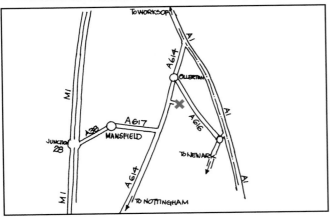

Sculpture: Peter Randall Page

Darrel Sherlock

I hope to achieve an inquisitive and emotional response to my work, exciting a visual and tactile curiosity. I enjoy working on the wheel, it provides a strong purity of form and the flexibility to explore.

The stoneware reduction firing process has proven to be the ideal method for glazing my work, creating a random element in the glazing. This is strengthened by the spontaneous way in which I apply slips and glazes to the piece, I aim to reflect the natural patterns found in stone and rock formations.

Following a degree from the Cardiff Institute of Higher Education, Darrel set up a studio in Cornwall, where he produces his individual work that quietly portrays elements of the landscape around where he lives.

Steve Tanner

Simon Hall

My current range of work is thrown in white stoneware with a green or purple volcanic glaze. The forms are inspired by metal garage paraphernalia; jugs, oil cans, trays and exhaust pipes. The glaze reflects the deterioration of the metal, softening the hard edges and turning something once straight and industrial into something smooth and organic.

The volcanic glaze is overloaded with silicone carbide, fired to cone 9 and crash cooled to fix the surface texture. Inside a smooth black glaze is applied to make using and cleaning more practical.

My time is spent between producing work and teaching pottery at local Nottinghamshire colleges, including Newark and Sherwood College, where I started potting before going on to take a BA (Hons) in Ceramics at West Surrey College of Art and Design.

Andrew Wynne

Using the traditional batik technique as a starting point I create contemporary free-hanging wall hung work, framed pieces, silk scarves and ties.

I have worked with batik for over ten years, learning from other artists and by constantly experimenting in my own work. I aim to create work, which exploits to the full the skills and knowledge that I have gained.

I like to experiment by combining techniques, developing ideas and constantly re-evaluating the work as it proceeds. By responding to the process in this way the starting point often becomes obscured as the work takes on a life of its own, as elements from the subconscious begin to affect the work; fragments of dreams, memories, music, conversation…

Steve Tanner

Sarah Dunstan

My work is a hand-built range of bottles, cups, spoons and teapots. They are a combination of oxidation and reduction stoneware, using porcelain along with a more textured clay.

Fragmented architectural details such as chimney pots, arches and railings are an underlying inspiration for my work, together with the forms and textures of metallic and material objects.

The porcelain pieces are decorated with several glazes, some having additional firings of bronze, silver or mother of pearl lustre, giving them a gem-like quality.

Sarah Dunstan trained at Cardiff Institute of Higher Education and Falmouth School of Art and Design. She is a member of the Craft Potters Association and regularly takes part in the ceramic fairs at Oxford and Rufford, where she was also artist in residence.

Some other Galleries in Eastern England

Felsted Studio
Braintree Road
Felsted
Essex
CM6 1XX
Tel: 01371 821 662
Email: felstudio@aol.com

Open Weds - Sat 11am - 4pm

To check extended times in December
please telephone 01245 237565

Pearoom Centre for Contemporary Craft
Station Yard
Heckington
Sleaford
Lincs. NG34 9JJ
Tel: 01529 460765
Email: pearoom@oden.org.uk
www.pearoom.co.uk

Open Mon - Sat 10am - 5pm,
Sundays 12noon - 5pm

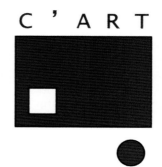

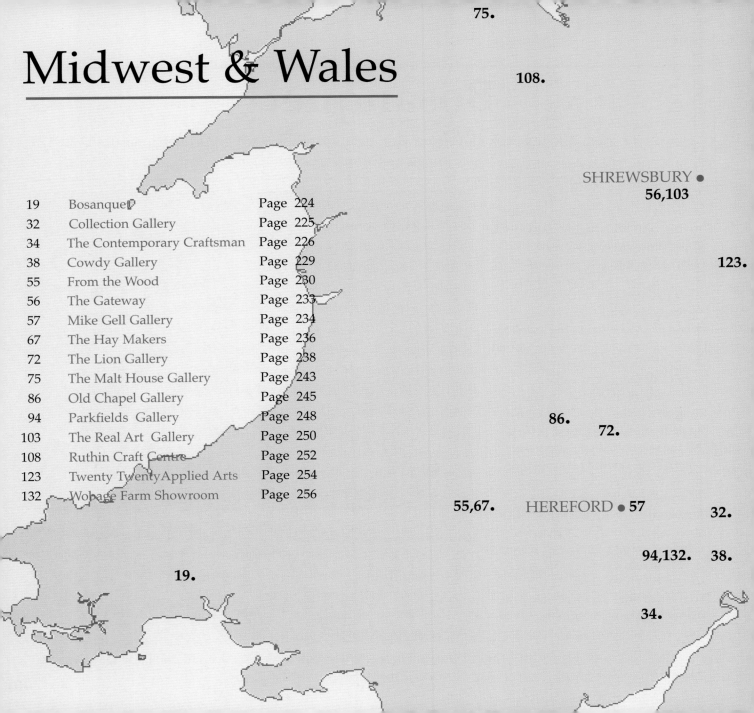

Midwest & Wales

75.

108.

SHREWSBURY ●
56,103

123.

86.

72.

55,67.   HEREFORD ● 57

32.

94,132.   38.

19.

34.

Bosanquet

♿

Hole in the Wall, Bridge Street, Haverfordwest, Pembrokeshire SA61 2AD Telephone: 01437 769178
Open Tuesday - Saturday 10am - 5pm

Bosanquet, a contemporary designer jewellery gallery, opened in July 2001 with highly individual, collectable and elegant work by thirty contemporary jewellers working in the UK. Some makers have national and international reputations, whilst others are relative newcomers to the jewellery scene. Pieces range from the one-off to small batch designs. owned by Sandra Bosanquet, it is the realisation of along-held ambition to open a gallery specialising in contemporary designer jewellery. All the work on display represents the makers' carefully considered use of the materials and range from precious metals to non- precious metals such as copper, brass, stainless steel, acrylic, carved cellulose acetate, laminated paper, porcelain and even embroidery. A former butcher's shop, its conversion into a gallery has opened a new chapter in the life of this very old building.

Joel Degen

Top right: Elizabeth Bone (Silver & gold) *Above:* Sarah Packington (Acrylic)

Bosanquet

Collection Gallery

The Southend, Ledbury, Herefordshire HR8 2EY. Telephone: 01531 634641

Open Tuesday - Saturday 10am -5.30pm, or by appointment

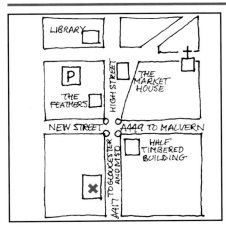

Collection in the historic and picturesque market town of Ledbury, offers a wide and lively selection of contemporary British craft and design. Between the cathedral cities of Hereford, Worcester and Gloucester,Ledbury is within easy reach of the Cotswolds, Wales and the West Midlands.

A large, light and airy showroom displays some of the best known ceramicists and jewellery which has contemporary appeal and is easy to wear!

Staff at Collection organise several themed or solo exhibitions each year. These are major events that take over the entire space. Please ring for details and invitations to private views. Collection is just five minutes walk from Ledbury's central Market House. Whatever the reason for your visit, you are welcome to take your time browsing. the gallery is guaranteed to show you something different, if you like it please join our mailing list and tell your friends.

The Contemporary Craftsman

0%

19 Church Street, Monmouth, Monmouthshire NP25 3BX.
Telephone: 01600 714527 Fax: 01600 714892
Open Monday - Saturday 10am - 5pm

The Contemporary Craftsman occupies a tall medieval building in the centre of the ancient border town of Monmouth. Surrounded by beautiful landscape, yet easily within one hour's drive of Cardiff, Bristol, Cheltenham and Hereford.

A range of both functional and decorative work in many disciplines is stocked, priced from a few pounds upwards to thousands, and is sourced from as far afield as the Orkneys, Channel Islands and Ireland.

The light and airy first floor Gallery features seven themed shows annually, with established makers promoted alongside unknown newcomers in an enjoyable mix and a friendly, informed atmosphere.

The Shop purchases small ranges of work from around one hundred makers, including

ceramics, glass, wood, furniture, baskets, jewellery, blacksmithing, calligraphy, leather, bookbinding, stone carving, painting, Sculpture and printmaking.

The Gallery is selected by the Crafts Council for the National List of Craft Shops and Galleries, and has facilities for interest free purchasing with the Arts Council of Wales' Collectorplan.

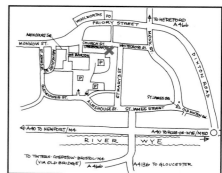

226

Janet Hamer

Ceramics has a tremendous potential for sculpture. I make clay structures from thrown pots and cut slices, then pattern the surfaces with oxides and glazes. Judging the final colours and effects of these fluid combinations after high-temperature fusion is an exciting challenge. The shapes and plumage of aquatic birds are a springboard for design ideas which balance sculptural inspiration with a chosen degree of naturalism.

I choose porcelain for sea and shore-line birds and stoneware for larger, sometimes garden, pieces. I fire in purpose-built propane gas kilns. For the lustrous copper-red on Grebes and Mandarins I fire in an outdoor kiln. During the hours of cooling I introduce lengths of willow and hazel which char under the work to create the necessary smoky reduction atmosphere. I exhibit widely and am co-author of 'The Potter's Dictionary.'

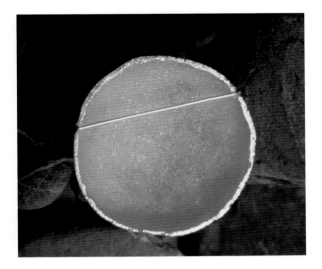

Katherine Smillie

Based in South Wales, I produce a range of Pate de Verre Jewellery, combining fused glass with 9ct gold, silver, gold and white gold leaf and silk threads. Each piece is unique due to the intricate process of firing the glass in moulds in a kiln over a 24 hour period.

I trained as a jeweller at Middlesex University, graduating in 1996. During my course I also studied modules in Glass and took the opportunity to study it further during an exchange to Australia in 1995.

I set up my workshop with the help of the Princes Trust in 1999 and was the recipient of the Harley Craft Prize in 2000. I am a member of the Contemporary Glass Society and Alloy, the Hereford Jewellers Group.

Jane Brooks

My work is concerned with journeying through landscapes. Intimate knowledge of an area plus the beliefs which have been woven around encounters with the natural world, are as intriguing in my visual response to the experience of place, as the more traditional representation of light and time in a landscape.

The mono prints express my interaction as an artist with the landscape, and are unique works.

Each piece is built up of layers of ink, collaged paper and dyed silk; the texture is achieved by including my hand made papers into image. Each print is worked and reworked passing through the etching press many times before it is complete.

Darren Yeadon

Kevan Hopson

The Contemporary Craftsman

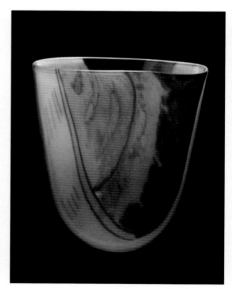

Pauline Solven

Cowdy Gallery

31 Culver Street, Newent, Gloucestershire GL18 1DB. Telephone & Fax: 01531 821173
*Open Tuesday - Friday 10am - 12.30, 1.30pm - 5pm, Saturday (April - December) 10am - 12.30 pm
and by appointment. Hours may vary - please phone to check.*

Cowdy Gallery specialises in studio glass - unique works by notable artists both established and emerging, as well as functional pieces by designer-makers.

The gallery is in a recently refurbished listed building, with 125 square metres of display space on two floors. It is located in Newent, an historic market town between Gloucester and Ross-on-Wye, 100 metres from the centre, on the B 4216 ,with private parking.

The gallery was established in 1989 by Harry Cowdy and his wife, glass artist Pauline Solven. Other artists shown include Colin Reid, Rachael Woodman, Ronald Pennell, Brian Blanthorn, Catherine Hough, Keiko Mukaide, Beatriz Castro, Sally Fawkes, Karlin Rushbrooke, Stewart Hearn and Bob Crooks.

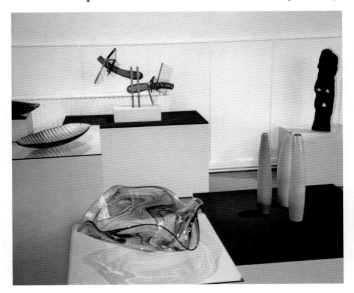

Cowdy Gallery

From the Wood

♿

Studio 6, The Craft Centre, Oxford Road, Hay-on-Wye, Hereford HR3 5DG.
Telephone: 01497 821355
Open 9am - 5.30pm seven days a week

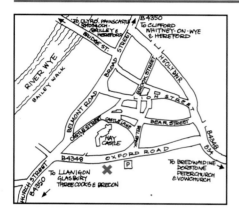

Hay-on-Wye nestles at the foot of the Black Mountains with superb views and breath-taking scenery the gallery is is a relaxing setting for visitors to browse.

Adjacent to the gallery is the workshop where the public can watch David Woodward a skilled wood turner, highly regarded among his fellow craftsmen,at work. 'From the Wood' hosted the first exhibition of the Association of Woodturners of Great Britain. Sixty-seven turners were selected to show more than one hundred pieces.

Our aim is to display, in shape and form, the most wondrous beauty of the wood.from John Sagar's furniture, and the magic of John Mainwaring's carvings - down to the wooden puzzles and toys - all are made to the highest standard. The quality of the work on show has attracted important collectors from various parts of the world. Aside from well known names like Bert Marsh, Don White and Jules

Tattersall, the gallery recognises new talent, such as Mark Hancock, Phil Iron,Rod Dunworth and Martin Pidgen whose work is now also collectable.

Hay-on-Wye has a lot to offer visitors, it has a wealth of second-hand bookshops, magnificent walks in the surrounding countryside, canoeing on the river Wye, and much more.

From the Wood

Bert Marsh

My life has been spent working with wood, and it is the love of it, coupled with a deep understanding of its ways, that has influenced all my work.

I select my materials from a wide variety of bland and exotic timbers, paying particular attention to natural defects, discolouration and grain malformations. Sensitive turning exposes the texture, colour and patterns that are enhanced by meticulous finishing.

Many of my vessels are functional, but I would prefer them to be judged for aesthetic elegance, craft and creativity, and hope that in time they will become collector's pieces.

I served an apprenticeship as a cabinet-maker, later for many years I was in charge of a workshop, designing and producing quality commissioned furniture. In 1965, I started teaching at Brighton Polytechnic, formerly College of Art, becoming responsible for all the furniture courses.

I have always felt a strong need to produce my own work. The decision to concentrate on it fully was made in 1982. Since then I have exhibited and sold my work widely all around the world.

Martin Pidgen

Martin Pidgen is known internationally for his excellent quality cord pulls in exotic and home grown timbers, his exclusive acorn design in English box and brown oak has been very popular over many years.

Also produced in many varieties of timber are nutmeg graters and pepper mills, square and diamond shaped bowls and platters complete the range of work available at a number of galleries throughout the UK.

Mark Hancock

I specialise in decorative and functional bowls and individual vessels using simple designs.

Most of my work is more an exploration of line and form than an effort at an artistic statement and it continually amazes me how each minute refinement of a curve or placement of a detail can alter the character of a piece.

This has evolved to my recent work with hollow vessels based around a vase design with exaggerated rims which are partly removed and shaped. For these I work mainly in sycamore with its subtle characteristics complimenting the simple flow and elegance of the forms. These forms are now recognised as my trademark and I was commissioned by the UK Government to produce work from this series for visiting heads of state.

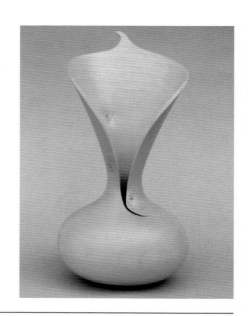

Rod Dunworth

I was born in Louth, Lincolnshire. Most of my working life being spent deep-sea fishing. When the fishing went into decline, I looked for another way to make a living. My pastime of Woodturning was that way.

I specialise in wooden fruit, using both British and exotic timbers, but also enjoy making one off bowls and platters.

Having my work accepted for several major exhibitions has been of great encouragement, and I now supply a few good quality galleries.

From the Wood

Gateway Galleries

♿

Gateway Education & Art Centre, Chester Street, Shrewsbury SY1 1NB.
Telephone: 01743 361120 Fax: 01742 358951 Email: gate-ed@hotmail.com
Open Monday - Friday 9am - 4.30pm, Saturday 10am - 12noon

Gateway Galleries is housed within the Gateway Education and Arts Centre, which is situated on the banks of the River Severn, near to Shrewbury's railway and bus station.

The public will find an exciting programme of contemporary art and dynamic crafts from leading British makers. In addition, there are several glass showcases in the foyer which offer high quality crafts for immediate sale.

The Gateway Education and Art Centre is a thriving centre, attracting around 200,000 visitors a year. It features a coffee shop, play group, adult education courses and private room hire. There is a pottery studio in the buiding, dedicated art rooms and a darkroom.

In addition, Gateway hosts dance, drama, celebrity lectures, the Children's Bookfest and the Visual Art Festival. It is also home of the Shrewbury and District Arts Association and the University of Birmingham in Shropshire.

Mike Gell Gallery

7 East Street, Hereford HR1 2LW. Telephone: 01432 278226
Open Tuesday - Saturday 10 am- 5pm

Mike Gell's Gallery for British Contemporary Jewellery has been open since 1997 and although slightly off the beaten track in the centre of Hereford, it continues to flourish, building a regular clientele.

There you can see the jewellery and silverware of about fifty makers, including Wally Gilbert, Martin Pugh, Teresa Samson, Andrew Marsden and of course Mike Gell, Sue Lane and Bronwen Tyler-Jones. Mike aims to show a wide range of the best of contemporary British Jewellery in a variety of media. Just come and look!

Mike, who runs this gallery, is self-taught and in his twenty ninth year as a maker. He is well known for his love of beautiful gemstones which he uses with startling simplicity to great effect. His

famous ringsets are often commissioned from his wonderful collection of beautiful diamonds and coloured stones, and his handmade chains are delicate and decorative. Mike is a Freeman of the Worshipful Company of Goldsmiths and is Chair of Alloy, Hereford Jewellers' Group, which he helped to found in 1994.

Ringsets by Mike Gell

Mike Gell Gallery

Sue Lane

Since graduating in June 2000 from Middlesex University, Sue returned to Herefordshire and is based in the Alloy jewellery workshop in Hereford. She sells her work in galleries through-out the country.

The range of jewellery Sue makes combines silver and gold to create work that has delicate and subtle qualitites, and uses very simple but strong lines and forms. The surface is given a soft matt finish which emphasises the contrast of the two colours of the metal. The range includes earrings, necklaces, rings and bracelets, and are all constructed with handmade parts.

Sue also makes one off larger vessels in silver and enamel, which are wallmounted and table standing, and reflect the same qualitites as the jewellery.

Bronwen Tyler-Jones

The inclusion of humour and animation is very important in all aspects of my work, along with function (no matter how small!). They are to be enjoyed, if they are able to make a person laugh or smile, then I feel I have achieved what I set out to do. No two pieces are identical, therefore they display a unique character which is further developed through the personality of the owner.

The inspirations for my creations are taken from a diverse and very varied range of influences such as a comedy, mechanical components, symbols, movement and text. Words and narrative derived from all areas play an essential role in the thought process and construction of my inventions; one word, phrase or title can spark off a whole range of ideas.

I like to think that they become precious to the owner on a personal level, through sentiment, memories and feelings, giving the piece a magical timeless quality.

The Hay Makers

St. John's Place, Hay-on-Wye, Hereford HR3 5BN. Telephone: 01497 820556
Website: www.haymakers.co.uk
Open daily 10.30am - 5pm (Mid - January - mid- February, Saturday, Sunday and Mondays only)

The Hay Makers is a co-operative group of professional designer makers, who are based in and around the world famous book town of Hay-on-Wye. The Gallery has traded successfully since 1989 as a permanent outlet for their work and has established a reputation for quality crafts at affordable prices.

The Gallery is always staffed by one of the following: Chris Armstrong, furniture maker; Pat Birks, potter; Caitriona Cartwright, stonemason; Dawn Cripps, embroiderer; Harry Franklin, sculptor; Pat Griffin, potter; Sue Hiley Harris, silk weaver; Maddy Jones, mirror designer, Victoria Keeble, silk

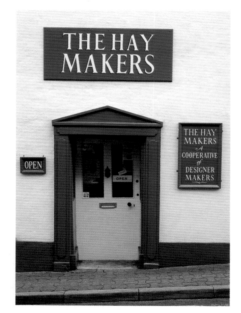

painter; Max Suffield, woodcarver and Nancy Sutcliffe, glass decorator.

There is always a broad range of work on display and visitors are able to meet and discuss the work with one of

In addition the Gallery organises a lively and varied exhibition programme for selected visiting artists a from Easter until Christmas.

Commissions are welcomed by all the makers.

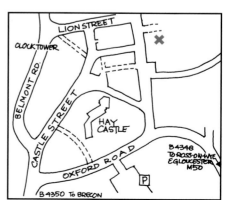

The Hay Makers

The Hay Makers

Embroidery Dawn Cripps
Stone Caitriona Cartwright

Silk painter Victoria Keeble
Silk weaver Sue Hiley Harris

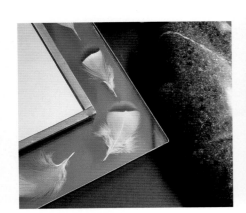

Sculptor Harry Franklin
Mirror Designer Maddy Jones

Wood   Chris Armstrong
Pottery   Pat Birks

Spoons Max Suffield
Glass decorator Nancy Sutcliffe

0%

The Lion Gallery

Lion House, 15b Broad Street, Leominster, Herefordshire HR6 8BT. Telephone: 01568 611898
Website: www.liongallery.co.uk
Open Monday - Saturday 10am -5pm all year
Closed Christmas, Boxing Day and Bank Holiday Mondays

The Lion Gallery was opened in direct response to the need by artists and craftspeople in North Herefordshire for a lively, self sufficient gallery space in the ancient market town of Leominster. Over 400 makers have now shown since opening in 1995.

The area is rich in makers of distinction and we show many of them through frequently changing exhibitions. You will find quality examples of contemporary ceramics, jewellery, turned and carved wood, all manner of textiles, glass, furniture and original prints shown alongside paintings, mixed media

Chris Noble

sculpture and photographs on regular display together with original items which are impossible to categorise. We also have one of the best collections of greetings cards in town.

Themed exhibitions, such as 'Some Body' and 'Fur,

Feather & Fin' bring in makers with national reputations from further afield, so please ring for details of our current programme. We actively promote the work of young craftspeople in their first professional shows.

Refurbished with the help of National Lottery Funding the gallery has been recognised by the Craft Council for inclusion on its National List of Craft Galleries. The gallery offers interest free credit on items between £100 and £1000 with the help of the Art Buyer's Credit scheme of West Midlands Arts.

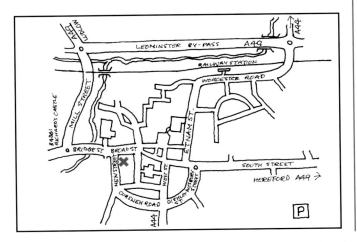

Chris Noble

Christopher Noble

As a printmaker for twenty five years I have used screenprinting as a medium to capture many fleeting aspects of my surroundings, but now I have developed using new digital media, exploring the exciting relationship between photography, printmaking and drawing. The subject matter has also changed to include working with the human figure, often my own, examining the ageing process, our place in nature and the subtle tricks memory plays on us all. I still enjoy the challenge of capturing the insubstantial permanently in ink.

The new processes have meant that images can be more experimental and challenging, produced in small, high quality editions using the best materials for lightfastness. I think of myself mainly as a craftsman as printmaking is basically a democratic process; accessible and literate; domestic and affordable.

Steve Chambers

Working in silver came about via wood and stone carving. With the contrast experienced creating sculpture in various scales leading to where I am today.

The Surrealist Movement, in particular the paintings of Dali and Magritte with their creation of 2-D illusions, has always interested me. This brought about the miniaturisation of everyday articles in my work. Using precious metals incorporated with texture and sometimes colour to create surreal jewellery, 'a dress on a dress'.

I find my work brings humour into jewellery which at times can be too serious, while sculpture is often so big that it is confined in situ. My way takes sculpture out of the gallery and onto the streets as accessible art.

Chris Noble

Jude Jelfs

I trained as a Fine artist, and became a potter when I married one! Over the last few years, I have returned to my roots, combining pottery with painting and sculpture.

My inspiration comes from all over the place. Many things spark it off: life-drawing, music, the thought that everyone you see walking down the street is naked under their clothes…this never fails to make me smile!

The pots are usually flat, almost two-dimensional slab-built vessels in earthenware or porcelain. I construct them like making clothes, using sheets of clay, and paper 'patterns'. I then paint them with slips, and glaze and fire them. They are usually functional as well as decorative, and can be used as jugs, vases, bowls. Although I am very serious about my work, it can just be enjoyed, and hopefully, amuse.

Jane Rocca

Jane has always been inspired by the perfect and beautiful shapes found in nature.

This collection of jewellery uses five different flower motifs. Each flower is individually cut out and beaten by hand which gives the silver sheet a softer and more natural appearance.

The range also includes small pieces of silverware, spoons, napkin rings, and candle holders.

Jane is a member of the 'Alloy' group of jewellers in Herefordshire, and regularly exhibits with 'Alloy Touring'.

Blake and Janette Mackinnon

We both trained as potters in London and now work from our studio just south of Ludlow.

What led to our joint involvement in ceramic jewellery I can't exactly say. No doubt an amalgam of things; the Bead Shop, a fascination with small natural forms, shells, beetles, crystals and an interest in the small precise products of the Electro porcelain industry. Playfully decorating a few small 13 amp tubes produced our first beads and hence necklaces. Since then we have evolved a variety of ways of making ceramic shapes suitable for necklaces, earrings, brooches, bracelets, and buttons. Larger objects available are small boxes and clocks.

What characterises our work is attention to detail, quality of materials and finish.

We accept design briefs and commissions.

Caroline Plumridge

Caroline's deep fascination with the sea, and the effects of light on and through water, stem from two years living in Cornwall. Now living and working in Hereford, where she obtained her HND in Design Crafts in 1996, visits to Cornwall are frequent, to gather inspiration and research.

The silk paper is made from unspun silk fibres, using a process similar to that of felt-making. These papers are then dyed and layered, to create images that evoke an atmosphere, reflecting light and movement.

Caroline has exhibited widely, both across the UK and, more recently, in Japan. She is a Licenciate of the Society of Designer Craftsmen and a member of the *Paperweight* group of paper artists.

Rozie Keogh

Rozie Keogh lives and works in Herefordshire. Her work takes two main directions: a range of costume jewellery including elaborate neck and head pieces and suspended wire sculptures.

Her main inspirations are an ongoing interest in the history of costume, fairy stories, winged creatures, myth and popular culture. The larger pieces often start with a particular garment worn in a story or by a character from film. Some of the work includes both darker and humourous elements.

The work, both sculpture and jewellery, is produced in various wires with inclusions of beads, sequins, semi-precious stones, pearls and textiles. Some pieces have elements taken from old garments, text or even insect wings. She uses many textile methods, such as knitting and stitching, in producing the pieces.

Rozie also works part time as one of the team who run the Lion Gallery.

Gosia Ksycka

The Malt House Gallery

Brookhouse Pottery, Brookhouse Lane, Denbigh, Denbighshire LL16 4RE. Telephone & Fax: 01745 812805 Email: frith@brookhousepottery.com Web: www.brookhousepottery.com
Open Monday - Saturday 10am -6pm Please telephone for Sunday details.

Situated in the beautiful Vale of Clyd, North Wales, and extended over the bank of the river Ystrad, the gallery is attached to the old woollen mill where the Friths have lived and worked for some thirty-nine years. Here are displayed significant pieces by David and Margaret as well as the range of their domestic and uniquely functional ware. David enjoys working on a large scale making jars, bottles, pitchers, platters and dishes. Margaret makes personal pieces in porcelain, which are carved or layered with coloured glazes in combination.

Traditional craftsmanship remains strong at the Frith workshop. A new wood kiln has added an extra dimension combining the exciting surface textures of wood effects with the

glazed surfaces. Intuitiveness and expressiveness play an important role, to find a depth of feeling that goes beyond mere technique.

The riverside garden provides a delightful setting for display of

plant containers, wall murals and water fountains.

The showroom is sign posted from the A525 to Ruthin Road, one mile from the town centre and is positioned about fifty yards down Brookhouse Lane.

David Frith

The richness of the North Wales landscape never fails to inspire me and I have valued living and working here. My work explores the thrown form -searching for that essence - a quality that survives time and where the traditional and contemporary meet. I use the techniques of the past with the eyes of the present. I hope the work shows an individuality and maturity that comes from experience, self-confidence and personal conviction about the current role of a craftsman and potter.

Margaret Frith

Working with clay never ceases to excite and each piece is an individual and still concerned with function. Decorative techniques involve high temperature reduction glazes used in combination. Sometimes there are several layers of glaze and pigments with wax masking to create colour separations and effects. The time spent glazing and decorating is considerable and often proves difficult - so it is with great trepidation that I approach the opening of the kiln. Guaranteed to arouse the emotions there is always plenty left to aspire to !

244

The Malt House Gallery

Old Chapel Gallery

East Street, Pembridge, Near Leominster, Herefordshire HR6 9HB. Tel & Fax: 01544 388842
Email: yasminstrube@yahoo.com Website: www.oldchapelgallery.co.uk
Open Monday - Saturday 10am - 5.30pm, Sunday 11am - 5.30pm.

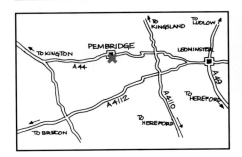

Old Chapel Gallery, Pembridge, is situated in a key position on the popular black and white tourist trail in the heart of rural North Herefordshire.

Established by Yasmin Strube in 1989 in the setting of a fine Victorian Chapel, the Gallery has gone from strength to strength and has established itself as a centre of excellence where casual browsers and serious collectors of contemporary art and crafts alike can find work by both established local and nationally-known artists and makers alongside innovative work by talented newcomers.

Comments in the visitor's book from all over the UK and overseas are testament to the pleasure given by a visit to this unique privately-owned gallery with its professional and friendly service.

Displayed in the downstairs gallery is an ever-changing kaleidoscope of craft: ironwork, a particular strength, garden furniture, contemporary furniture, wood turning and carving, three dimensional work often using recycled or natural material, fine hand-blown glass, sculpture, ceramics, jewellery and textiles with a strong accent on knitwear. Yasmin started in the craft world as a knitter and has always had a special interest in finding makers and including top knitters in her exhibition line-ups. Exhibitions are held seasonally four times a year in the upstairs gallery, usually mixed media, which provides the opportunity to introduce new young makers alongside well-known names.

Pembridge is an interesting village with many fine black and white houses, a fourteenth century church with a famous free standing bell tower. On a practical level, there are several shops and businesses including a village store, garage, two inns and public car park and toilets. The gallery is in East Street in the centre of the village. Most major credit cards are accepted and the gallery will arrange carriage for larger items and will organise special commissions with the makers. The Gallery is included in the 1999 National List of Craft Shops and Galleries.

Paul Margetts

I have been forging metals for the past twenty five years, and my passion for designing and creating pieces in this wonderful material is as strong as ever. Having undertaken a traditional blacksmithing apprenticeship and subsequently enhanced my design skills with a period at Birmingham Polytechnic; I thus benefit from the combination of a sound practical background and a vivid imagination. I firmly believe that all craftwork should have a sculptural quality and even the simplest pieces must have the ability to intrigue. My work ranges in size from the inexpensive domestic items to large civic sculpture .

I have exhibited my work at the Old Chapel since the gallery's early days and I have enjoyed a positive relationship between the customer, Yasmin and myself. My gallery work typically includes candlesticks, bookends, clocks, fire irons, bowls and sculpture, and occasionally larger pieces of garden ornament.

Mary Rose Young

Mary Rose Young throws beautiful, elegant pieces of pottery. This would be enough for many artists but Mary Rose goes further. Hand made roses and jewels adorn the surface of teapots vases and plates, while rich deep colours and bright gold are mixed in a tapestry of decorative designs.

Her startling pieces have won her a world-wide reputation. It would be difficult to find an important city that did not have a gallery representing her ....and Pembridge is no exception.

Top Right: Jane Charles (glass)
Brian Griffiths (furniture)
Centre: Mary Ann Rogers
Bottom: Deborah Scaldwell

Parkfields Gallery

Parkfields, Pontshill, Ross-on-Wye, Herefordshire HR9 5TH. Telephone: 01989 750138
Email: info@parkfieldsgallery.co.uk Website: www.parkfieldsgallery.co.uk
Open 7 days a week 10.30am - 4.30pm

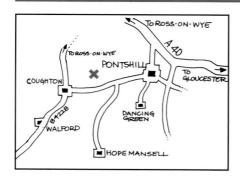

Such is the success of the concept behind the original Parkfields Gallery, that not only can you visit Parkfields house, which accommodates the purpose built gallery and artists studios: you can also take a short drive to their latest venture in Ross-on-Wye,- 'Parkfields in Town' at 4, The High Street. In both cases you will be treated to a diverse and extensive range of the highest quality art and contemporary crafts, together with a newly developed 'sculpture trail', set in the glorious ten acres surrounding the carefully restored Georgian building that houses the original gallery.

The themed, multi media exhibitions that run throughout the year at Parkfields Gallery include works from established local artists and craftspeople, together with the very best of work from across the UK. There are also working studios, where you can chat freely to the artists in residence.
At Parkfields in Town, the display can range from unique pottery, bronzes and glassware to quirky jewellery or stunning handmade furniture.

Both venues encourage you to browse in a relaxed manner so that you can fully appreciate the many and varied works on display. Parkfields Galleries encourage you to join their mailing list so that they can keep you informed about their latest developments, exhibitions and private viewings.

Parkfields Gallery

Kathy Lewis

Kathy found it difficult to select one image to illustrate her work, as her subject matter is so varied. Her paintings range from still life to architectural aspects, but can include items as diverse as an old leather suitcase to a collection of beetles. One of Kathy's most popular styles is putting together a montage of images to illustrate a theme.

Kathy's inspiration comes from many different sources but shape, colour and texture will be an important feature, together with her 'trademark' image of strong tonal contrasts.

She always travels with her sketchbook and camera, constantly looking for new ideas, but admits that she is delighted to have her studio at Parkfields Gallery: "I find the peaceful atmosphere and beautiful surroundings are so conducive to creativity". She also enjoys chatting to people visiting the gallery and studios and is always happy to discuss her work with visitors.

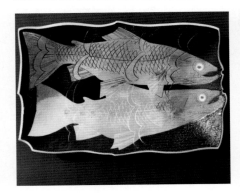

Frank Hamer

Centre: Adrienne Craddock

Carol Mather

The Real Art Gallery

Meadow Place, Shrewsbury, SY1 1PD. Tel: 01743 270123. Email: realartgallery@lineone.net
Open Tuesday - Saturday 10am - 5.30pm and Sundays 11am -5pm.
If travelling a distance please telephone to check opening times

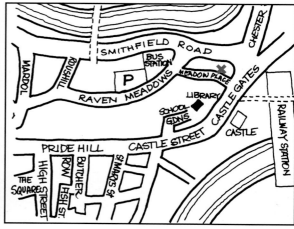

The Real Art Gallery is set in an attractivlely converted, part mediaeval building within the historic river loop of Shrewsbury town centre.

The wealth of artistic talent throughout all corners of Britain is the gallery's cornerstone, giving a diverse vitality to this collection. The thriving visual art culture of Shropshire is also demonstrated in a rich supply of contemporary art and quality craft from local makers.

The gallery has a continually changing display of art on two floors, including paintings, sculpture, glass, ceramics, metalwork, furniture, photography and designer jewellery.

To complete the day, a warm welcome awaits all in the wonderful coffee shop. Here you can settle down to a cappuccino, relaxing in soft armchairs or have a three course meal accompanied with wine or a selection of beers, whilst surrounded by fabulous art. With the use of vibrant colours and contemporary furniture our coffee shop exudes an atmosphere suitable for artistic inspiration.

The Real Art Gallery

Mel Mars

Mel Mars studies glass at Stourbridge College. He is excited by the magic of glass, its immediacy, fluidity and sensuality. His work exploits the way that the hot liquid glass solidifies at a particular moment in the making process. He is concerned with colour as a structural part of his contemplative large blown pieces.

Such pieces rely upon balance between controlled and natural forces.

Mel is represented in a number of public and private collections in this country and abroad. He enjoys working to commissions. When not travelling and lecturing abroad he lives in Shropshire. He is an Associate of the Royal Birmigham Society of Artists.

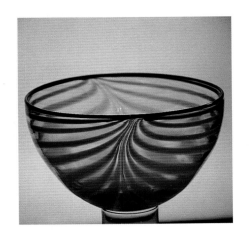

Victoria Dark

Victoria Dark graduated with a BA Hons., Bath Academy of Art and a MFA., Southern Illinois University. Very early on in her ceramics career, she specialised in the technique of slipcasting and working with porcelain. Over the last fifteen years she has produced an extensive range of delicate vessels, developing simple elegant forms, which could then be transformed by the Raku process.

Each piece is unique and has a fine network of lines, being rich in textures and depth of colour, which include metallic lustres of copper and gold. She applies many applications of different glazes to achieve a rich diversity of surface; moreover, an intense investigation into Raku has enabled her to discover the beautiful qualitites that are found in this process. She has exhibited extensively in England and America.

Ruthin Craft Centre

The Gallery, Park Road, Ruthin, Denbighshire LL15 1BB. Telephone: 01824 704774 Fax: 702060
Open SUMMER Daily 10am - 5.30pm, WINTER Monday - Saturday 10am - 5pm, Sunday 12 - 5pm

North Wales' Premier Centre for the Applied Arts is situated in the medieval town of Ruthin, in the picturesque Vale of Clwyd.

The Gallery at Ruthin Craft Centre is included in the Crafts Council's National List of Craft Shops & Galleries for showing the best of fine crafts by contemporary Designer-Makers from the British Isles. It is a modern Gallery with an exhibition space and retail area with contemporary craft for sale under the same roof.

The exhibition programme runs all year round and consists of changing temporary exhibitions, many of which tour, aiming to show the breadth of excellence in the applied arts, through a stimulating and diverse selection of innovative contemporary work.

Also at the Centre are Independent Craft Studios, a Gallery showing framed work, a Restaurant and Tourist Information Centre. There is free admission to the whole of the Centre, ample car parking and accessible facilities.

Virginia Graham

Everyone has objects and possessions that they are passionate about. Often they are not valuable in monetary terms, but are simply mundane, everyday things that evoke memories and experiences. I make teapots and associated pieces because they are the ultimate in terms of collectible ceramics. I am fascinated by the way that they are collected and displayed behind glass, never to be used for fear of betraying their new found status. I use a combination of slip casting and hand building techniques to reference utilitarian ceramics such as Cornishware, Mochaware and blue and white porcelain. Open stock transfers and metallic lustres are the finishing touches to create pieces that not only marry industrial processes with handmade ceramic traditions, but also have the potential be be collected and displayed.

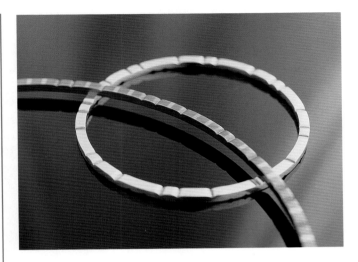

Kathleen Makinson

I have worked in North Wales for a number of years producing jewellery in various materials. Ideas are drawn from research, and developed through precise drawings which reflect my early training in illustration at the Royal College of Art. An ongoing investigation of contemporary architecture informs recent designs.

My work is mainly geometric in character and through carefully considered use of materials, mainly precious metals, each one-off or small batch design is precise and understated. When worn, jewellery will be continually in movement so that even a simple bend or fold in a geometric form will reflect constantly changing light and shade. It is fascinating to explore economical means of achieving maximum effects, sometimes inlaying silver with coloured golds before folding, striving to achieve interesting effects by simple means.

Twenty Twenty Applied Arts

0%

3 High Street, Much Wenlock, Shropshire TF13 6AA. Telephone: 01952 727952
Open Tuesday - Saturday 10am - 5pm or by appointment

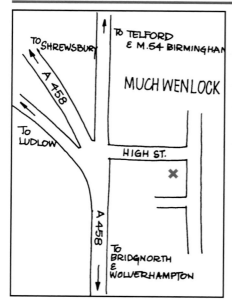

Tom Foxall

Twenty Twenty was established in 1997 by tapestry weaver Meabh Warburton. As Meabh's work is small in scale she is also able to use the gallery as her studio.

At any one time you can see the work of around fifty makers, including Duncan Ayscough, Kathryn O'Kell, Tony Gant, Sarah Packington and Gilly Langton. We specialise in ceramics and jewellery and also show wood, glass and some textiles. Each month two makers are highlighted in our 'In the Window' showcases.
Last year we were accepted for inclusion on the Crafts Council's national list of shops and galleries and also West Midlands Arts 'Art Buyers' Credit Scheme'.

Duncan Ayscough

All work is produced using techniques relating to the potter's wheel. The work is coated with fine layers of terra-sigalatta (fine clay particles) and then exposed to one of a range of surface carbonisation techniques. All work is subsequently polished with beeswax and occasional additions of gold-leaf are made to heighten the visual impact of the work.

The movement of form and structure provided through the use of the potter's wheel remains for Duncan a constant intrigue. It is the fluidity of the process that he intends to reflect in the product; control and chaos are of equal importance in the production of form and the consideration of surface.

Duncan lives and works in the village of Bethlehem, West Wales and is a professional member of the Crafts Potters Association of Great Britain and the Society of Designer Craftsmen.

Kathryn O'Kell

I make relief woodcarvings, using mainly English lime. The colours, shapes and movements of birds are my main inspiration although other images do sometimes appear: deer, foxes, badgers and otters are current projects for a new primary school in Oxfordshire.

I very rarely make preliminary designs, preferring to let a piece develop intuitively, letting the wood itself suggest the final image. The colours are achieved using mainly thinned-down acrylic paints and the judicious use of sandpaper and wire wool.

My carvings vary in scale from small, domestic pieces to large, architectural panels. I have made commissions ranging from commemorative pieces for a Lincolnshire village hall to a series of large panels for Royal Caribbean Cruise Liners.

Wobage Farm Showroom

Crow Hill, Ross-on-Wye, Herefordshire HR9 7QP. Telephone: 01989 780 233/495
Open Saturday & Sunday 10am -5pm all the year, Thursdays & Fridays April 1st-Sept 30th
(Other times please telephone for appointment)

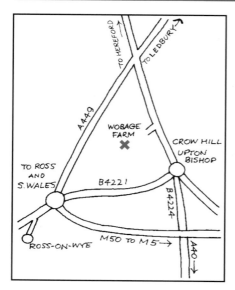

In 1977 Michael and Sheila Casson moved to Wobage Farm which lies on the B4224 Hereford road out of Upton Bishop. The late eighteenth century sandstone farm buildings have been converted into craft studios for nine craftspeople working individually and sharing facilities. There are six potters, Michael and Sheila Casson, Patia Davis and John Alliston, Petra Reynolds and Jeremy Steward. Clair Hodgson is a jeweller and her sister Lynn Hodgson a wood carver and furniture maker. Ben Casson also designs and makes furniture.

All the work in the showroom is made on the premises with the exception of pots from France made by Andrew and Clare McGarva, who worked here for ten years. The makers supply a wide range of items in size and price.

Wobage Farm Showroom

Andrew McGarva

Joel Degen

Clair Hodgson

Ben Casson

John Alliston

Lynn Hodgson

Wobage Farm Showroom

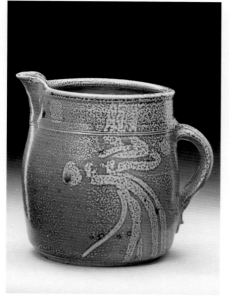

Michael Casson

Patia Davis

Sheila Casson

Petra Reynolds

Jeremy Steward

Some other Galleries in the Midwest and Wales

Bowie & Hulbert

5 Market Street

Hay- on-Wye

Hereford

HR3 5AF

Tel: 01497 821026

Fax: 01497 821801

Email: info@hayclay.co.uk

Open Mon - Sat 10am - 5.30pm

Sunday 11am - 5pm

Countryworks

Broad Street

Montgomery

Powys SY15 6PH

Tel: 01686 668866

Open Mon - Sat 10 am - 5.30 pm

Sun 1.30 - 5.30 pm

Mission Gallery

Gloucester Place

Maritime Quarter

Swansea

SA1 1TY

Tel & Fax: 01792 652016

Open daily 11am - 5pm

Oriel Mostyn Gallery

12 Vaughan Street

Llandudno

LL30 1AB

Tel: 01492 879201

Fax: 01492 878869

Email: post@mostyn.org

www.mostyn.org

Open Mon - Sat 11am - 6 pm

Spectrum Gallery

27, Maengwyn Street

Machynlleth

Powys

SY20 8EB

Tel: 01654 702877

Email: art@spectrumgallery.co.uk

www.spectrumgallery.co.uk

Open Mon - Sat 10am - 5pm

West Wales Arts Centre

16 West Street

Fishguard

Pembrokeshire

SA65 9AE

Tel/Fax: 01348 873867

Email:

westwalesarts@btconnect.com

www.home.btconnect.com/WEST-WALES-ARTS/

Open Mon - Sat 10am - 5.30pm

Sun by appointment

Central England

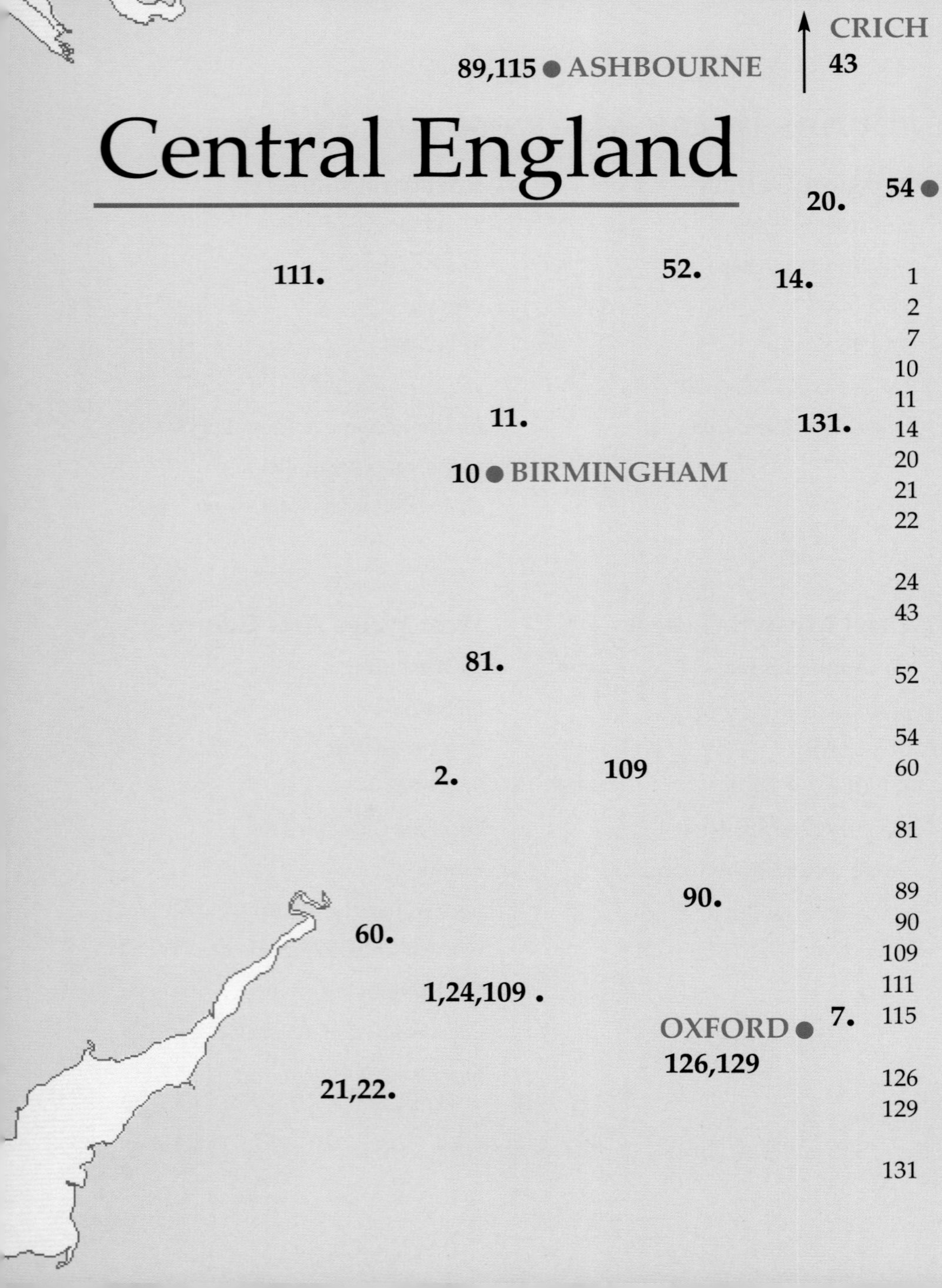

89,115 ● ASHBOURNE

↑ CRICH
43

20.

54 ● NOTTINGHAM

111.

52.

14.

11.

10 ● BIRMINGHAM

131.

81.

2.

109

90.

60.

1,24,109 .

OXFORD ● 7.

126,129

21,22.

andersongallery

96 High Street, Broadway, Worcestershire WR12 7AJ. Telephone & Fax: 01386 858086
Open Daily 10am -1pm & 2 - 5pm.

Owned by the writer Ronald Anderson and his wife the painter, Christine Barnett, the subtle blend of the old and new is the defining feature of the Anderson Gallery.

Considered by many to be the most exciting art gallery outside the West End of London, this spacious and airy gallery, located in the beautiful Cotswold village of Broadway, offers the visitor the widest possible choice in a varied annual programme of exhibitions.

From Whistler to Sickert, Ben Nicholson to John Piper; together with the best of British contemporary art, are all to be found in this Broadway gallery.

As members of the British Crafts Council, other specialities include ceramics and jewellery, sculpture and furniture. Whatever your budget and whatever your taste you can be sure the Anderson Gallery will provide the answer.

Anderson Gallery Broadway

261

andersongallery@burford

142, High Street, Burford, Oxfordshire OX18 8QU. Telephone: 01993 822093
Open Daily 10 am - 5pm

Based on the same philosophy as the Broadway gallery, (see previous page) the new Burford Gallery opened in May 2000. What makes it different from the parent gallery in Broadway is its sheer size. Once the home of a supermarket the andersongallery @ Burford displays one of the largest and most diverse selections of art and crafts in the country.

Art in Action Gallery

♿

Waterperry, Near Wheatley, Oxfordshire OX33 1JZ.
Telephone: 01844 338085 Fax: 01844 339883
Email: office@waterperrygardens.fsnet.co.uk
Open Tuesday - Sunday April - October 9am - 5pm, November - March 9am - 4.30pm

Housed in a restored eighteenth century barn the Art in Action Gallery is situated at Waterperry Gardens. The gallery opened in October 1994 and is a natural extension to the Art in Action Festival held in July each year. With a friendly atmosphere visitors are encouraged to browse; the aim being to make high quality crafts accessible to all.

The varied collection of work on display is constantly changing and a number of special exhibitions are held throughout the year. Within the landscaped grounds there is free car parking and a licensed restaurant.

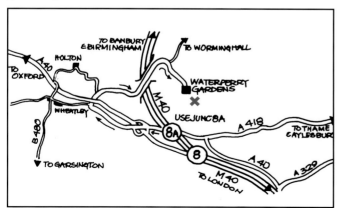

Art in Action Gallery

Linda Heaton-Harris

Linda trained as a teacher, studying English literature and History, becoming interested in Ceramics whilst at College. Her sculptures are influenced and inspired by a lifelong love of animals and birds.

In the past her work has fallen into two categories: handbuilt pieces, demonstrating a more simplified stylistic approach, and extremely detailed individual sculptures.

She has recently added a more flowing style of work, concentrating on the form and movement of the subject. In the sculptures a variety of techniques and clays are used to produce a range of textures, various oxides are used in order to retain the fine detail.

Her sculptures have sold worldwide and have also sold at Christies Wildlife Auction.

Marian Watson

Marian Watson studied Fine-Art Painting at St. Martins School of Art in the late sixties and then turned to jewellery making in the seventies.

Her work has a freedom, which is obtained by using traditional skills in original ways, and it has a timeless quality. She works in silver and gold,(often using combinations of the two metals) and beautiful stones.

Each piece is unique and comfortable to wear and she exhibits in galleries throughout the country.

Her workshop is now near Oxford, and inspiration comes from her garden, the museums in Oxford, walking the hills in Shropshire, and travels to North Africa, Italy and New Zealand.

Abdul Abbas

Art In Action Gallery

Isabella Whitworth

Isabella Whitworth originally trained as a graphic designer and spent several years in publishing and the toy industry. She 'discovered' textiles while travelling in India and Indonesia and began painting on silk in the late 80s, when she was living on the Isle of Skye.

She works on various weights of fabric and her technique involves a hand-painted build-up of several layers of dye, generally held by gutta resist. She maintains recurrent design themes, often based on studies from nature, and is also inspired by mythology and folklore.

Recently, Isabella has been working with wax as a resist, producing scarves with more abstract textures and forms. A love of drawing and colour are consistently at the heart of her work.

Martin Barfoot

Lucy Butterwick

Lucy Butterwick lives and works in Oxford. She makes simple handbuilt forms decorated with vivid glaze and lustre. Silver and gold bands feature in her ceramics and are about simplicity, continuity and support. Colour is an important driving force and shapes are often rounded and tactile. Visits to Australia, New Zealand and Mexico have greatly influenced her work.

She has produced four main series: *Sacred Spheres* (red and orange orbs); *Heart as Vessel* (turquoise and lilac bowls); *Green Wisdom* (green and black asymmetrical forms); and *Latin Blood* (black, red and gold burnished ceramics). She has received a City & Guilds Medal for Excellence for her ceramics, a Southern Arts setting up grant, and travel grants to help develop her designs. Her work is exhibited in a range of galleries in the UK.

Artfull Expression

23/24 Warstone Lane, Hockley, Birmingham B18 6JQ
Telephone: 0121 2120430 Fax: 0121 2365146
Open Monday - Friday 10am -5pm and Saturday 10am - 4pm

Artfull Expression was opened in a Victorian building in the heart of Birmingham's Jewellery Quarter in 1995 to provide a showcase for contemporary designer-makers in jewellery and other crafts. We aim to be an alternative to the very traditional jewellery shops which surround us.

Most of the jewellery we stock is silver, but other materials are represented - copper, brass, wood, ceramics, plastics and slate. Some of the jewellers have their workshops in the building. Repairs and commissions can be undertaken.

As well as jewellery we sell clocks, mirrors, prints,

paintings, small sculptures (in bronze and in ceramics) and greetings cards.

Artfull Expression was included among the 'top fifty places to go in Birmingham'

in The Independent's 'Best of Birmingham' supplement (17.2.2001) - "a perfect example of the attractions to the discerning shopper of the Jewellery Quarter".

Artfull Expression

Michele White

Each unique gemstone inspires its own design. The shape and the markings of semi-precious stones can be enhanced by the sensitive use of the metal. Silver and 18 carat gold together compliment each other. The silver can be oxidised, brushed to a soft finish, or highly polished to give different effects, and highlighted by the warm colour of the polished gold.

Trees often feature in my work. I feel a particular affinity to the natural world and love the grandeur of trees. Many of the gemstones I use have markings which are reminiscent of landscapes. They often look as though they have been painted by an artist, but are completely natural. To compliment these I have established a way of forming trees by reticulation; fusing wire and saw pierced metal without the use of solder.

Penny Gildea

I love the combination of precious metal and glass, the combination of these two materials creates an almost limitless medium of colour and texture on objects that can be functional as well as delicate and decorative.

The traditional techniques of cloisonne, basse taille and champleve show off the relationship between transparent enamels fully and lately I have begun to use handmade kumihimo braids in silk instead of traditional chains to compliment the finished pieces.

The range of my work includes jewellery, small objects such as bowls and boxes as well as whistles.

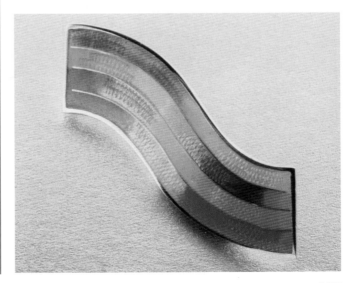

Anna de Ville

Anna de Ville has her work shop in the heart of the Birmingham Jewellery Quarter. She exhibits and sells her work throughout the British Isles.

Her jewellery is distinctive in its use of contrasting oxidised and polished silver, with an emphasis on surface detail. The zig-zag has become a personal motif.

Much of Anna's work is inspired by fish, birds and animals. Her latest designs include flower and vegetable forms taken from her beloved garden.

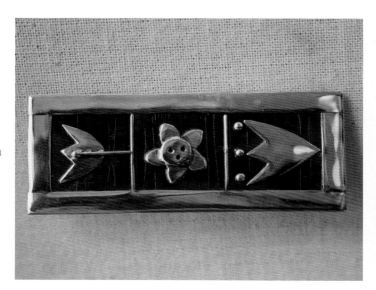

Katherine Campbell-Legg

Katherine's work is a subtle combination of silver and 18ct gold, employing a variety of techniques including rolling, stamping, hand-engraving and inlay. She is influenced by natural forms, printed textiles, graphic images and geometrical shapes. These elements are put together to create wearable contemporary jewellery.

Artifex

Mitchell Centre for Art & Craft, Weeford Road, Sutton Coldfield, Birmingham B75 6NA.
Telephone: 0121 3233776 Email: sales@artifex.co.uk Website: www.artifex.co.uk
Open every day 10am - 5pm

Artifex contemporary art and craft gallery is housed within a set of sympathetically converted farm buildings, situated in a peaceful rural area, and yet near the town centre of Sutton Coldfield, only five minutes away by car.

Partners Nigel Bates and Ross Fenn established the gallery in 1993. Their aim is to provide a West Midlands showcase for the very best in British contemporary art and craft.

The 3,000sq. ft of gallery space displays some of the finest pieces of contemporary furniture, glass, jewellery, metalwork, ceramics and textiles being made today, with an emphasis on innovative, high quality work.

There is also a large area devoted to paintings, all originals, featuring

small groups of work by about twenty artists, as well as substantial 'solo' exhibitions.

A furniture commissioning service is available, including personal consultation and professional high quality drafts of design proposals. Artifex also offers an interior design, as well as exterior garden design service.

Permanent displays are constantly updated, with work from two hundred artists and crafts people on show at any one time, as well as a programme of ongoing exhibitions.

Interest free credit available.

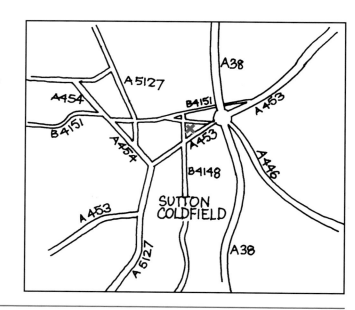

Eryka Isaak

Copper, aluminium and steel become encapsulated in glass through the fusing process carried out in a kiln. the high temperatures cause the metals to change colour when used individually or in different combinations. These colour variations can be predicted to a certain extent but there is a definite element of chance involved which makes each piece unique.

Using simple icons made from foil, sheet mesh and wire, I create glass hangings: from delicate pendants to floor-t -ceiling installations. The clarity of the glass captures the incredible colours of the metals and allows the pieces to be viewed from both sides.

Mike Inch

Andrew Varah

Having lived and worked abroad for twelve years, architecture has been my major influence. Each culture has influenced a theme or detail I wished to explore.

Now, having four talented cabinetmakers working for me, I wish my workshop to produce pieces which really are superb examples of furniture. The cost must be such that any prospective client must feel he or she has excellent value and that no one could better our craftsmanship. My pieces must stand the test of time and be appreciated in the next century and thereafter. I should like to be known for executing very complex commissions, and perhaps for the fact that in many pieces I build a secret compartment, giving the client twelve months to find what has been hidden, before I retrieve the hidden object and reveal the secret opening.

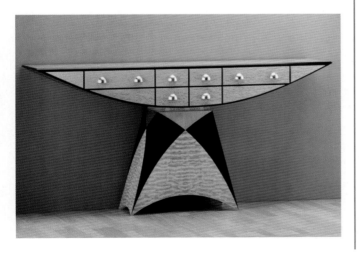

Blandine Anderson

Blandine Anderson established her studio in Devon in 1989. Since that time, she has exhibited in Galleries throughout Britain and now has work in collections world-wide.

Her Ceramics and Paintings are centered on the natural world, which provide an ever changing variety of colour, texture and mood. Some are simple pieces based on the study of single creatures. Others are more elaborate, inspired by myth, legend and folklore. These invite the viewer to explore their literary reference and symbolism. None of the work is ever repeated, although themes and ideas may be reworked several times.

The Beetroot Tree

South Street, Draycott, Derbyshire DE72 3PP. Telephone: 01332 873929
Email: thebeetroottree@ukonline.co.uk Website: www.thebeetroottree.com
Open Wednesday - Sunday 10am - 4.30pm and Bank Holidays (during exhibitions)

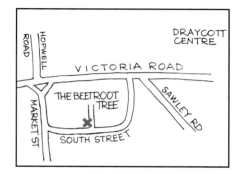

'Beautiful gallery- inspiring exhibitions'
'Every exhibition offers something new and exciting'
'Peaceful and refreshing but progressive'.

The perfect setting for exhibitions is found in a converted Jacobean Barn with dramatic beams, beautiful lighting, a landscaped garden and artist studio, all suffused with a distinctively tranquil ambience.

We select contemporary decorative and applied arts and design-led crafts for each of our exhibitions. Always giving scope for both professional and domestic buyers in search of unique, creative work.
Contact Alysn for full details and a current programme of exhibitions, workshops and events or visit our regularly updated website.

Alysn Midgelow-Marsden

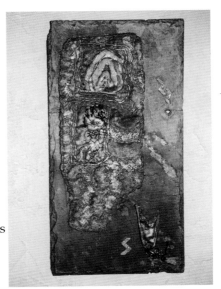

Looking for sumptuous surface textures in textiles with paper thread, metal, glass, shells, stone etc.? Then visit my studio at The Beetroot Tree Gallery.

Inspired by the myths and symbols of several cultures past and present and by the art of children, these desirable works tell a story.

All my work is unique and takes several forms including large hangings and clothing, framed and mounted work, work mounted on slate, mirrors, books and cards.

I use a wide range of contemporary textile and mixed media techniques including dying, painting, burning fabrics, adding stitching and embellishments.

I frequently work to commission with textiles and special occasion clothing as well as dance-theatre sets and costumes. In all these cases the design and techniques are developed following close consultation with the client.

Pat Hazzledine

What a load of rubbish! My collections of driftwood, shells, bones, feathers and rusty metal are my 'treasures', and are the very stuff of my craft. Everything I find has had a previous life. I take my found objects and give them a new life. I make assemblages, constructed as free standing sculptures or wall hung reliefs, and decorate them with bright acrylic paint markings. The works have resonances of Native American totemic art.

I also make watercolour and collage greetings cards, drawing for inspiration on landscape and ancient standing stones, brochs, and menhirs.

My host gallery is The Beetroot Tree Gallery, but I live and work on the island of Shapinsay in the Orkney Islands.

The Bottle Kiln
Contemporary Art and Craft

High Lane, West Hallam, Derbyshire DE7 6HP. Telephone: 0115 932 9442
Open Tuesday - Sunday 10am - 5pm

The Bottle Kiln Centre for Contemporary Art and Craft is built on the site of a former pottery, and comprises a set of beautifully restored and reconstructed buildings including an unusual bottle-necked kiln. It was designed and developed by potter Charles Stone and his two sons, and now houses the gallery, an excellent card and gift shop, a decorative accessories shop, a buttery serving superb home-cooked food and a Japanese tea garden.

The gallery features the work of seven or eight painters working in a range of media and styles from abstract to figurative, but all favouring imagination, originality and a love of the natural world. Displayed amongst the paintings are a selection of studio ceramics and glass. We believe in crafts which display integrity, and define this as a pleasing harmony between medium and function. Inside the kiln itself is a display of handmade British jewellery by over twenty stylish and original makers, shown off in nine purpose-built cabinets, interspersed with other crafts in ceramic, glass and metal; surely one of the most imaginative re-uses of an old industrial building to be found!

Lunches are served daily and make a visit to the Bottle Kiln a treat for both body and soul.

0%

Opus Gallery

34, St. John's Street, Ashbourne, Derbyshire DE6 1GH. Telephone: 01335 348989
Open every day from 10am -5pm except for Sunday.

Opus is the sister gallery to the Bottle Kiln page 274, and opened in June 2000. A much smaller space than that at West Hallam, it none-theless contains not only the distilled best of the Bottle Kiln but some exciting and different work as well, particularly at the more contemporary end. It specialises in ceramics, glass and metalwork, with a changing monthly exhibition of paintings.

A selection of work which may be seen at both galleries:
From Left: Vivienne Ross, Jolene Smith, Simon Shaw & Charlotte Mowlson.

Opus Gallery

275

Brewery Arts

Brewery Court, Cirencester, Gloucestershire GL7 1JH. Telephone: 01285 657181
Fax: 01285 644060 Email: admin@breweryarts.freeserve.co.uk
Open Monday -Saturday 10am -5pm (Closed Bank Holidays)

Brewery Arts is situated in Cirencester, a market town in the heart of the Cotswolds. The converted Victorian brewery is at the core of this historic town, with ample parking in the nearby Brewery Car Park.

The shop, which is on the National List of Craft Shops and Galleries, is part of a multi-disciplinary arts and crafts centre. The centre also has a theatre, coffee house, education programme and gallery, which exhibits craft and applied arts from national and internationally recognised artists. There are also sixteen resident craft workers on site running independent businesses. Further details can be found on the following pages.

An emphasis, in the craft shop, on new makers combined with the more established names in wood, metal, glass, ceramics, jewellery, toys and textiles creates an exciting and informal atmosphere with ever changing work. People are encouraged to browse and enjoy the regular programmes of small scale shows which further increase the range of work on display.

276

With knowledgeable staff on hand to discuss the makers and processes involved, Brewery Arts continues the tradition of promoting and encouraging the enjoyment of crafts with which the Cotswolds have long been associated.

Brewery Arts has a main gallery which shows a number of high profile touring exhibitions throughout the year. The education department is linked with the gallery and offers one-off workshops connected with specific exhibitions, regular adult classes and children's workshops (during school holidays).

Phone for a quarterly brochure listing current events.

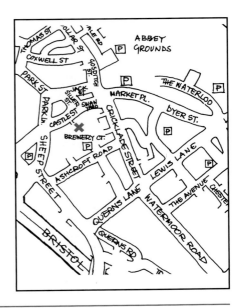

Both photos Sandra Ireland

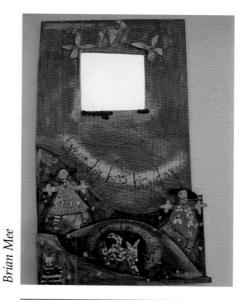

Brian Mee

Hilary Mee

The enjoyment of drawing is carried through into the production of a piece. Each stage of the process is open to change, whether it be form, colour or ornamentation.

The highly flexible medium of paper lends itself well to being humourous and childlike with the application of colour and line becoming both dramatic and theatrical. There seem to be few limitations using these materials. I am often invited to participate in themed exhibitions, this leading to unexpected images becoming part of the range.

Part of my week is spent designing pieces for clients who have specific ideas, a room in which they would like a large clock or mirror on a particular theme or colour, gardening being a favourite at the moment, also jewellery being sought in the same manner, this culminating in a highly personalised range of pieces, which also creates interesting and lively work.

David and Rosemary Ashby

David and Rosemary Ashby have worked together for the past eleven years. After meeting at college in Bath where they studied ceramics and illustration respectively, they have continued to evolve and expand on their range of quirky ceramics, including birds, vases, clocks and jewellery.

Throughout their work there is a fascination with miniature intricate detail and surface texture and markings. Carved windows often feature precious little nuggets with pebble shapes being a particular recurring theme. All the pieces are decorated with coloured slips in subtle muted shades, sometimes embellished with gold lustre.

Although precise influences are impossible to pinpoint, a love of the seashore in Devon where they set up in business and the wild limestone landscape of the Yorkshire Dales where they now live are both inspirations.

Simon Easterby

Brewery Arts Resident Makers

Sandra Ireland

Michelle Ohlson - *Workshop - 7a*

Sarah Brooker - *Workshop - 1*

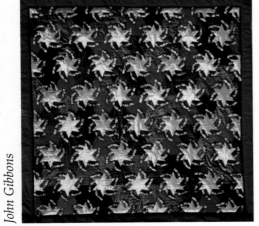

John Gibbons

Esther Barrett - *Workshop - 9*

Loco Glass - *Workshop - 2*

Sarah Beadsmoore
Workshop - 3

It was while working for a sailing club in Devon, twenty years ago, pursuing my first career as a cook that I knew that I wanted to weave! I was lucky enough to return to college and completed three years Textile Design at Derby College of Higher Education. I became a Resident Craftworker at Brewery Arts in 1984 and have never regretted my decision! Most of my production is in silk scarves, as it is such a beautiful and versatile fibre and is easily dyed. My weaving techniques are simple, concentrating on colour and texture, sometimes combining cotton or linen with the silk. I also make throws and cushions, often to commission and am working on a new line of household linens to include table mats, napkins and hand towels.

Dorothy Reglar
Workshop - 6

I am a garment designer/maker with an enduring passion for antique textiles from different cultures. I enjoy using fabrics made with natural fibres, and I am particularly concerned with fine stitching details, texture and colour, simplicity and comfort.

Working with small groups of silk producers, natural dyers and weavers in South East Asia has not only reinforced and expanded these interests, but has put the experience I have acquired through my fashion career to a practical and beneficial use. I enjoy the exchange of ideas and 'know how' I share with these skilled women and the result is beneficial to us all.

Sandra Ireland

The Textile Studio

Workshop - 7

LIZ LIPPIATT
HUGH & SOPHIA BLACKWELL

Designers, dyers, printers
and makers of
amongst other things…
dyed & printed devoré
velvet
silk, satin & organza
dip dyed
pashminas
digitally printed velvet
scarves
& cushions,
scented pillows &
nosegays,
jewellery bags.
bucket bags &
shoppers,
exotic feathery
hairclips & ties
devore window panels
& banners
quotation cushions,
digitally printed
classic reproductions,
bolsters, pouffes
& pillows, velvet skirts
& floaty
georgette tops.

Pam Harrison

Workshop - 9

My work is a reflection of memories; remembered fragments of my life, thoughts, walks and journeys; responses often depicted through an integration of direct observation and symbolic imagery. I have an inherent interest in surface texture and the subtlety of edges, which reflect strongly in my work, creating a variety of layered, tactile elements.

Inspiration comes from a wide range of sources - aged andweathered surfaces, the natural world, coast and land forms, doodles, icons, paintings. Recurrent themes explore concepts of contrast and hidden depths, the notion of equilibrium and dysfunction, a sense of 'broken unity'.

I love to work spontaneously with mixed-media incorporating hand-made papers, paint, collage, print, drawing, stitching, found objects. I aim to capture or evoke a sense of place.

Louise Parry - Workshop - 12

Louise has been producing highly imaginative jewellery since 1987, during which time she has developed a large range of pieces using metals such as silver, gold, bronze, copper and niobium.

As well as being influenced by her surroundings when creating new designs, Louise takes inspiration from architecture, painters such as Kandinsky, Klee and Miro, and also tribal art. She adores the combination of bright colours with metal - whether emeralds with gold or niobium with silver.

Quality and design are both of paramount importance regardless of the materials used. Louise's work appeals to both young and old and is very affordable.

One-off pieces of jewellery can be commissioned from Louise's Cirencester workshop - wedding and engagement rings are a speciality. Louise also supplies shops and galleries throughout the United Kingdom.

Cetta Di Lieto - Workshop - 3

During and since my degree in Ceramics at Loughborough I have continued to enjoy painting and drawing, which has been reflected in my approach to making ceramics. I work using simple forms either made by press moulding or slabbing. Making the form is like making a canvas to paint on.

I work with light coloured clay so that the slips, engobes, and stains are intensified and the contrast between them and the clay body can become part of the surface treatment. Working in a painterly way using a variety of techniques, I can be spontaneous and each piece is individual.

Inspiration for my ceramics comes from a variety of sources including Mediterranean colours and light, architecture, Italian frescos and landscape.

Burford Woodcraft

144 High Street, Burford, Oxon OX18 4QU. Telephone: 01993 823479
Website: www.burford-woodcraft.co.uk
Open Monday - Saturday 9.30am - 5pm, Sunday 11am - 4.45pm

Enjoy an opportunity to browse in the relaxed and friendly atmosphere in one of only a handful of galleries specialising in wood. Surrounded by the beautiful architecture of the Cotswolds BW is at the top of the High Street of this old wool town, looking down into the Windrush Valley.

It is here in this listed building with oak beams, that contemporary British Craftsmanship in wood has been successfully promoted for over twenty years. The ethic remains the same - work is selected carefully by Robert and Jayne Lewin from sixty-seven British designer makers for its good design, quality of finish and originality. The skill and talent displayed encompasses the unusual, creative and with more than a hint of fun. The natural beauty and diversity of wood, the smell and the unique touch bind the extensive collection together through carving, furniture making, sculpting and turning.

The one-off pieces, furniture (Robert is one of the designer makers), mirrors, sculptures, jewellery, bowls and platters coexist with boxes, desk and kitchen ware, jewellery boxes, small accessories, games, toys and much more. Commissions are welcomed and regularly sought. An exhibition is held each Autumn.

The reputation BW has for a wide range of handmade British contemporary work is excellent. The commitment it has providing pieces that are of a high quality, designed and created with inspiration and lovingly made, is strong.

Furniture by Robert Lewin

Graham Lane

I spent a year at Rycotewood - one of the country's leading colleges of furniture design and craftsmanship - which provided a springboard for a career change to furniture designer and maker. The year was highly successful, during which I enhanced my making skills and discovered a hidden talent for design.

Working mainly to commission for private clients, I design and make contemporary furniture of the highest quality. My work has been awarded prestigious Guild Marks from the Worshipful Company of Furniture Makers.

I draw inspiration from architecture and many of my pieces have an Oriental influence. Solid timbers and decorative veneers, home grown and from around the world, are carefully selected to display the natural grain and colour of the wood.

John Mainwaring

One of the most exciting things about sculpture is how many new avenues there are waiting to be explored. Technology has a large part to play in this; although it is not always something an artist likes to admit. New tools and methods make it easier and previously unattainable results more accessible. The internet also has great potential for the craftsperson.

I enjoy making the individual pieces such as the cormorants (pictured) although it is still satisfying to make the animals and bird forms I am so used to. I find that working on a form I am familiar with allows my mind to plan the next piece.

Helen Johnson

Ecstatic elephants, extravagantly coloured fish, cats in hats and dancing figures appear in my work on the theme of 'The joy of Life'. Clocks, mirrors and furniture are made in my own contemporary style as one-off or limited edition pieces.

Making up a new design and seeing it for the first time after removing the masking tape is a great joy. Each item is unique as every piece of veneer is different.

Forms are freely sawn from MDF and plywood and the marquetry veneer cut and assembled by hand, ensuring a high quality of craftsmanship. The items are finished by hand sanding, sealing, waxing and buffing. The wood continues to change colour over the years and this natural ageing process is, for me, part of the charm of the medium.

Ralph Williams

Ralph Williams was born in Hertfordshire in 1940 and now lives in Cornwall. He is a self taught artist/craftsman, his carvings reflecting a life-long interest in the natural world and his chosen medium.

For a time he worked at the Department of Ornithology of the Natural History Museum and subsequently for several years in forestry, before devoting all his working hours to carving about 25 years ago. He collects and seasons most of the timber himself, keeping larger stocks of favourites such as Walnut, Yew, Laburnum, Plane and Oak.

In recent years he has supplied many carvings to be awarded to winners of competitions run by the BBC Wildlife Magazine.

Don White

Since moving to North Cornwall in 1997, and been relatively free of the constraints of raising a young family it has been my intention to place more emphasis on creating individual pieces rather than to continue as 'the maker' of salad bowls, which has been the bulk of my production for over 20 years. Carving, texturing and colouring are techniques that I have touched on during the period but have been unable to devote enough time to explore to its full potential. It is now time to satisfy my soul. My ambition now is to live long enough to enjoy the immense wealth that this new work will inevitably bring.

Crich Pottery

Market Place, Crich, Derbyshire, DE4 5DD. Telephone: 01773 853171 Fax: 01773 857325
Website: www.crichpottery.com
Open Daily 10am - 6pm but phone first if coming far, to check.

Crich Pottery, Gallery and Workshops are located opposite the bakery in the village Market Place in Crich, on the edge of the Peak Park, four miles south of Matlock, twelve miles north of Derby (M1 J28)

David and Diana Worthy have lived and worked at Crich Pottery for over twenty

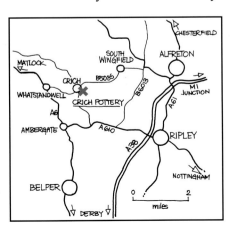

five years. The premises consist of the Workshop, house, stables (now self-catering accomodation) and Gallery.

All the buildings, arranged around a courtyard, have been converted from old farm buildings, circa 1800.
The Gallery, which is open to the public, sells the full range of Crich Pottery, plus the new Life Force work of Diana Worthy, together with paintings by William Barber and Daniel Alexander.

Diana & David Worthy

Diana & David produce an extensive range of stoneware ceramics, handthrown on the Potter's Wheel, and indiviually applied with rich colourful stoneware glazes; their recipes evolved empirically by Diana over the years in the workshop.

Her intense love of colour was there from childhood, but developed in her postgraduate years at the RCA when she worked in glass and acrylics, and later whilst a freelance Designer at Denby, where she discovered Derbyshire, and a 'handwriting of landscape' evolved into ceramic surface, with images drawn freehand directly into the glaze.

The robust oven-to-tableware collection includes mugs, jugs, teapots, bowls, plates etc., and interior accessories such as lampbases, planters and waterfeatures. They also make a luxury bathroom hand-washbasin with matching tiles and drawer-knobs.

Diana Worthy

These pebbles, hilltops and landscaped squares are pure escapism from years of production line pieces, and return me to the abstract lines of blowing grass which defined my drawing when I left the RCA.

Always a beachcomber, the pebbles, or Dinosaur Eggs, as I like to call them, relate to the landscape geologically, combining different influences from the lines on the actual pebbles with the flora to be found in the dunes - allowing for artistic license !!

I love to work 'graphically' around a satisfying form, and relate the one to to the other, and these new pieces have reminded me how much fun you can have with clay.

The colour variation I can apply to these pebbles by 'drawing' with the spray gun is such a refreshing change from the requirements of our production line.

Ferrers Gallery

0%

Ferrers Centre for Arts and Crafts, Staunton Harold, Ashby de la Zouch, LE65 1RU.
Telephone: 01332 863337 Website: www.ferrersgallery.co.uk
Open April - October, Tuesday - Saturday 11am - 5pm. October - April, Tuesday - Sunday 11am - 5pm

Set amidst a beautiful country estate in the heart of England is the former Georgian Stables of Staunton Harold Hall. The stables have been sympathetically converted into a thriving Arts Centre with workshops, tea-rooms and the Ferrers Gallery.

We are in the old Granary, where on three floors you will find an eclectic selection of work covering all the major disciplines by accomplished British craftsmen, and young emerging makers in ceramics, glass, ironwork, jewellery, prints, textiles and wood from about three hundred makers. customer and the maker.

First floor

We offer a vibrant exhibition programme, details of which can be sent on request.

We usually show five exhibitions a year, sometimes themed, very often mixed media, but always beautifully displayed and well worth a visit. Consistently selling furniture we are well versed with dealing with commissions and welcome the opportunity to provide a link between the customer and the maker.

Jonathan Eadie

Jonathan Eadie is the designer and chief maker of all the products crafted at Belltrees Forge Limited.

An artist in his own right, Jonathan is able to create from metal what others can not imagine possible. With free-flowing shape and a subtle sense of fun, his designs create decorative, yet functional, pieces of furniture and decorative accessories including candlesticks, sconces, lighting and wine racks.

These age-old skills involve heating, hammering and twisting the white-hot steel and then forming it into Jonathan's eye-catching, contemporary designs. Finally, each piece is highly polished to accentuate the natural textures of the steel and then coated in a light, protective lacquer.

With the popularity of his work growing, opportunities for apprentices to learn the traditional skills of blacksmithing are becoming readily available at Belltrees Forge.

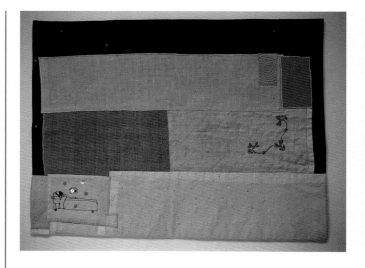

Michelle Holmes

My new textile pictures continue my interest in spaces of pattern, inhabited by line drawings of figures. I have used colour more widely and strongly than my previous 'sandstone' pieces to produce work which describes the sense of awe I feel when I look at landscapes or the sky - the vastness and the variety.

My figures are drawn with a grey shiny thread like pencil onto backgrounds of varying textures. The stitches sit on the surface and light plays with the texture of the thread. This can be emphasised by experimenting with stitch length and density. It is a very spontaneous process. It is tricky to undo so I have to work with my mistakes. I also use hand stitching, beads and applique.

Pamela Burrows and Oliver Vowles Burrows

After studying sculpture and fine art Pamela turned to jewellery making with a sculptural emphasis. Working with her husband designer-jeweller Christopher Burrows, their work was shown widely in Europe and the USA and in touring exhibitions in Japan and Canada. Pamela ceased making jewellery on the death of Christopher in 1982, spending the next few years with her young son travelling and working in other areas of art and design. Returning refreshed to jewellery and metal work, Pamela's work is now exhibited at galleries across the UK and in collections in Europe and Australia.

Her son Oliver, who studied at Falmouth Art School before a period at a design studio is developing his own distinct style and has joined Pamela who works from her home close to some of the wildest coast and cliffs of North Cornwall, where the boldness of the landscape echoes her interest in form and structure, while her love of travel brings the visual difference, change and excitement which combine to create a continuous development in her work.

Tom Petit

I was initially intrigued by Glass Blowing, while participating in a weekend class at a Studio in Cornwall over a school holiday. I became fascinated by this molten material, which could be fashioned into a diverse range of forms from the truly classical to the widely organic.

Five years of Higher Education led to working and exhibiting in not only the United Kingdom, but also Europe, Canada, New Zealand and Australia.

My Glass work varies from the elegant twists and curves incorporated into the stoppered bottles, in my 'Mono' range, to the delicate layers, which make up the abstract depiction of a landscape in my 'Moors' range.

Glass is extremely tactile - Go on touch it!

Brian Hollingworth

Observation and the recording of observation are the most important skills used in my work. Without these, I would not have the knowledge needed to design and make my sculptures.

I have been gifted with the ability to have a total view of my work before I begin. An idea will take months, if not years, to formulate in my imagination.

When I am ready to begin work on a new piece I have a clear vision of the completed sculpture. The blocking of the basic form is the most important stage of my work; it is then that I turn my personal vision into form. If a sculpture is going to be right, I will know almost immediately as the form takes shape beneath my hands.

Top: Brian Hollingworth
Centre: Exhibition floors
Bottom: Pamela Burrows

Focus Gallery

108 Derby Road, Nottingham NG1 5FB. Telephone: 0115 9537575
Open: Monday 10am - 5.30pm, Tuesday - Saturday 9.30am - 5.30pm

Founded in 1971 to provide "an alternative to high street mass production," Focus Gallery has brought contemporary arts and crafts to the East Midlands for over thirty years. A change of ownership in 1995 did nothing to diminish the unique combination of a wide choice of craft products in an accessible and welcoming atmosphere and has resulted in much new work being introduced.

Situated on the fringe of a busy city centre, Focus has a reputation as the place for different gifts and cards in a street where "the unusual and curious are commonplace." The gallery is housed in an attractive listed building with two large downstairs display areas which provide plenty of exhibition space and a ground floor shop where customers complain of being spoilt for choice!

Large selections of the work of over one hundred and fifty makers are featured, including pictures and paintings, ceramics, jewellery, glass, wood and metal sculpture, and a large range of handmade cards. The bustling location provides a wide and varied audience for featured makers. Focus retains its integrity and its difference through the consistent quality of its selection and the unique knowledge of artists gained through the relationship built up, often over many years.

If Focus Gallery has a predominant theme it comes perhaps from sharing in a celebration of landscape, countryside and the "sense of place" that inspires so many craftspeople in the materials they use and the images they present whether realistic, abstract or even fantastic.

David Withnall

David Withnall has made his living full-time as a ceramic artist for over twenty years. His early success with functional garden and conservatory pieces has recently allowed more sculptural work to evolve. Every pot is an individual sculpture and these pieces have found a particular following with flower arrangers world-wide, a creative use that David feels adds to the integrity of his work. His influences stem from a celebration of landscape and mythology: the paradox of the process of creation and disintegration visible in nature, in the Derbyshire countryside for example. He seeks to present the perfect shape in contrast with the natural fissure or fault found in nature. The rustic colours and textures hint at the primeval.

Elaine Thompson

Elaine has a degree in mathematics and gave up a full time occupation with computers to allow time to pursue her interests in arts and crafts.

She took up woodcarving as a hobby and with this came an interest in pyrography and a desire to produce original work in this medium. She particularly appreciates the grain of the wood and has aimed to use pyrography to enhance the figuring of the wood rather than detracting from it. The drawings are imaginatively integrated into the grain patterns already existing in the wood making every picture unique. "Every piece of wood is different. I may spend hours looking at the wood to see what it suggests to me before starting work on it. It's impossible to have two pictures the same".

The Gloucestershire Guild Gallery

Painswick Centre, Bisley Street, Painswick, Gloucestershire GL6 6QQ. Telephone: 01452 814745
Email: info@guildcrafts.org.uk Website: www.guildcrafts.org.uk
Open Tuesday - Saturday 10am - 5pm, some seasonal opening variations

The Gloucestershire Guild of Craftsmen was established in 1933. Now in its 67th year the Guild still holds to the same high excellence that has earned it an international reputation for the quality of the work of its members.

As a fitting development at the start of the new Millennium, last year the Guild established its first permanent base and gallery in Painswick, the village long associated with our summer exhibitions.

The members of the Guild are selected to become associates for two years and only become full members after an appraisal by the full Guild.

Visitors to the gallery can enjoy and purchase from a range that includes ceramics, wood-turning, jewellery, glass, paper marbling, textiles, printmaking, furniture, hand made cards and much more!

The Gloucestershire Guild Gallery

*MONTPELLIER

Contemporary Art

8 Chapel Street, Stratford-upon-Avon, CV37 6EP. Telephone: 01789 261161
Open Monday - Saturday 9.30am -5.30pm

Montpellier Gallery has been established in the heart of Stratford-upon-Avon since 1991. It is Crafts Council selected for its quality and can be found near the centre of the town opposite the Shakespeare Hotel. Set in a 400 year old building, the gallery comprises three adjoining rooms, opening to a delightful tiny courtyard which floods the rooms with natural light.

We have built a strong reputation for the contemporary works we show - whether ceramics, studio glass or contemporary jewellery, pieces are always selected using a discerning eye for their quality, originality and form. In fact the Gallery has been host to leading craftsmen and the work of artists for over 25 years, having previously been owned by Peter

Dingley, a leading Craft dealer specialising in, amongst others, Lucie Rie.

Whilst maintaining these traditions, we now include contemporary paintings, original printmaking and a diverse range of sculpture in

bronze and other materials. The gallery is strongly committed to promoting an awareness of the originality of the hand-made process in all media.

Montpellier Gallery regularly features exhibitions of work by individual artists and

Montpellier Contemporary Art

crafts people, or shows a variety of media sharing a theme. Between exhibitions, the varied displays represent a selection of the finest work by new and recognised makers, bringing fresh expectations along with the continuity from earlier traditions. We find there is a ready responsiveness and enthusiasm for new talent, together with a loyalty and appreciation for established names. This mix gives the gallery visual excitement, colour, and a refreshing stylistic diversity.

The Gallery is run by Peter Burridge, a trained jeweller/silversmith and an established artist-printmaker in his own right, bringing his broad knowledge of the Fine Arts and Crafts to create the Gallery's breadth of choice and selection. We are a member of the Independent Crafts Galleries Association, and also have a number of long-established relationships with artists from France and Italy.

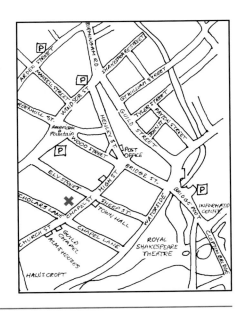

Nick Mackman

During her formative years, Nick Mackman developed a great love for animals, especially dogs. Initially, she began expressing this admiration on canvas. Then in 1990, on a Foundation course, she was to discover the wonders of clay. In 1992 she began an HND course specialising in animal modelling, during which time she worked as Rhino keeper in Chester Zoo.

"This inspirational experience allowed me to get involved with a variety of animals and to watch, touch and study the nature of these animals intimately. When making an animal, I first consider the character of the animal, such as the pride and grace of a giraffe, and then try to emulate this through its stance, movement and expression." The clay body is T material, the strongest clay type, with paper pulp which gives a strong but lightweight result. Occasionally, she uses papier mache on delicate extremities as it lends itself well to clay and has the great advantage of being unbreakable.

"I aim to enlighten people to the beauty, humour and tenderness of those animals that are largely seen or represented as purely aggressive, dangerous or ugly. Above all I hope that humankind will feel the individuality of each animal and appreciate its intrinsic beauty".

Claire Seneviratne

'The way is like an empty vessel that yet may be
drawn from'   (LAO-TZU - 3rd Century B.C.)

This 'silence' or 'stillness' is not just a void empty
space but has an energy, a wisdom, a feeling of
totality. It also presents itself in the natural world.
Sunlight shimmering on quiet seas, forms sculpted by
the elements and washed up on beaches, evoke an
omnipotence that feeds the inspiration for my work.

I imagine how the ebbing tides influence the surface
of shells and rocks while burnishing my own vessels.
I am searching for this timeless quality. Violent smoke
firing in woodshavings and sawdust produces ancient
contrasting effects with flashes of metallic lustre and
can create a calming and energising resolution.

Peter Layton

Trained in ceramics, Peter was captivated by the
immediacy of glassblowing, and in 1976 set up the
London Glassblowing Workshop.

His approach is experimental and his pieces seek to
express the magic of glass, its sensuality and fluidity.
As an inveterate beachcomber much of his work is
inspired by shells and pebbles, lichen patterns, found
objects and places visited. Recent works explore the
theme of ice and snow; exploiting the way glass
freezes at a particular moment in the cooling process.
Such pieces record intention and accident, a process
partly controlled, partly natural, in the endeavour to
create objects that express more than purely
functional or decorative qualities.

He is considered one of the finest glassmakers
working today with work in major public and private
collections throughout the world.

Alasdair Neil MacDonell

Inspired by the classicism of antiquity, African and Tribal art, Alasdair Neil MacDonell makes a wide range of ceramics that are unmistakably contemporary. Faces are a central theme but he makes frequent references to architecture.

The complex surface patterns that he creates are derived from found objects, packaging and industrial scrap. A search through the hundreds of moulds in his studio may reveal textures from squashed frogs, breakfast cereals and a host of other unlikely sources.

"My studio contains so much resource material that I need never repeat myself, and I am adding to these resources all the time. The discovery of a discarded wrapper can launch a new range of ideas".

Alasdair is a professional member of the Craft Potters Association.

Michael Storey

Michael has been creating and casting his own bronze sculpture for over twenty years. Specialising in smaller, more affordable items, Michael also produces hand blown glass and bronze combinations.

Galleries throughout Australia, the USA and the UK represent this artist.

"Many people who eventually become artists often experience difficulty in life until an outlet for their expressiveness is found.

I really enjoy being in a creative environment. Of particular interest to me is the physiological illusion' some how' imparted to an inanimate sample of bronze that then becomes a living breathing entity. The same applies to a flat canvas that is transformed into a spatially alive atmosphere".

That 'some how' - is what the magic is all about.

Oxfordshire Craft Guild Co-operative ♿

7 Goddards Lane, Chipping Norton, Oxfordshire OX7 5NP. Telephone: 01608 641525
Website: www.ocgcraftshop.co.uk

Open Monday - Saturday 10am -5pm (closed Wednesday & Sunday)

In 1994 the Theatre at Chipping Norton approached the Oxfordshire Craft Guild with the idea that a small room opposite their Box Office could become a craft shop. After some deliberation, and help from ICOM, a group of around twenty Guild members set up a co-operative to run a shop.

The co-operative has steadily increased its turnover during these seven years, selling crafts that range in price from under £10 to over £500. Although most of the work is by potters and jewellers, we have mixed media work, and members working with pewter, glass, wood and textiles. We provide a portfolio for commissions, to promote the work of those who do not have sufficient space to display large pieces.

The shop is staffed on a rota by members, helped by some generous volunteers and an enthusiastic coordinator. Our profile is enhanced by featuring members as 'Craftsperson of the Month'. We also participate in Oxfordshire Artweeks in May, and link with other local crafts people on a Christmas trail.

Oxfordshire Craft Guild Co-operative

Oxfordshire Craft Guild Co-operative

Jane Hanson

Jenny Hassan (*Papier maché*)

Left: Maurice Bourne *Above:* Peter Clark

Oxfordshire Craft Guild Co-operative

Gilly Whittington

Clare Wratten

Chris Townsend

Hannelore Meinhold-Morgan

Tom Neal

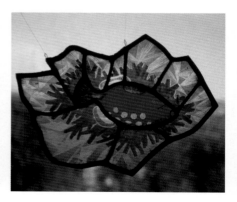

Margaret Cullen

Oxfordshire Craft Guild Co-operative

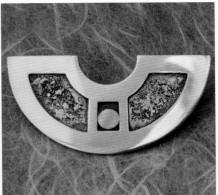

Annik Piriou

Audrey Stockwin

Edith Holt

Pauline Payne

Rosemary Zeeman

Maryon Phelps

Shire Hall Gallery

Market Square, Stafford, ST16 2LD. Telephone: 01785 278345 Fax: 01785 278327
Email: shirehallgallery@staffordshire.gov.uk Website: www.staffordshire.gov.uk
*Open Monday & Friday 9.30am -6pm, Tuesday, Wednesday & Thursday 9.30am - 5pm,
Saturday 10am - 5pm*

The Shire Hall Gallery is an important visual arts venue located in Stafford's Market Square. The magnificent eighteenth century Grade II listed Court building, with its magnificent classical pillars and plasterwork hosts a number of temporary exhibitions each year. Visitors can view exhibitions of fine art and craft across the whole spectrum of creative work, produced by contemporary artists from many different cultures.

The Gallery's Craft Shop is listed on the National List of Craft Shops and Galleries, and represents many leading British craftspeople. High quality jewellery, ceramics, glass and other craft works are carefully chosen and displayed in a specially designed setting.

Why not join the Friends of the Gallery scheme and enjoy benefits such as discounts on purchases from the Craft Shop, invitations to

exhibition private views and priority booking for events?

Access details:
*Level access from the street
*Chairlift to the Courtroom

Shire Hall Gallery

(limited access) & coffee bar.
*Accessible toilets with baby-changing facilities.
*Induction loop system in main gallery spaces.
*Guide/hearing dogs are welcome.

304

Daryl Harber

I make jewellery, but do not consider myself a Jewellery Maker. Similarly, my clock and frame designs are not the work of one formally trained in these fields. Arriving at Craft Design via Graphic Design, Illustration and Sculpture, my ignorance of conventional craft methods leaves me unconstrained to experiment freely with my designs. I work mainly in photo-etched nickel silver, brass and copper, beaten, polished, patinated and relieved to produce a variety of finishes which are often combined to interesting effect. The infinite variation of the Natural World is a constant inspiration, with a fascination for the art and culture of the Ancients often in evidence. I aim to create original designs in which aesthetic considerations and functionality are integrated. If they occasionally make people smile, all the better.

Robert Meadows

Pat Armstrong

Pat Armstrong is a potter who favours thrown classical-shaped pots in three very different raku finishes - coloured crackle glazes, black and white burnished naked raku and copper-fumed vessels. The crackle finishes give an aged appearance which works well on the simple forms. The copper-fumed work is inspired by her fascination with fire and flames, and the technique 'paints' fiery pictures directly onto the pots.

Simon Shaw

I studied at Wirral College of Art and Design and at Braintree College, Essex. I have enjoyed employment at many workshops both in the UK and abroad, I established my present workshop in my native Merseyside in 1988.

The work is thrown in a stoneware clay with additions of raku and porcelain strips or coils. I rarely turn work, except bowls and some platters. The work is bisque fired to 1000°C and glaze fired at approximately 1200°C. I vary the glaze firing temperature and glaze application to achieve subtle variations in the dry, matt glazes.

Plans for 2001/02 include producing more raku work and helping build, develop and produce work from Anagama type kilns.

Malcolm Sutcliffe

I started making glass back in the mid seventies and I have always enjoyed making bowls. I like to keep the shapes simple and spend a lot of time adding and blending the colours to achieve a layering and depth of one colour over another.

Then I take most of the colour off again in the sandblasting process, the elephant bowls in particular have to be treated with great care so as not to take too much colour away when doing the shading.

Each piece is a challenge to try and get it to be how I imagine it should be in my minds' eye.

Shire Hall Gallery

Salt Gallery

♿

4 Bear Court, 38 Lower High Street, Burford, Oxfordshire OX18 4RR. Tel: 01993 822371
Email: saltgallery@btinternet.com Website: www.saltgallery.com
Open Thur - Mon 10am-4.30pm (Other times by appointment)

The Salt Gallery can be found in a picturesque Cotswold stone courtyard garden accessed from the High Street via a stone built archway, part of the premises of the Wren Gallery(original paintings).

The space occupied by the gallery, which in a previous life was partially a stable, is surprisingly light and airy benefiting from three sunny cottage windows and items are displayed in an uncluttered way.

We specialise in British Studio Pottery & Glass and cater for both the serious collector and the casual visitor alike.

Ceramics, despite the gallery name, are not limited to salt and soda glaze.We inlcude work by Steve Harrison, Rebecca Harvey, John Leach, Emily Myers, Ruthanne Tudball, Gilda Westermann & Clare Wratten amongst others. The glass we offer is by Norman Stuart Clark and Siddy Langley. In both cases we like to offer a range of items in both design and price.

Bridget Wheatley Contemporary Jewellery

38 Cowley Road, Oxford OX4 1HZ. Telephone: 01865 722184 Fax: 01865 79058
Website: www.bridgetwheatley.com
Open Tuesday - Saturday 10am - 5.30pm

The shop is twenty minutes walk from Oxford City centre on the increasingly popular and vibrant Cowley Road. It is a light and airy showroom for the work of many designer/makers, alongside Bridget's own ranges of unique jewellery.

Bridget opened her shop in October 2000. There is a welcoming atmosphere

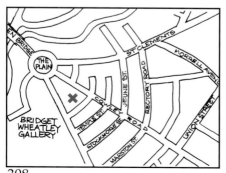

within a working environment. The shop is a haven of creativity and innovation, even the displays which are made on the premises are original.

The jewellery is from an eclectic group of artists. It is diverse in design and materials. The individuality of each designer is immediately striking. The collections continue to evolve.

Bridget Wheatley Contemporary Jewellery

Bridget Wheatley

I am inspired by medieval and celtic art. The essence of my work is simplistic with attention to detail. I enjoy using irregular shaped freshwater pearls and richly coloured gemstones combined with gold and silver. Bigger pieces of silver are hammered and embossed with 18ct gold and have a tactile quality.

I graduated from Birmingham School of Jewellery in 1984. Since then I have designed and produced a wide selection of jewellery. After humble beginnings, I was able to open my first shop 'Uniikki', a shared venture, in 1995. There I gained enough experience and confidence to branch out on my own. It is a pleasure to offer a diverse selection of other peoples work and to continue with my individual ideas, together with a bespoke service.

All photos on this page by Paul Freestone

Jessica Briggs

My work continues to develop exploring the possibilities for creating pattern and texture on silver.

Through a series of low-tech techniques pieces are textured, formed and decorated with gold which is fused to the silver surface.

Simplicity and ease of wear are important elements in my jewellery, as is the quality of the finished piece.

Each piece is individually worked, and design ideas are adapted and refined throughout the process of making.

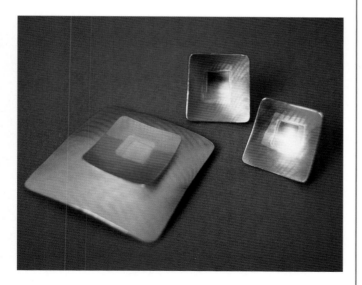

Gina Cowen

Found along the shoreline, these sea 'jewels' are transformed from bottles and other discarded glass objects, worn down over the years to frosted translucent pebbles by the constant surge and ebb of the tide. Most common are shades of green, pale aqua, brown and white. More rare are dark blue, pink, red, purple, orange, even yellow, bringing delight to any finder. They are carefully drilled and strung into necklaces - like solid water - bracelets and earrings, or bezel set in rings (in silver or 18ct gold). They are worked in a way that captures their natural shape and luminosity and look wonderful against bare skin or natural fabrics. The sea glass is formed in places of beauty and timelessness, qualities which stay with the jewels when worn.

Annik Piriou

I studied Fine Art at the Ruskin School of Drawing and Painting in the 1960's. By the 1980's I had turned to making jewellery.

I use simple tools, modern versions of those used by jewellers through the ages. Working mostly in silver I decorate in various ways; indenting with steel punches, which I make myself; oxidisation to provide a contrast. I add 18ct gold detail and also semi-precious stones. I am still fascinated by the process of making - how a piece, partly worked, blackened and unprepossessing, is transformed into a desirable object.

I work out my designs both on paper and while working, allowing a constant evolution. I wish my work to be strong, beautiful and wearable and recognisable as mine.

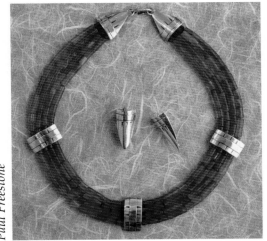

Paul Freestone

Jenifer Kilgour

Shona Fidgett

Shona Fidgett graduated from Duncan of Jordonstone School of Art in 1997, and has based herself in her home town of Glasgow, setting up her workshop in the west end of the City.

Taking inspiration from architecture, she produces a wide range of jewellery using geometric forms in bold clean-lined pieces, enjoying working predominantly in silver, using 18ct yellow gold for precious detailing.

Since graduating she has successfully established her name, supplying her work in various outlets, galleries and exhibitions.

The jewellery has a broad range of wearers who appreciate the elegant simplicity of the designs. Each piece is individually hand crafted and finished off with an emphasis on quality.

Verandah

♿

13 North Parade, Oxford OX2 6LX. Telephone: 01865 310123
Open Monday - Saturday 10am - 5.30pm

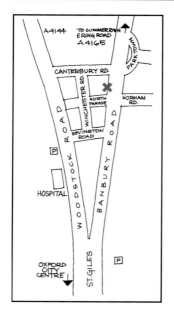

Verandah, an exciting gallery opened in 1998, is owned, run and 'manned' by five local designers. The gallery displays a rich mixture of ceramics, jewellery, glass and textiles. New work is sourced constantly from makers throughout Britain, a selection of whom are featured in our entry. Exhibitions of featured artists during the year add to the diversity of Verandah.

North Parade, well worth the ten minute walk from Oxford city centre, offers great eating places, unique specialist shops and a most beautiful laundrette! And there's easy parking for an hour or so in the neighbouring roads.

Verandah

Verandah

Left: Sue Binns
Right: Lorna Jackson-Currie

Jan Fryer

Sophie Thompson

Whitemoors Gallery

♿

Shenton, Near Nuneaton, Warwickshire CV13 6BZ. Telephone: 01455 213350
Open Monday - Sunday 11am - 5pm. Winter months 11am - 4pm.

Whitemoors Gallery is part of Whitemoors Antique Centre in the conservation village of Shenton on the Leicestershire and Warwickshire border.

Surrounding the gravelled courtyard car park is a carefully restored collection of farm buildings dating back to the seventeenth century. The Gallery used to be the stables and the huge timbers supporting the Granary above date back to Elizabeth I, when they were used for maritime purposes, then subsequently returned to the Shenton Estate.

Whitemoors was the camp of Henry Tudor and the whole area is known for 'The Battle

of Bosworth '.The Centre has landscaped gardens and a licensed tea room.

The Gallery exhibits mainly 'one off' pieces from well known makers as well as newcomers to ceramics and glass, with a seasonal change over on a continuous display basis. There are also original paintings, etchings, silkscreen prints and limited edition prints always available.

Whitemoors Gallery

A corner of the gallery showing work by the following makers, whose work is regularly displayed at Whitemoors:

Pat Armstrong - *Raku ceramics*

Chris Carter - *Porcelain 'cycladic' pots*

Carlos Versluys - *Ash glazed and carved stoneware*

Berenice Kate Alcock - *Porcelain spiral pots and raku wall masks*

Siddy Langley - *Blown glass*

Jean-Paul Laudreau - *Sgraffito and lustre decorated bowls*

Stephen Thompson - *Dancing clocks and jugs*

Paul Young - *Traditional English Country Pottery*

Some other Galleries and Shops in Central England

Roundhouse Gallery
The Firs
Foston
Derbyshire
DE65 5DL
Tel: 01283 585348
Open
Mon - Fri 1 - 5.30 pm, Sat
10 am - 5.30 pm

Traffords
Digbeth Street
Stow-on-the-Wold
Gloucestershire
GL54 1BN
Tel: 01451 830424
Email: anthony@
traffords.sagehost.co.uk
www.
traffords.sagehost.co.uk
Open
Mon - Sat 9.30am- 5.30pm
Sun 10am - 4pm

Warwick Gallery
82 Regent Street
Royal Leamington Spa
Warwickshire
CV32 4NS
Tel: 01926 422833
www.art-is-a-tart.com
Open Mon - Sat
9.30 am 5.30pm

Warwick Gallery
12 - 14 Smith Street
Warwick
Warwickshire
CV34 4HH
Tel: 01926 495880
www.art-is-a-tart.com
Open Mon - Sat
9.30 a.m - 5.30pm

WWW. ?

Research for the recent second edition of Second Steps (for more details see back cover flap), revealed that there are now numerous craft related websites.

Some show selected crafts others show all who want to be promoted. Is this the way forward for buying crafts? Any comments would be welcome; good sites which you have discovered, how did you find them, do you buy from the internet or not etc.?

Sites which took space in Second Steps:

www.Allegria.co.uk

www.craft-connections.com

www.craftselect.co.uk

www.getsomeart.com

There are many, many more and your feedback would be appreciated. Information received may be used in the next edition of Second Steps, it should be addressed to the Craft Galleries office (see page 422), thank you.

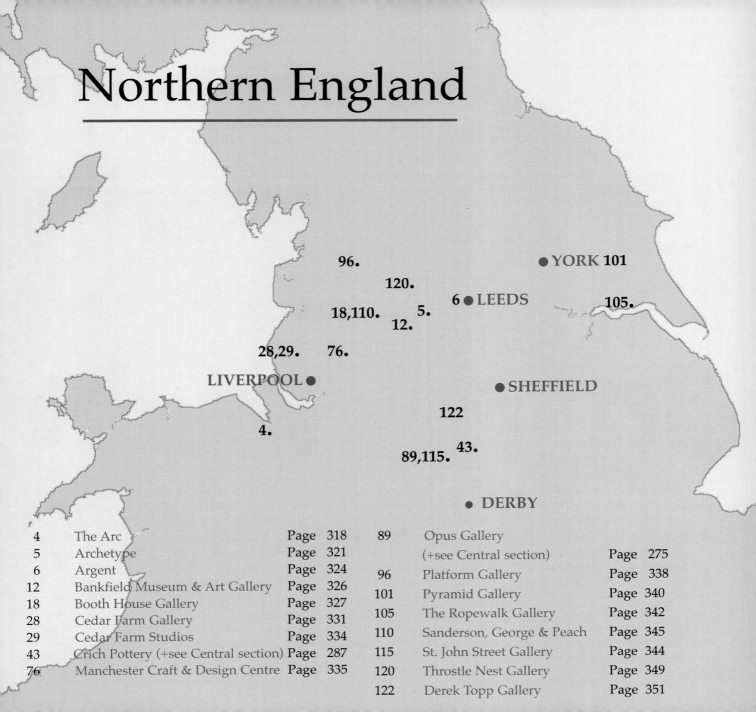

Northern England

96.

120.

18,110.

12.

5.

6 ● LEEDS

● YORK 101

105.

28,29.

76.

LIVERPOOL ●

4.

● SHEFFIELD

122

89,115.

43.

● DERBY

The Arc

4 Commonhall Street, off Bridge Street, Chester, CH1 2BJ. Telephone: 01244 348379
Open Tuesday - Saturday 10am - 5pm

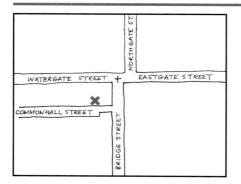

Chester is one of England's most beautiful cities and compactly contained within its medieval wall, it is also one of the easiest to explore - even in the rain. The Arc, housed in an 18th Century warehouse and only a few steps from the Central Cross, is both shop and gallery. Alongside beautifully made and useful traditional crafts, from bookends and horn spoons to scrubbing brushes, you will also find a spread of the very best contemporary ceramics, glass, textiles and jewellery.

Everything is chosen with an eye to the skills that reveal the qualities of a chosen material; light through glass, glaze on clay, the grain and weight of wood, the curve of acrylic, spun pewter. Jewellery is selected for wit and wearability, fashion and decorative textiles for the glorious richness of colour, imagination and different techniques.

New work is explored through the exhibition programme 'Changing Places' which allows us to show work from the degree shows as well as established makers. Among recent additions we have Liz Lawrence and Kyra Cane, potters; Blowzone, glass; Wallace and Sewell textiles. Always in demand, are Sally Reilly, Richard Pheathean, Gail Klevan, Julie Sellars, Nick Munro and Bert Marsh among many others.

Last - but the reason we are here - we thank new customers who seek us out and most especially, those who return.

The Arc

Sally Nicol-Blair

Sally Nicol-Blair specialises in creating limited edition and one-off contemporary designs on fabric, which combine hand painting, dyeing and some silk-screening to enhance designs, with rich use of colour to give an impression of depth and structure.

Sally uses luxurious silk fabrics, ranging from velvet to fine chiffon, that are chosen for their interesting textures and weight. Work includes scarves, ties, cushions, throws, wall panels, framed pictures and scented pillows which are both functional and decorative.

Monica Boxley

Monica trained in jewellery design at South Thames College in 1999 after a long career in teaching. In just two years, she has developed an astonishingly diverse collection of bold contemporary pieces with a unique blend of style, elegance and originality.

Much of her exquisite silver work is hollow-formed and textured using a variety of techniques including etching and milling. The tactile surface patterns are derived from a wide range of natural forms such as marine, plant and animal life, giving them character and depth. For added richness, many pieces are oxidised and embellished with semi-precious stones and subtle gold detailing.

Dramatic pieces such as glass bead multi-strand wire necklaces and bracelets are imbued with her imaginative use of lively colour - and these are also available with rock crystals and other semi-precious stones.

Monica works from her studio in a converted 19th century stable block in Isleworth, West London and her jewellery is sold and exhibited widely around the country.

Sarah Vernon

I originally studied graphic design and after twelve years in magazine publishing, I left the BBC in 1997 to pursue a more creatively fulfilling career.

Morning walks with my dog on the beach have proved beneficial, not only do I gather driftwood and shells for use in my work but the daily activity of the Thames estuary's fishing boats, cargo ships and racing yachts are currently my source of inspiration.

I enjoy the playful qualities of clay as I like to rip, stretch and draw in the rolled out slabs, and paint and splash the finished boats with coloured slips. The free and spontaneous style I have developed means that each piece has individuality and I hope an element of fun.

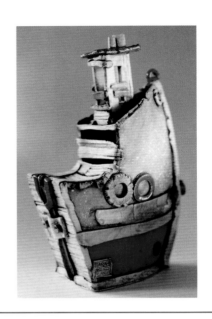

John Jelfs

I have been potting full time since leaving Cheltenham College of Art in 1971. From the very start the work that excited me most was that of Bernard Leach and his life long friend, the Japanese potter Shoji Hamada. I have always wanted to make simple pots that rely on subtle form and rich glazes. My pots are all handthrown and are often altered whilst still on the wheel. I make my glazes (which are mainly Eastern in origin) from materials local to my studio, ie, wood ash, limestone and local iron bearing clay. The pots are stoneware fired in gas kiln.

My hope is that people who come upon my pots will enjoy them as much as I did making them.

Archetype

36 Byram Arcade, Huddersfield HD1 1ND. Telephone: 01484 532550 Fax: 01484 861619
Email: info@archetype-gallery.co.uk Website: www.archetype-gallery.co.uk
Open Tuesday - Saturday 10am - 5.30pm

Archetype is located conveniently in central Huddersfield's Victorian Byram Arcade, enjoying rapid access from both railway and bus stations.

The gallery exhibits a wide range of contemporary crafts, featuring both internationally established designer/makers and emerging new talent.

Work is offered for sale within the context of a rolling showcase programme, allowing for a frequently changing selection of items in a variety of media. In addition to the exhibition programme, Archetype hosts a core group of popular makers whose work is

available on a regular basis. Every effort is made to cater for all tastes and price ranges.

Established in May 2000, Archetype is fast gaining a reputation as the place to find an exciting choice of unique, design-led jewellery, ceramics, glass, textiles, wood, prints, metalwork and photography. Hand-made cards are a particular speciality.

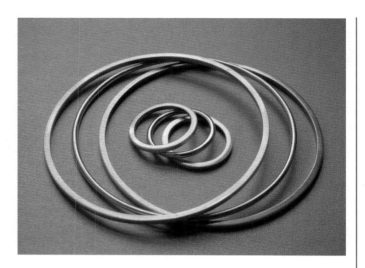

Julie Pratt

After studying various craft disciplines Julie soon realised working with precious metals was her main area of interest. Her contemporary jewellery is classical and yet simple in style with inspiration coming from such forms as the line and the circle. Most of her design reference comes from architecture and nature in which these shapes are infinitely represented. Repetition and grouping is also a factor in her designs. All her range is hand fabricated from a combination of sterling silver and gold, the two materials creating more choice within the range.

Born in Yorkshire, Julie has had her own business since graduating in 1998. She successfully sells her work at several leading galleries in the North of England.

Ian Clarkson

I love wood! As a result I collect wood on a somewhat obsessive scale - always with a mind to what could be made from it - a bowl, a hollow form, plain or natural edged; using the natural finish of the wood or staining or ebonising it. The most important factor in producing a quality product, though, is form and I aim to achieve flowing curves that mirror nature and enhance the beauty of the raw material. I almost always use British timbers for my bowls, hollow forms and sculptural pieces, but also employ colourful laminates and small pieces of exotic timbers for jewellery pieces.

Inspiration comes from a variety of sources - particularly some North American, Australian and European artistic turners, sculptors and ceramicists.

Maureen Collier

Natural forms like shells and leaves are the main focus for my ceramic pieces. I have made extensive exploration into the use of paper clay. The mixture of clay and paper fibres allows great flexibility and enables me to create very delicate forms. My work is predominantly porcelain collaged with handmade paper and found objects and mounted into box frames. I studied at Bretton Hall College at the University of Leeds where I graduated in 1997 with a BA Honours degree and an MA.

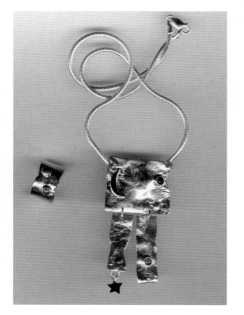

Sally Ratcliffe

After working for several years on costumes for a Rep Theatre, a move to Sheffield released Sally from one creative atmosphere into another. Inspired by the beautiful scenery and natural forms around the countryside, Sally embarked on her jewellery interest which quickly blossomed into a full-time career. Two children later she finds the odd sleepless night does wonders for inspiration! After working at home for twelve years, starting to talk to herself a little too much, she is now waiting for the new Yorkshire Artspace studios to be completed which will maybe add even more dimensions to an already wide range of designs…watch this space!

Argent

16 Thornton's Arcade, Leeds LS1 6LQ. Telephone: 0113 247 0085 Fax: 247 0085
Open Monday - Saturday 9.30am - 5.30pm, Sunday December only

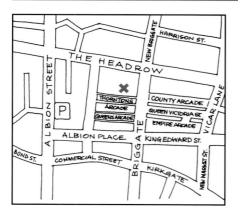

Situated in one of Leeds' oldest arcades, Argent is a bustling contemporary shop. Representing a variety of jewellery designers, ceramicists and glassmakers, we are notably renowned for our collections of exquisitely designed and handcrafted ranges. We are constantly sourcing new talented designers at trade fairs and exhibitions from both Britain and abroad. We carry a wide range of styles catering for all age groups, tastes and pockets. Increasingly, a large proportion of our custom comes from the wedding and engagement ring sector. The cross-section of materials used throughout these ranges include platinum, gold and silver in varying combinations and in isolation. In contrast to the traditional approach from the high street jewellers, we encourage customers to browse in an informal and relaxed atmosphere, promising a courteous, professional service at all times. Our current brochure represents a selection of our gold and platinum ranges and is available on request.

Genevieve Broughton

Originally trained as a painter, I am a self-taught jewellery designer, who developed technical skills whilst working for a large jewellery manufacturer. I now design and produce jewellery in small batches from my West Yorkshire based workshop.

My recent work is influenced by minimalism and has an emphasis on the serial production of designs which develop through subtle shifts. I am exploring themes of repetition with simple geometric shapes and the way these different forms fit together. I contrast colours and textures using silver and gold with polished and matt finishes, to create simple, elegant designs. I am also interested in the tactile qualities of jewellery and often incorporate moving pieces in my work, which make it interesting to wear and play with, as well as aesthetically.

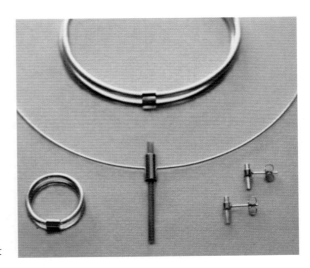

Tony Clare

On leaving school I worked in retail jewellery, gaining a number of qualifications and becoming more interested in the design and making of jewellery. This lead to a four year course in 3D design (jewellery) at Medway in Kent, including work experience in Canada, America and Europe, after which I spent a year as the in-house designer goldsmith in Denia (Alicante) Spain.

After returning to the UK in the mid 1980's I set up my own workshop, specialising in 18ct multi-coloured gold and platinum jewellery. I hand make each individual piece with a satin or textured finish which allows the contrasting colours to pick out the details, from simple bold stripes to the more complex patchwork effect.

Bankfield Museum & Art &♿ Gallery

Akroyd Park, Boothtown Road, Halifax HX3 6HG. Telephone: 01422 354823
Fax: 01422 349020. Email: bankfield-museum@calderdale.gov.uk
Open Tuesday - Saturday 10am - 5pm and Bank Holiday Monday, Sunday 2pm - 5pm

Set within an Italianate mansion, Bankfield Museum is the former home of textile mill owner Edward Ackroyd. The museum houses an impressive, internationally renowned collection of textiles, both historic, contemporary and from around the world.

Set within the sumptuous mosaics and textiles of Bankfield Museum you will find a display of contemporary and historic crafts in The Marble Gallery.

Jerry Hardman-Jones

Bankfield Museum also houses extensive collections.Highlights include a rare collection of Balkan Costume collected by 20th century traveller Edith Durham, The Duke of Wellington Regiment permanent exhibition, Toy Gallery and an extensive collection of contemporary baskets and textiles by leading international and British designer makers.

Sculpture by Lucy Casson

Booth House Gallery and Robison Ceramics

3 Booth House, Holmfirth, Huddersfield, West Yorkshire HD9 2QT. Telephone: 01484 685270
Email: jim.robison@virgin.net Website: www.booth.cjb.net
Open Saturday and Sunday 1- 5pm, Weekdays please ring to check.

Booth House Gallery houses a unique combination of exhibition spaces with the studio ceramics practice of Jim Robison. Housed in an early nineteenth century barn, the massive wood beams, natural stone walls and wood floors are a perfect setting for art work, sculptural ceramics and studio pottery.

The scenic locations around Holmfirth provide the backdrop for the TV series 'Last of the Summer Wine' a clear idea of the dramatic hillside placement of this gallery.

The continuous display of work by many of the country's leading artist potters provides a

feast for the eye and exceptional choice for that special gift or one's personal collection.

Signposted approximately one mile west of Holmfirth town centre, (both on the 635 Greenfield Road and the 6024 Woodhead Road) small lanes lead into a generous car park, splendid views and exciting art and crafts - well worth the effort.

Visitors will find Jim (an elected fellow of the Craft Potters Association for many years) well placed to discuss all aspects of ceramics, the people and processes involved and possible commissions. His attached studio is open for viewing works in progress.

During the summer months, there is an opportunity to learn skills during week long ceramics courses. Evening visits for larger groups may also be arranged.

Jim and his wife Liz have planted the beginnings of an outdoor sculpture garden on the site. They have celebrated twenty seven years in this family business and whatever your interest in ceramics, enthusiasts and customers alike will find a warm welcome at the Booth House Gallery.

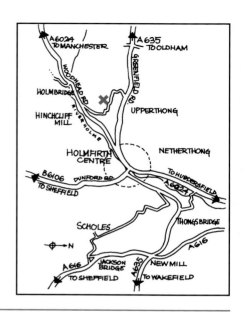

Above: Chris Jenkins

Right: Jim Robison

Centre: Maureen Collier

Booth House Gallery & Robison Ceramics

John Egerton

Since the mid sixties I have been making and selling pots in the North East based in the Whitby area. My work is mainly thrown oxidised stoneware, fired in an electric kiln. I make individually decorated, domestic and one off pieces of a functional nature. I make simple, traditional shapes out of preference, decorating each piece by drawing through the glaze after it is first applied. Living as I do by the coast, my designs often include fish and fossils but also birds and an assortment of plant forms. I have been a member of the NPA for the last seven years and have exhibited regularly with this group. I sell mainly through galleries in the North.

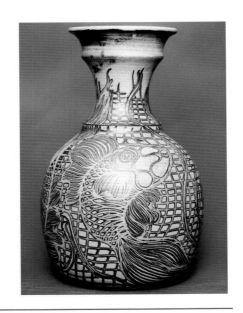

David Frith

Margaret Frith

The richness of the North Wales landscape never fails to inspire me and I have valued living and working here since I started my workshop with Margaret some thirty five years ago. My work explores the thrown form searching for that essence, a quality that survives time and where the traditional and contemporary meet. I use the techniques of the past with the eyes of the present. Pieces are individual, often on a large scale, and include platters, bottles, ginger jars, store jars, pressed and extruded dishes. I like flat surfaces which enhance innovative decorative techniques. The glazes are rich and lush with wax motifs, heavy overglazes and trailed pigments. I would hope that the work shows an individuality and maturity that comes from experience, self confidence and personal conviction about the current role of a craftsman and potter.

Willie Carter

Willie started his first workshop in Farndon aided by a Crafts Council, 'setting up' grant. Here he developed a range of mainly thrown, highly decorated domestic stoneware.

Decoration has always been a compulsion and each pot is individually brush decorated with a variety of animals and fish. His designs have a free, yet precise quality produced by oriental brush. He has spent many years developing glazes and techniques, consequently his pots are soft yet vibrant in colour.

Over the years, a love of modelling in clay has resulted in the evolution of handbuilt raku animal sculptures. These figures have a free flowing quality which captures the creature's character and ranges from bisons and beagles to a complete bridge of elephants !

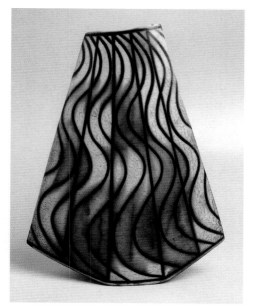

Jacqui Atkin

My work is inspired by the observations of form in every day life and especially in nature. I see pattern in everything, everywhere and although form and pattern must be integral to the work, I often feel that I am really most interested in creating a surface to decorate when I am making the pieces.

Working with clay has a profound effect on my life. The focus required acts to balance and heal the stresses of everyday life, but I find it difficult to articulate an opinion about what I do beyond this. I work with clay because I cannot imagine doing anything else, and because I love it. For this reason I do not apply meaningless titles to the works. I hope they speak for themselves, use their own language to convey the sense of joy that goes into their making.

Booth House Gallery & Robison Ceramics

Cedar Farm Gallery

Back Lane, Mawdesley, near Ormskirk, Lancashire L40 3SY. Telephone: 01704 822038
Email: info@cedarfarm.net Website: www.cedarfarm.net
Open Tuesday - Sunday 10am - 5pm and Bank Holiday Mondays

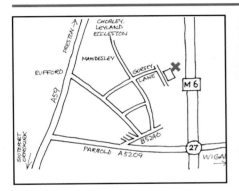

Cedar Farm is in the peaceful village of Mawdesley, not far from the surrounding towns of Ormskirk and Chorley. The Gallery, established in 1987, is housed within a sympathetically restored barn which provides an ideal setting for a wide selection of contemporary crafts ranging from ceramics and glass to wood, textiles, jewellery and cards.

The Frame Shop, alongside the gallery, carries a wide range of artists' materials, originals, prints and etchings and of course picture frames plus a bespoke picture framing service.

Further converted buildings, known as 'Cedar Farm Galleries' offer a selection of fascinating specialist shops and a cafe.

An exciting new development on site is art@cedarfarm which consists of nine studio spaces for art and design based businesses. Visitors to the site have an opportunity to view work being made by some of the most creative designers in the region and work can be purchased or commissions discussed.

Regular exhibitions are also held in the broad glazed arcade promoting British art and craft, both local to the area and from around the country.

Katy Kirkham

My work has developed from the enchantment I find in everyday life. Starting with the characters I met at college (and friends), I wanted to capture peoples personalties, celebrating their birthdays, holidays and hobbies.

I am very influenced and inspired by wonderful countryside and the wealth of images that I am so lucky to be surrounded by at my home.

I use bright colours and exciting patterned fabrics to colour peoples lives when they receive one of my greetings cards.

Sarah Jane Brown

Still using the combination of shiny and rusty tin, this new collection is loosely inspired by views of the landscape from hilltops - with rows of houses, towers, trees with birds and dogs in the garden.

The use of text in the form of poems brings together the variety of themes:

From the top of the hill I can see
For miles and miles all around me
Row of houses one, two, three
Dog in the garden.
Bird in the tree.

Christine Cummings

Christine trained in ceramics at Lancashire Polytechnic and her final show consisted purely of pig studies. It was the beginning of a whole new world of sculpture inspired by the animals on the farm where she spent her childhood.

The research and inspiration for her work is achieved with constant observation, photography and sketching of rare breeds and farm animals. She finds it more satisfying to capture the 'warts and allness' of a big floppy sow than the cuteness of a piglet.

She enjoys stretching her styles; producing clean smooth pig sculptures, free formed angular goats, strutting cockerels and curious chickens. The sculptures are made in a mixture of crankbodied and stoneware clays. Raku and smoke firing finishes naturally compliment the final pieces.

Liz Riley

Liz Riley has been making a range of table and decorative ware under the name of Love Unlimited Ceramics since 1988.

Most of Liz's work is thrown white earthenware which is then hand painted, scraffitoed and finished with the trademark candy stripe handles. The pots are then bisque fired before being dip glazed and fired again. Liz's work is highly coloured with a BIG sense of fun. Inspiration comes from, life, love, food, language, people and colour in no particular order.

Cedar Farm Studios

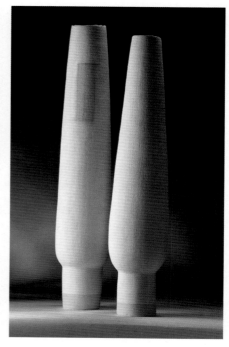

Julie Langan

Phillipa Halliwell

Mary Brown

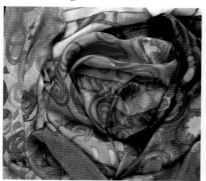

Joanne Eddon

Derek Noble

Julie Massam & Sharon Kelly

Manchester Craft & Design Centre

17 Oak Street, Northern Quarter, Manchester M4 5JD. Telephone: 0161 832 4274
Fax: 0161 832 3416   Email: manager@craftmcr.demon.co.uk Website: www.craftanddesign.com
Open Monday - Saturday 10am - 5.30pm, Sundays 11am - 5pm throughout December

Located in Manchester City Centre's Northern Quarter, Manchester Craft & Design Centre is at the hub of a growing innovative and artistic community. It is the largest combined retail and production centre for the Northwest's top designer makers and is one of the few places in the UK open to the public where contemporary goods are both individually produced and sold on the premises. Formerly a victorian fish market, the centre now houses two floors of shops ranging from jewellery, sculpture and textiles to ceramics and clothing design. Many of the artists at Manchester Craft & Design Centre exhibit at prestigious trade fairs, such as Chelsea, Top Drawer and Birmingham NEC . All work is the centre is for sale and individual commissions are welcomed.

Manchester Craft & Design Centre regularly collaborates with other artists and organisations in a number of annual arts events. There is also a varied programme of selling exhibitions of work from both leading national and international contemporary makers. Exhibitions change quarterly and continue to excite and provoke in a relaxed, informed atmosphere.

Visitors can buy work directly from the thirty makers working in the centre's shops. Hungry shoppers can then relax and enjoy a delicious meal or just a cake and coffee in the open-plan cafe.

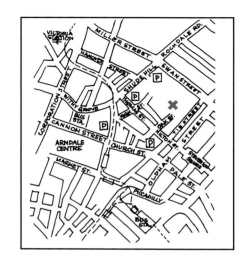

Len Grant

Left: Colette Hazelwood
Right: View of Manchester Craft & Design Centre

Manchester Craft & Design Centre

Tara Kirkpatrick

I produce complimentary ranges of jewellery. The pendant shown is one version from the wrapped cage collection. The designs came about by studying lampshades and the way light reflects from them. What I have tried to achieve is something that can have another dimension, whether it is the clothes worn beneath the jewellery or the openness through an earring. Then I developed the pointy version. This is concaved to add reflection back in the direction of the observer. Having wire wrapped around gives the opportunity of using silver or gold. I like the mixture of the two metals - with silver's wonderful reflective quality and the luminous colour of gold.

From my workshop in Manchester Craft & Design Centre I sell direct to the public, make commissions and wholesale nationwide.

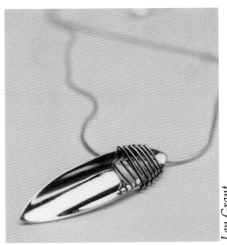

Len Grant

Tone van Krogh

I trained at the National College of Art, Design and Teaching in Blaker, Norway and Manchester Metropolitan University, where I graduated in 1995.

My work is predominately handthrown with handbuilt details added to each piece.

The range of work include candlesticks, boxes, bottles, vases and vessels in vibrant colours.

The impressions from Norway are continuously becoming a greater source of inspiration for my work. The glazes reflect the colours of the southern coast line; the skies and the sea in contrast to the sandy beach, the rocks, hills and trees.

My choice of forms is strongly influenced by both the folk tales (with castles and secret shrines) as well as the traditional designs such as the butter 'tine'.

The fusion of traditional influence and humour gives the products individuality and a contemporary expression.

Platform Gallery

Station Road, Clitheroe, Lancashire BB7 2JT. Telephone: 01200 443071 Fax: 01200 414556
Email: platform-gallery@ribblevalley.gov.uk Website: www.ribblevalley.gov.uk
Open Monday - Saturday 10am - 4.30pm

The Platform Gallery is situated in the historic market town of Clitheroe in the heart of the Ribble Valley. We are in a prime position in a refurbished railway station building, which was originally completed in 1870.

Since 1994 it has provided a valuable and exciting space for artists and makers to exhibit their work.

We host a regularly changing programme of contemporary crafts exhibitions and a retail area where high quality work is available for purchase.

The gallery offers the arts purchase scheme (TAPS). This interest free credit scheme encourages the purchase of arts and crafts work from practising artists.

The gallery was awarded a lottery grant and was upgraded in 2001. We now house an education/workshop facility and have improved all aspects of our exhibition and retail areas.

The Ribble Valley Sculpture Park is nearby. Situated on a riverside, it provides an idyllic setting for the sculptures.

Louise Swindells

I paint with watercolour onto calico and then embroider with fine thread using the stitches like drawing. I take landscape and buildings as subject matter. I only use hand stitching and it takes many hours to complete a piece.

The pictures are produced upon the kitchen table in-between looking after my family and going to concerts and the theatre. I am also a member of Embroidery 2000 based at Gawthorpe Hall near Burnley, the home of the Rachel Kay Shuttleworth Embroidery Collection.

My training was in Textile Design at Manchester Art School. I have work in a number of private collections both here and abroad and have exhibited work in various galleries throughout the country.

Ellen Darby

Ellen Darby studied jewellery and silversmithing at Leciester Poly before returning to Salford, where she first set up her jewellery workshop. She has lived in the Ribble Valley for the last fifteen years, continuing to develop her work and outlets. She now exhibits at a number of galleries mainly in the North as well as taking on individual commissions.

Her work has evolved over time from more intricate designs in polished silver to simple forms using textured effects. The combination of matt finishes and polished silver detail contrast well and the added use of semi-precious stones give the pieces more colour and interest.

Ellen aims to produce jewellery which is aesthetically pleasing, wearable and affordable whilst drawing on inspiration from her romance with nature.

Paul Kenney

Platform Gallery

Pyramid Gallery

43 Stonegate, York YO1 2AW. Telephone: 01904 641187
Website: www.pyramidgallery.com
Open Monday - Saturday 10am - 5pm, Sundays 11am - 4.30pm

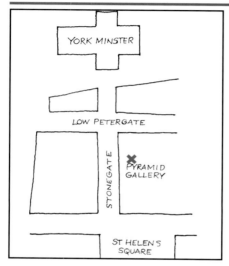

Pyramid Gallery was first established in York in 1980 and has been listed as a Crafts Council Selected Gallery since 1991. Pyramid is a delightful gallery, housed in a National Trust owned 15th century building on one of Yorks finest mediaeval streets close to the south door of York Minster.

Privately owned by Terry and Elaine Brett, Pyramid stocks and exhibits work by over 100 British artists and craftmakers, many of whom are among the most respected makers within their field. Quality of workmanship is one of the most important criteria for the selection of work, but this does not exclude the inclusion of many new makers.

Pyramid Gallery has four display areas. The front and back of the shop include work by up to fifty designer jewellers, plus studio ceramics, sculpture, studio glass, clocks and mirrors. the two first floor galleries are used for exhibitions of ceramics, glass and sculpture. The wall spaces display a continuous exhibition of framed original prints by printmakers including Brenda Hartill, Anita Klein, Alan Stones, Helen Hanson and local artists.

Pyramid Gallery's philosophy is to offer the visitor affordable hand made crafts and works of art in a friendly, welcoming atmosphere. All visitors are invited to add their names to our mailing list.

Pryamid Gallery

Tom Sutton

Working with smooth stoneware clay, I produce painted ceramic reliefs based on building facades, particularly those I have observed in Venice.

What interests me is the way surfaces of buildings show the effects of time and the elements in the form of peeling stucco, crumbling brickwork and weather-stained paintwork.

Window and door openings play an important part in the work with this being emphasised by the inclusion, usually of a figure or a curtain blowing.

I use acrylics rather like watercolours: thin washes of paint laid one over the other.

Unlike watercolours, however, acrylics, when dry, are insoluble in water and thus impose their own discipline on the work.

Influences include the writing and drawings of John Ruskin and the paintings of Edward Hopper.

Sarah McDade

I am inspired by the endless creative possibilities when hand-building figures and faces in clay. Subjects are observed from many facets of life, sometimes serious, often humourous.

Using a blend of slab building and modelling, each character is individually constructed in a grogged stoneware clay, before decorating with brushwork and sponged patterns in a variety of underglaze colours and oxides.

I also enjoy exploring shape and form using the female figure, and am currently developing a new range of terracotta pieces that will complement my existing range of designs.

Pryamid Gallery

341

Ropewalk Contemporary Art & Craft

0%

The Ropewalk, Maltkiln Road, Barton Upon Humber, North Lincolnshire DN18 5JT
Telephone & Fax: 01652 660380
Email: the-ropewalk@supanet.com Website: www.the-ropewalk.com
Open Tuesday - Saturday 10am - 5pm, Sunday 10am - 4pm

In the shadow of the Humber Bridge situated in the historic market town of Barton upon Humber this former Rope factory lends itself well to its new use. Ropewalk Contemporary Art & Craft opened in April 2000 offering two galleries, artists' workshops, print making and dark rooms, a bespoke picture framing service and The Waterside Heritage Display. One gallery has a six weekly changing programme of touring exhibitions and selling shows whilst the craft gallery has an ongoing exhibition of quality and diverse craft work from in excess of eighty makers.

Andrew McNaughton

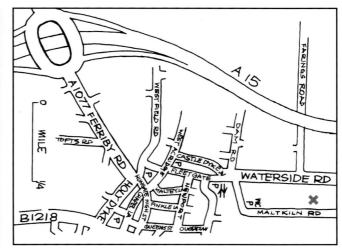

Ropewalk Comtemporary Art & Craft Craft

Stuart Walsh

I make a wide range of both oxidised stoneware ceramics and raku pottery. I have developed a series of pink, purple, red, blue, turquoise and bronze stoneware glazes, which feature, on my studio range of wheel-thrown bottles, bowls and jugs.

My figurative work is derived from drawn objective, historical and futuristic sources and is constructed using thrown forms, modelled features and slip casts of found objects sometimes impressed in paper-clay to enhance the surface textures.

By using the raku-fired process of flame and smoke, I can extend the range of surface decoration into lustres or carbonised textures. I use a grogged white clay with copper, cadmium and cobalt glazes to make full, round decorative bottles and bowls. My workshop is in Louth, Lincolnshire.

Andrew McNaughton

Wendy Wai-Ying Chan

My work combines traditional techniques with modern materials, and marries diverse mixes of yarns with vibrant colours. Hand framed machine knitted bags are finished with intricate macramé woven handles. The materials are simple and luxurious throughout: pure new wool, wool and silk blends, wash cotton linen.

Scarf fabrics blend natural yarns of wool and silks, with man-made fibres such as lurex and floss rayons, giving an illuminating and sensual feel to the designs. Each macramé designed fabric bag has been enriched with exclusive finishes on the handle pieces or strapping. Colours range from soft urban ecru blues to dazzling mixes in neon. Their intricacy in combining knitting with macramé and crochet is a reflective yet novel approach to fashion, textiles and the crafts.

St. John Street Gallery

50 St. John Street, Ashbourne, Derbyshire, DE6 1GH. Telephone: 01335 347425
Open 10 am - 5.30 pm Tuesday - Saturday and Bank Holiday Mondays

Ashbourne's St. John Street Gallery is spread over three floors of a spacious Victorian building, which was for many years the town's Magistrate's Court. It is now the region's premier venue for Contemporary Fine Art and Craft.

We specialise in Contemporary painting, and hold regular shows of work by artists of national repute. We also stock, amongst others, ceramic sculpture by Paul Smith, steel sculpture by Miles Halpin and wire sculpture by Astri Utvik - Bleasdale.

Our eclectic range of Crafts in various media includes, glass by Ingrid Pears, Linda Addison and Tom Petit, Ceramics by Tony Laverick, Stephen Thompson, Diana Parker and Evan Rutherford. We also have a stylish licensed café in our large and airy first floor gallery, where we serve drinks and food, most of which is freshly prepared on the premises.

Top Right: ceramics by Tony Laverick, clock by Stephen Thompson, glass by Tom Petit and ceramic sculpture by Paul Smith.
Top & Below: paintings by Kathryn Matthews and bronzes by Garry Barker

Sanderson, George & Peach

0%　　39 Station Road, Holmfirth, W.Yorkshire HD9 1AB. Telephone: 01484 684485　　&

Open Tuesday - Saturday 10am - 5pm

Owners Debbie George and Catherine Hill constantly aim to present and promote the work of designers and craft workers in a unique yet accessible way. Being two double fronted Victorian shops, the building has many superb original features that have been carefully, yet simply restored to provide a sympathetic backdrop to the many and varied works on display.

Having first opened in April 1996, the Gallery expanded into the second shop in November 1998. The new space is slightly simpler in its design, offering a large space for solo exhibitions of both wall work and sculpture.

Based in Holmfirth, an area brimming with artists and craftspeople, the gallery

represents and supports many local artists including a variety now working in its many studio spaces. Regular exhibitors include Jane Muir, John Maltby, Jane Strawbridge, Mick Kirkby-Geddes and Jo Aylward.

Famous for Last of the Summer Wine, Holmfirth is also rapidly emerging as a cultural centre. New additions to its many attractions are the new theatre, a restored cinema and a number of restaurants and cafe bars. The regeneration of the village is to include an arts trail along the riverside that runs right through the village, passing the gallery.

Visitors to Sanderson George and Peach frequently express their delight at its discovery, and once visited, they return again and again.

Major exhibitions are held four times a year. Work ranges from painting, printmaking and photography, through designer furniture in the new wing, to sculpture, ceramics, jewellery and textiles.

We offer a free commissioning service on behalf of our regular artists.

Andrew Sanderson

Brendan Hesmondhalgh

Brendan's work has always been inspired by the different form, movement and characteristics of animals. Large life-like ceramic sculptures of dogs and other wiry creatures; a snapshot of a lively stance. He makes animals as he sees them through his own personal experience.

Each piece is individually crafted using slabs of fibre reinforced clay wrapped in a paper armature. In this way, wrinkles and folds in the skin can be readily incorporated into the shape. The wet flexible clay can be pushed out from the inside to form the fullness of a belly, the line of a rib or the undulation of a muscle.

He does not strive for anatomical perfection but rather exaggerates certain features that express the essence of a character and movement.

Sanderson, George & Peach

Jo Aylward

I live and work in Holmfirth, renting a studio at Sanderson, George and Peach Gallery. The Yorkshire landscape is a constant inspiration, but I draw much of my imagery from the things that surround me in my home and studio. I have a fascination for ceramics, and enjoy the influence of faded and worn ceramic surfaces on the colours and textures I choose in my work. My passion for plants and flowers leads me to include them in my still life paintings, often in an obscured and minimised way.

My primary interest is in exploring the relationship of object to environment. My paintings act as a holding space in which it becomes unimportant for me to present objects as real, my emphasis being on the creation of a painted space.

Olivia Brown

Olivia is an exceptionally talented artist with skills in many different media. Her ceramic dogs, all with names and characters from dogs she has worked with, are often complimented by her mixed media drawings, paintings and screenprints. Olivia's ceramic pieces start with extensive drawing and painting of the subject, followed by the construction of a wooden frame padded with paper to form the hound's shape. 'T' material clay, often grogged, is then built around the frame and left to dry before firing up to three or four times to reach the required surface effect or colour.

Olivia's travelling installation of a 1960's hair salon for dogs, provides a perfect backdrop for some of her more comical pieces in hairnets and salon capes.

Judith Rowe

Working in an idyllic setting on Eel Pie Island in the middle of the Thames, Judith Rowe produces pieces in response to the places she has visited. Judith's aspiration is to create pots that are evocative of the special times she has known. Her distinctive pieces, decorated with stripes of blue or green, are either painted or topped with her characteristically long legged birds. Judith's earthenware pieces are for domestic use, and as such are delightfully functional. She especially likes the idea that people will use and appreciate her work every day and that it will enrich any home or garden.

Left: Jane Strawbridge
Above: Martin Rees
Right: Jane Muir

Sanderson, George & Peach

Throstle Nest Gallery

Old Lindley, Holywell Green, Halifax, West Yorkshire HX4 9DF. Telephone: 01422 374388
Open Tuesday - Sunday 10am - 5pm (except Christmas)

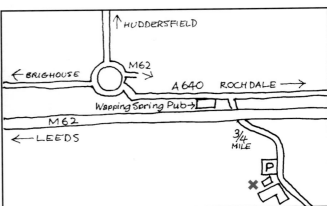

With trepidation, in 1984 we opened the doors of our renovated two hundred and fifty year old stone barn. Happily ten years on in 1994 we extended, by rebuilding over old farm buildings. The new space facilitates coffee making etc. and Previews.

A loyal nucleus of makers supply regularly, but for new Exhibitions we often go further afield. Regular displays show the highly skilled, the new and innovative, the practically sound, humorous or often just the beautiful. We attempt to keep prices sensible.

The gallery nestles in a lovely green valley, minutes away from the accesible M62 (East & West)

Throstle Nest Gallery

Andrew Hague

Pam Lumsden

Pat Kaye

Don Glanville

Barbara Ward

derek topp gallery

Chatsworth Road, Rowsley, Matlock, Derbyshire DE4 2EH
Telephone: 01629 735580, Mobile: 0410 189953 Email: info@derektoppgallery.com
Website: www.derektoppgallery.com
Open 10am - 5pm daily

Set amongst the rolling hills of North Derbyshire, the small village of Rowsley is situated on the edges of the Peak District National Park, and the Duke of Devonshire's rural estate, with its magnificent Chatsworth House.
The village is also close to Elizabethan Haddon Hall and the thriving market town of Bakewell.

In this setting the derek topp gallery was established in 1995 intent on offering, under one roof, the widest possible range of contemporary applied art, within the ongoing criteria that everything is hand made in Britain, and of the highest quality and artistic integrity. The artists, many of whom are listed on the Crafts Council's Index of Selected Makers or are recipients of its Setting-up Grants, have been chosen from across the length and breadth of the country for their skill, flair and imagination.

derek topp gallery has, since 1997, been selected for inclusion on the Craft Council's National List of Shops and Galleries. This national list is compiled from Regional Arts Boards recommendations, following inspection of the gallery. Quality of stock, the display arrangements and staff knowledge are all factors taken into account.

The gallery is also a member of the Independent Craft Galleries Association.

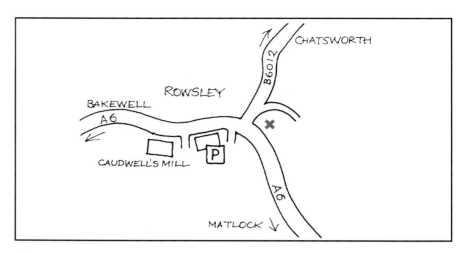

The gallery's web-cameras linked to its Internet site allow customers to view specified items of current stock on line.

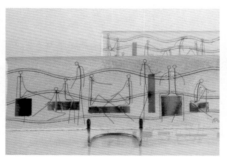

Above: Kevin Wallhead

Photo: Adam O'Meara

Right: Georgina Dunkley

Left: Rebecca Buck

Stephen Brayne

derek topp gallery

Georgina Dunkley

Georgina studied ceramics at the University of Westminster (Harrow 1993-1996). During this time she developed ideas based on natural patterns. Looking closely at ammonite textures, she imagined them unwinding and growing upwards - this formed the basis for her unique ceramic lamps she makes today.

Originally starting life as oil burners, these curvaceous creatures evolved into elegant electric lights with delicately thrown ceramic shades. There are currently two styles of lamp base, the original with its ammonite inspired, highly textured finish and the more recent smooth surface base with painted resist decoration loosely based on leaf veins.

Due to her methods of working, no two lamps are ever the same, making each piece individual. She has a wide range of sizes and colours and welcomes commissions.

Georgina Dunkley

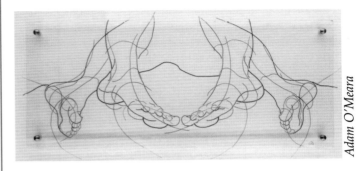

Adam O'Meara

Kevin Wallhead

The sensual and unique properties that lie within glass enable images to be created with the use of inclusions. Like line drawings, strength of line, form and tone can all be constructed. I feel there is an added attraction in depicting only part of an image, this permits the viewer to use their personal ideology to interpret what lies beyond the realms of the composition.

This personal ideology has led to the introduction of stick people, simple images that can be drawn even in childhood. Even these can arouse different responses when perceived by individuals.

Recycled materials are used wherever possible.

Mikaela Bartlett

I create elongated figures - people, dogs, cows and other animals, stretching their limbs giving each body more expression while adding a touch of humour. My work becomes more illustrative with this process.

The figures are grouped onto hills and into boats, seemingly searching or exploring by land or sea or continuing their journeys on animals such as cows, elephants or horses. Each piece has a story to tell, left to the imagination of the viewer.

I use paper clay for my figures while stoneware is used for boats and hills. Each piece is detailed with slips and oxides, a selection then mounted into wooden frames.

Jan Watson

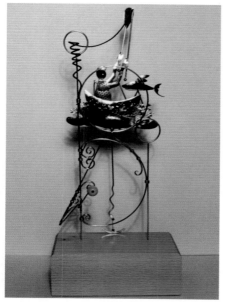

Jan Watson started working in metals in 1994, exploring the pure and flowing forms that can be created with metals such as copper, nickel and brass, often using various decorative effects on the metal surfaces.

Initially Jan worked on jewellery pieces followed by a natural progression to moving pieces which was encouraged by his wish to experiment with a third dimension, an element not always available in his previous work and fuelled by his long standing interest in mechanical movement.

His brooches and kinetic sculptures are inspired by nature, animal forms, both in reality and the more surreal. He creates pieces of artistic beauty often with the added element of humour, working the metal to achieve character and individuality. Quality of design and workmanship is paramount in all that he produces.

derek topp gallery

Some other Galleries in Northern England

Bluecoat Display Centre
Bluecoat Chambers
School Lane
Liverpool
L1 3BX
Tel: 0151 709 4014
Fax: 0151 707 8106
Eamil: crafts@bluecoat.u.net.com
www.
bluecoatcrafts.merseyworld.com
Open: Mon - Sat 10am -5.30pm

Godfrey & Watt
7 Westminster Arcade
Parliament Street
Harrogate
N. Yorkshire
HG1 2RN
Tel: 01423 525300
Open Mon- Sat 10am - 5.30pm

**Williamson Brown
(Contemporary Jewellery)**
20a Clayton Road
Jesmond
Newcastle upon Tyne
Tyne & Wear
NE2 4RP
Tel: 0191 281 8273
Fax: 0191 281 8287
Open Mon - Sat 10am - 5pm

**Craft Centre & Design
Gallery**
City Art Gallery
The Headrow
Leeds
W.Yorkshire
LS1 3AB
Tel: 0113 247 8241
Email: ccdg-art-leeds
@pop3.poptel.org.uk
www.craftcentreleeds.co.uk
*Open Tues - Fri 10am - 5pm,
Sat 10am - 4pm*

**Priors Contemporary Fine
Art & Crafts**
1st Floor
7 The Bank
Barnard Castle
County Durham
DL12 8PH
Tel: 01833 638141
Email: mark@priors.co.uk
www.priors.co.uk
*Open
Mon - Fri 10am- 5.15pm, Sat 10am-
5.30pm, Sun 12 - 5pm*

William Sissons
23 Market Place
Helmsley
York
YO62 5BJ
Tel: 01439 771385
www.sissonsgallery.co.uk
*Open :
Daily 10am - 6pm, Sun 12 -6pm*

Lake District, Tyne & Wear & Scotland

8,27.

EDINBURGH ●

97 ● GATESHEAD

49,87.

68.

128 ● KENDAL

121.

art.tm

20, Bank Street, Inverness, Scotland, 1V1 1QU. Telephone: 01463 712240 Fax: 01463 239991
Email: info@arttm.org.uk Website: www.arttm.org.uk
Open Tuesday - Saturday 11am- 6pm

Situated on the banks of the River Ness, in the centre of Inverness, art.tm is the Highlands' leading venue for contemporary visual arts and the countrys most northerly Crafts Council approved outlet. Established in 1986 to provide printmaking facilities and a gallery for artists, it has subsequently developed into an organisation involved in all areas of arts activity.

Crafts in the Highlands of Scotland have historically been practiced out of necessity - the product of functional life. Basketry, woodwork and the textiles industry; revolving around knitting, tweed and felt, are all examples of indigenous crafts still thriving today. art.tm seeks to support these traditional crafts as well as encourage the development of innovative contemporary craft. The ground floor of the gallery is a dedicated crafts exhibition space stocking the work of up to twenty makers at a time. The space also holds the 'off the rail' and 'on the shelf' display areas which show the work of Highland makers on an exhibition basis.

David Churchill/Arcaid

Allison Weightman

East meets west-coast of Scotland in Allison Weightman's hand built ceramics.

Self taught, and specialising in the Japanese technique of Raku firing, she lives and works on the remote Highland peninsula of Scoraig. She exhibits throughout the UK, and has undertaken public commissions.

Her hand built vessels are treated in various ways, some textured, some burnished and carved. She views her ceramics as an evolutionary process, letting the pieces have a voice of their own. "Sometimes I feel like a medium as the forms seem to have a will of their own. Raku is now part of my existence. The contemplative calm one obtains (before the frenzy of activity, once the kiln is opened), makes the link between the 14th and 21st century Raku-ist. The state of mind is still the same."

David Body

David trained at Twickenham College as an illustrator and worked for ten years in various advertising and design groups in London. He moved to Caithness in 1977 and set up his pottery business with his wife, Sally. Since 1986 they have been based in John O'Groats.

David says of his work, "In Caithness the landscape and weather are all pervasive and dominate my work. My forms lean in the wind, are textured like stone and reflect the colours that surround me." He uses a variety of making techniques including throwing, extruding and hand building to produce individual ceramics and tableware, reduction fired to 1300°C. He also makes a limited amount of soda fired pots but aims to increase this range in the future.

art.tm

Castle Gallery

43 Castle Street, Inverness IV2 3DU. Telephone: 01463 729512
Email: castlegallery@aol.com Website: www.castlegallery.co.uk
Open Monday - Saturday 9am - 5pm

The Castle Gallery is situated in the lee of Inverness Castle, in the heart of the city. The building dates back to the early eighteenth century and during extensive renovations, wattle and daub was exposed. The premises now provide three separate gallery spaces on two floors for the display of contemporary paintings, sculpture, hand-made prints, ceramics, glass, wood and jewellery by leading artists from Scotland and throughout Britain.

As well as changing exhibitions, the Castle Gallery houses a permanent collection of diverse and distinctive works by artists such as Blandine Anderson, Diana Barraclough, Tiziana Bendall-Brunello, Eoghan Bridge, David Carter, Sarah Cox, Irma Demianczuk, Marianne Forrest, Dave Goodsir, Majolica

Works, Maureen Minchin, Alice Palser, Phoenix Hot Glass, Shakespeare Glass, Julian Spencer, Malcolm Sutcliffe, Anna de Ville and Arie Vardi.

Our friendly and welcoming environment makes the Castle Gallery an ideal place to browse, enjoy and buy the best in contemporary art.

Castle Gallery

Joel Chester Fildes

Clockwise from top left : Majolica Works,
Maureen Minchin, Blandine Anderson & Eoghan Bridge

Dexterity

Kelsick Road, Ambleside, Cumbria LA22 OBZ. Telephone: 015394 34045
Email: dext@btinternet.com
Open Every day 9.30am - 6pm (Closed Christmas Day and Boxing Day)

Ambleside, set among the lakes and mountains of the Lake District National Park, is a major holiday centre but also welcomes many day-trips visitors from Liverpool, Manchester, Leeds, Newcastle, etc. Opened in 1988, Dexterity sells work by established and new artist/crafts people from all parts of the UK.

Domestic, decorative and sculptural ceramics feature strongly, utilising the full range of making, firing and glazing techniques. Our designer jewellery uses a wide range of materials including silver, non-precious metals, slate, glass and textiles. Two dimensional work includes paintings,

Andrew Morris

collage, limited edition etchings, lithographs and screenprints, also ceramics and large turned wooden sculptures. Blown and cast glass, papier-mache, turned and carved wood, automata and textiles are also shown. Commissions can be

arranged. A full framing service is provided.

No gallery can match the selection of craft books and magazines (including out of print and secondhand) we stock and mail.

Ellen Graubart

Ellen Graubart works from objective reality and from imagination. Her printmaking has consisted mainly of etchings, but recently she has become interested in the making of collagraphs, which offer endless opportunities for exploration and invention. A collagraph is a print taken from a matrix of things glued together, i.e. a collage. Any material which can be glued to a base (such as card), will take ink, and will survive the pressures involved in being put through a press, can be used. The medium demands a radical simplification of images (unlike etching, which offers the possibility of realism). This exciting challenge involves inventing new languages for conveying visual ideas.

Sue Bartholomew

The inspiration for my pottery reflects my love of ancient pots and the classic shapes of early Greek and Roman pottery. I combine these shapes with texture reminiscent of weather-worn rock surfaces. Other pieces have texture influenced by patterns on textiles and Islamic tiles. Dry glazes are used in earthy tones and muted blue/greens.

I spent many years making pots in Australia and returned to my native Cumbria in 1994, eventually setting up a studio in Ambleside.

My latest work explores the use of textured and patterned slabs to create platters and wall pieces.

Dexterity

Gwen Bainbridge

I work with both Bone China and Porcelain, using slip-casting and hand-building techniques.

The porcelain allows me to explore colour using glazes to experiment with 'cocktails' of oxides, to produce vibrant colours and texture, which alter as they wrap around the form. In the hand-built work I use various impressed techniques to give a 'textile' quality reminiscent of historical embroidery in fashion accessories, particularly from the Elizabethan period.

I turn plaster models on a lathe, produce the moulds and slip-cast the forms in both Bone China and Porcelain. I use a variety of resist techniques alongside lamination of coloured slips to explore and emphasise the translucent qualities of the body.

Christopher Holmes

Pauline Yarwood

I work in the Lyth Valley, Cumbria, overlooking the River Gilpin. I like the variation of working with different clays and produce a range of work in porcelain, flecked stoneware and craft crank. I love the rawness of grogged clay and keep glazing on this work (bowls, dishes, tall vases) to a minimum. I also love glazes with a cool, stone-like quality and use a wide-firing dolomite and tin glaze which I fire to 1260°C. This gives a beautiful dense white, especially on porcelain. I decorate quickly and stop at the point at which I am about to make another mark.

Having always been addicted to throwing, I now find handbuilding equally satisfying and am currently working on a range of larger functional pieces.

MiSuLi -
Lucy Myfanwy Jepson & Damian Carl Naylor

These artists base their work on natural elemental patterns and textures, blending corroded surfaces with contemporary linear and sculptural forms. Bark, barnacles, lichen and textured rock, interpreted using silver, brass, bronze and copper are featured in their main collection 'From The Earth'. Inspired also by abstract and tribal art, the work has developed an ethnic, organic style.

Organic chemical processes produce exciting mottled colours and finishes with an archaeological, unearthed and ancient quality. Complementing chosen pieces with Baltic and Tibetan amber, Egyptian paste, glass, wood, clay, semi-precious stones and rare excavated 1000 BC. African beads, they create jewellery with a unique and individual appearance.

Other collections feature the use of colourful abstract enamel and contemporary silver, selling through galleries and private commissions.

Emma Grover

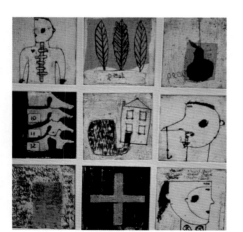

Emma uses a wide range of symbolic imagery in her work, which draws on personal experience and is narrative in content. Oddly transformed figures, animals and objects inhabit her image world. This other world defies interpretation; it is at once absurd, sinister, disturbing and humourous.

She works in a wide variety of printmaking processes including etching, collagraphs, screen and mono print producing unique prints and small editions.

Emma trained first at Falmouth and then Manchester obtaining a Masters degree in printmaking in 1991. She exhibits nationally and has received several awards including, in 1999, the prestigious Michael Rothenstein Trophy awarded by the Printmakers Council.

Work held by: Cupola Gallery, Sheffield. The Craft Centre and Design Gallery, City Art Gallery, Leeds. Artichoke Print Workshop, London.

Susan Bruce

At Lowestoft College in 1987, where Susan was a student, she became very interested in the forms made by domestic potters, such as teapots, coffee pots, bowls and jugs. During this time her own work was very traditional, but over the years throwing had been replaced by some handbuilding, and the work has developed in new directions. The inspiration for her designs comes from her study of bird and plant life. Each piece has an original design from Susan's drawings applied in clay to the work. Mermaids, exotic looking birds, ostriches, fish, stars and sailing boats from a fantasy land are the images she currently uses.

A blue colour wash is applied to the areas that are to remain matt, selected areas are glazed, and finally gold and mother of pearl lustres are applied for the third firing.

Linda M. Caswell

I came to porcelain whilst still at college, and continue to revel in its complexities and possibilities. Never one for an easy life, I work with colour in the clay itself, and not as surface decoration. This brings its own constraints and making methods.

My porcelain agateware is a contemporary use of a traditional technique. Instead of mixing clays of differing colours, I work in porcelain alone: colouring some of the porcelain and mixing the coloured with the white to create my patterns. I enjoy this combination of part control and part happenstance: I decide the colours, the quantity of colour and create the patterning, but then a random element takes over - beyond my control. The work is made in a series, but no two pieces will be identical.

Syl Macro

The constant factor in my work is the inspiration of pattern and texture in landscape. My college training in dual disciplines, ceramics and illustration, lead to my fascination with the use of imagery in clay.

Living and working in the Pennines has heightened my awareness of the changing colours and textures of hills, woods and moorland. I spend periods drawing and photographing before beginning a sequence of making derived from these observations.

My pieces are built up in areas of clay, which have previously been coloured and textured in a variety of ways - such as impressing, marbling, and printing with coloured slips. The design is worked flat, then formed in moulds. Recently, larger scale work is being developed in the form of wall and floor panels, and table tops.

Jennie Gill

Jennie Gill designs and manufactures her jewellery from her studio in the heart of Sheffield's 'Cultural Industries Quarter'. 'Persistence Works' is the country's first purpose built artspace, home to over sixty makers and artists.

"I work mainly in silver and gold, I collect precious and semi-precious beads, which, when incorporated into my work, justifies the vast amounts of money I spend on them.

Lost wax casting is a technique I use a lot to produce the shapes I use, I like taking everyday objects, casting them in precious metals, giving them a new identity.

In 2000 my range of cast 'sweeties & chocolate drops' were highly commended by the British Giftware Association".

Inexteriors

Bishops Court, Main Street, Corbridge, Northumberland, NE45 5LA
Telephone: 01434 634746 Fax: 01434 634745 Email: Artefacts@supanet.com
Open Tuesday - Saturday 10 am - 5 pm Sunday 10 am - 4 pm

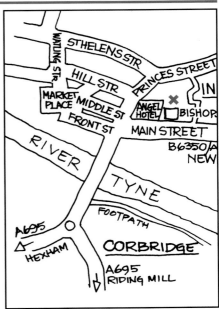

Inexteriors opened its doors in June 2000 in the historic Roman village of Corbridge.

The gallery is a beautiful room with polished wood floor and white painted walls, the perfect setting to view the various crafts and paintings on display.

There are wood carvings entitled 'Tree Spirits' from Huw Storey, Raku bowls and vases from John Scott. Hand forged wall sconces, lights and furniture by Bill Roberts.

There is an ever changing exhibition of original paintings and etchings. The hand sculptured water features made from ceramic and copper enhance the tranquil ambience.

0% Old Courthouse Gallery

Market Place, Ambleside, Cumbria LA22 9BU. Telephone: 015394 32022 Fax: 015394 33022
Email: andrew@oldcourtgallery.demon.co.uk
Open Daily 9.30am - 5.30pm (Please ring to confirm if travelling a distance)

Established in 1994, two expansions and eight years later, we have evolved into one of the largest contemporary arts galleries in the north of England.

Changing our mix of objects means that the gallery is constantly stimulating for our regular clients, who often travel for up to two hours 'just to look' as well as for our first timers, which Ambleside supplies in plenty. The comments are always the same, "what a splendid surprise…," "what beautiful things…".

We cover a full spectrum from large furniture and sculpture to small specialised

Old Courthouse Gallery

Tony Richards

368

collectable pieces. Our jewellery collection has expanded to include work by over forty exciting jewellers including Alan Vallis, Paul Spurgeon, Jeremy Hicks, Michael Carpenter and Sarah Sheridan and incorporates platinum, gold, silver and acrylic.

Some of our contributors have been with us since the beginning, steadily being added to over time with new and established makers and artists.

Tony Richards

Blowzone

Blowzone is Iestyn and Beverley Davies. They established their studio in 1993 having spent time working in the glassmaking industry and as tutors. They each bring a different but complimentary approach to glass making. Iestyn's work specialises in the application of hot gathers onto the surface of hand blown glass. Beverly, meanwhile, experiments in cold working techniques, specifically sand engraving through layers of coloured glass.

They have developed a wide range of work from functional vases, bowls and glasses through decorative paperweights and sculptural pieces to the limited editions.

'Virtu' and 'Meridian'
Working with one of the countries last great glasscutters Roger Sidaway, Blowzone have created these two limited edition ranges that bring together the old and the new, a fusing of the traditional and contemporary.

Virginia Dowe

Virginia has always had a fascination with dogs, ever since growing up alongside 'Tolly', a very loveable and energetic Irish setter/labrador mix. He has been the main inspiration for her work, along with 'Polly', her mums springer spaniel cross labrador, whose big paws, big ears, very springy and ever so slightly neurotic nature make her the perfect artists muse.

Since graduating from the University of Wolverhampton in 1997, Virginia has set up an open studio in Northamptonshire.

Her dogs begin their lives as extruded tubes of hand-built clay, which are then manipulated into the animal form. Once dried and fired, the dogs are placed into a brick pit and set light to, resulting in a very natural and unique finish.

Tony Richards

Chris Brammall

I have had a great deal of success over the last six years designing and making contemporary forged steel clocks, mirrors and candlesticks for the gallery market. However, more recently, my work has evolved and become more focused on the public art commissions that now take up the majority of my time.

I intend to compliment this move with a new direction towards furniture design. Along with the limited production gallery pieces and public art works, this will give me a well rounded, broad spectrum of work.

Old Courthouse Gallery

Ronnie Fulton

The long summers spent messing about in boats at my grandparents in Lochgoilhead still inspire me and conjour images. Many of the stories I have imagined, some are composite and some could even be verified, but why bother? I am a potter not a journalist.

Where I work I overlook the North Channel to Northern Ireland. This ever-changing view, stories from old fishermen (research often happening in the pub), books and Radio 4 help provide even more stimuli.

Most work is a combination of throwing and handbuilding. The work is decorated with various coloured slips and alkaline copper glazes to create a rich surface. Recycled or found objects are often incorporated onto the work after firing. I enjoy making with clay and hope that this is reflected in the work.

Tony Richards

Tony Richards

Anthony Scott

My work is inspired by Celtic mythology, although viewed from the perspective of animals rather than humans.

Animals played a central role in the Celtic myths. The ancient tales are full of accounts of shape changing. The Celts believed that the spirit world of animals often impinged on and influenced the human world and I have tried to convey this feeling in my work.

While they can represent a bygone age, animals also possess a sense of timelessness since they are unaffected by changing fashions. Animals have appeared in art from the earliest cave painting to classical sculpture to modern times and I would like to think I am continuing with my own development of this tradition, to offer something completely unique.

Rob Whelpton

Rob Whelpton makes highly decorative raku fired pots. Having been brought up by the sea and subsequently living in the country, the pots are, unusually for raku, intricately decorated using fish, animals, birds and people as their theme. Designs are drawn into the clay using a scalpel, coloured using slips and metallic salts which is very time consuming. Some pots are further embellished with gold leaf after firing.

Melanie Adkins

Melanie designs and creates one-off ceramic sculptures of animals produced with humourous qualities, all of which capture the true essence of animal behaviour. They depict an extensive selection of mannerisms and characters found within the animal kingdom. Each one is hand made and glazed. They are unique in both form and personality.

The pieces are made using Earthstone clay. After forming the body of the animal separately, the legs, feet, head and tail are created and added. Gradually layers of clay are built up creating the features and bringing the character to life.

Influences stem from closely observing animal mannerisms whilst working at the RSPCA, giving Melanie an inexhaustible research vocabulary for the development of present ranges and the introduction of new ones.

Tony Richards

Old Courthouse Gallery

Paul Barcroft - *Hothouse Glass*

I specialise in niche contemporary studio art glass, considered designs with rich textures incorporating precious metals and lustres, which are both decorative and functional and range from distinctive drinking glasses through to visual 'one off' pieces.

Glass-Scapes
The concept behind these pieces is the delightful tensions and dynamics created from the changes in colour, line and surface decoration. The central strata, like band of Zebra stripes, is used to separate the upper and lower blocks of colour.

The forms, suggesting a pebble like quality, have two sides with a larger surface area that encourages the viewer to examine them in an almost two-dimensional way and enforces the concept of an abstract statement, whilst still retaining a three-dimensional form.

Larissa Kay Philbin

Conroy

Conroy employs a philosophical approach to design and manufacture, working sensitively with natural materials to provide a considered, well made, quality product with a sense of individuality, at an affordable price.

Conroy comprises of two designer/makers; Chris Conroy and Larissa Kay Philbin, a husband and wife team. They bring complimentary elements to the partnership from their respective three dimensional design backgrounds in furniture and jewellery. Both have an eye for proportion, believe in attention to detail and share a passion for natural materials.

The distinctive visual style achieved results from a set formula combining sensitivity, applied processes and characteristics inherent in the materials. Using these elements creatively ensures that each product retains its own unique identity.

Maureen Minchin

Having spent a year moving and setting up a new studio, Maureen now works on the very west coast of Scotland, in northern Argyll. Currently she is still mainly producing earthenware pots, though this could change as she adapts to her new surroundings.

The domestic pots are thrown in terracotta clay, sprigs (small pieces of impressed clay) and handles attached, then dipped in a cream slip when leather hard. Once a pot is firm again the slip is drawn into with a sharp tool (sgraffito) then left to dry. After being fired to 950°C, the pots are decorated with underglaze colours, glazed and glostfired to 1140°C under light reduction.

Her style of pottery lends itself to personal commissions and Maureen is happy to undertake such work.

Tony Richards

Norman Stuart Clarke

I am first and foremost a painter, the image is the message and the form is the vessel that carries it. As long as I can remember I have been painting, and during Art School I was using hot glass as a medium for my imagery.

Several themes have developed over the years and became 'Icons' with an integrity that I revere.

The blue moon on scarlet sky, the archetypal wave symbol and the lone tree image have been with me for years. This idea of a 'single image' decoration for my glass sprung instinctively from my painting. To define a surface and then suggest something beyond, to question ideas of reality, time and illusion. These things have been important for me, but the joy of glassmaking and image creation are at one with my walk through life to find a way and to follow.

Tony Richards

Tim Atkinson

Where does the time go! A few more years have passed and I am now incorporating new materials in to my furniture such as African Slate, Parchment Stone and Bronze inlay. Having unusual colours and texture these materials complement the natural wood perfectly.

This development has added a new dimension to design ideas, not to mention even more job satisfaction. Hopefully this pleasure will be conveyed to the collector who will have many years of joy from their pieces.

The success I have had in the past few years has enabled me to expand into a new studio work-shop and invest in new 'Felder' machinery.

Above: Susan Clough *Centre:* Anthony Blakeney
Top: Lilian Busch

Portcullis Craft Gallery

0%

7 The Arcade, MetroCentre, Gateshead, Tyne & Wear, NE11 9YL. Telephone: 0191 4606345
Fax: 0191 4604285 Email: j.milburne@libarts.gatesheadmbc.gov.uk
Open 10am - 8pm Monday, Tuesday, Wednesday & Friday, 10am - 9pm Thursday,
9am - 7pm Saturday and 11- 5pm Sunday, Bank Holidays 10am - 6pm

Established in 1989 and in its twelfth year of operation, Portcullis Quality Crafts Gallery is situated in Gateshead Metro Centre, Europe's largest out of town shopping and leisure complex.

Portcullis is a Crafts Council selected gallery operated by Gateshead Metropolitan Councils, Libraries, Arts and Information Service, most recognised for commissioning the Angel of the North sculpture by internationally renowned sculptor Antony Gormley.

The Gallery shop displays a constantly changing range of high quality contemporary crafts by crafts makers throughout Britain. The gallery specialises in ceramics, glass and jewellery and holds regular exhibitions throughout the year.

All work displayed in the gallery is for sale and Portcullis is able to offer interest free credit though Northern Arts' arts purchase plan scheme.

Portcullis also offers a selection of unusual gift ideas and hand made greeting cards. The gallery is located on the Upper Level Red Mall, next to the Mediterranean village in Gateshead MetroCentre.

Portcullis Craft Gallery

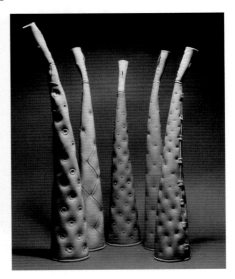

Above:
Iain Henderson

Top Left:
Emma Johnstone

Top Right:
Abigail Davies

Left:
David Booker

Right:
Jane Charles

The Tinners' Rabbit

48 Market Street, Ulverston, Cumbria LA12 7LS. Telephone: 01229 588808

Email: chris@tinnersrabbit.freeserve.co Website: www.awtc.org.uk

Open Monday - Saturday 9.30am - 5.30pm

Since opening in December 1997, the Tinners' Rabbit has gone from strength to strength and has now acquired additional premises next door, The Tinners' Rabbit Two! This gives three times the hanging space, six artists' studios and a greatly improved picture framing workshop.

The original workshop resembled a 'Dickensian garret', but nonetheless Chris has built up a thriving bespoke framing service of some renown. Exhibition contracts and customised frames are produced as well as the 'run of the mill'.

Each month the gallery has a small one-man show for artists and makers from as far afield as Devon, Ireland and Scotland.

A bookshop has now been added to paintings, drawings, ceramics, textiles, jewellery, turned wood, sculpture and greetings cards.

Tinner's Rabbit

All photos David Briggs

Above: Ronky Bullard
Below and bottom right:
Local views by Martin Procter

Spongeware: Nicholas Mosse,
Brixton & Eden Potteries

Wave Contemporary Art & Design

20 Kirkland, Kendal, Cumbria LA9 5AD. Telephone: 01539 736975 Fax: 01539 737600
Email: wavegallery@hotmail.com Website: www.wavegallery.co.uk
Open Monday - Friday 10am - 5pm, Saturday 9.30am - 5.30pm

Wave, established 1999, has a fresh approach to contemporary art and design. It is run by Paul Henderson and his partner Jo Casey, a designer/maker (featured overleaf). Wave shows the finest quality work, in three rooms, by over fifty artists- the majority of whom are recently established. Wave has a large selection of jewellery in precious metals, beautiful studio ceramics, blown glass, mixed media paintings, and a wide range of handmade furniture. You will find everything from a hand made card to a dining table or sofa.

A commissioning service is available and wave holds a database of artists, so if the piece you are looking for is not on show it can be made especially for you. Wave is Craft Council listed and also registered with Northern Arts' Purchase Plan, which means purchases over £60 are available on interest free credit, subject to status.

Jo Casey

Jo graduated from Manchester Metropolitan University with a first class degree in 3-D design in '98. Since then she has set up her studio with the help of her partner, Wave.

Her work ranges from porcelain vessels (as pictured) and wall plaques to larger hangings and lighting, in aluminium, which can be commissioned to fit any space. Jo's work is inspired by many things including architecture, every day objects and the qualities of the materials she uses. Her work is constantly evolving as she likes to be experimental with techniques and scale. Wave is an ideal place to see any new developments as the gallery is always the launch pad for a new range. Jo finds this particularly valuable as she can benefit from direct feedback from her customers.

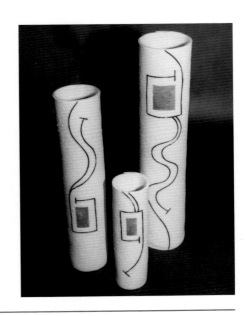

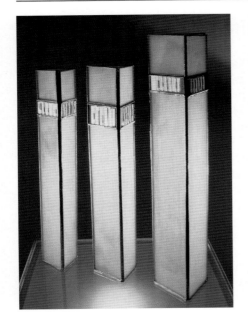

Fatima Zohra

Fatima is a graduate from the University of Wolverhampton with an Honours Degree in glass design. She specialises in contemporary glass design, using various glass making techniques i.e. blown glass sculpture, kiln formed glass, architectural glass, surface design using acid etching techniques.

Fatima is an innovative designer maker with an enviable client list and a developing reputation for cutting edge contemporary glass design. Lighting, wall screens, constructed glass vessels, architectural panels, blown glass sculptures, mirrors, clocks and obscure commissioned works are all uniquely designed, and hand crafted to the highest quality.

Inspiration for works is derived from a variety of different sources e.g. modern architecture, Islamic architecture, Islamic calligraphy, marine life and the natural world.

Clients and representation include international corporate art companies galleries, private clients and specialist outlets.

Sarah Stafford

Sarah graduated in 2000 with a first class honours degree in Jewellery Design from the London Guildhall University.

Her work combines silver with translucent resin and has evolved from a fascination with leaves, plant structures and the effect of light upon surfaces. She is constantly developing her ideas and introducing new work to the collection. The most recent addition being jewellery that resembles clusters of cells or bubbles constructed from precious metals with oxidised or gold leaf details.

Sarah has already exhibited at Lesley Craze Gallery, Sotheby's, Leeds City Art Gallery, Goldsmiths' Fair, Dazzle and Chelsea Crafts Fair amongst others. Collections of her work can be found in various selected galleries throughout the UK.

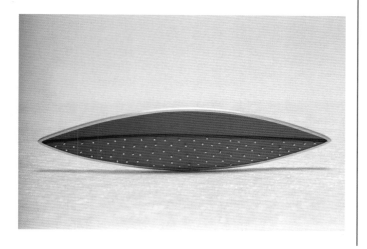

Bernard William Joseph Daniels

On completion of a HND in Design and Make at Burnley College and receiving a design award from Lancashire Enterprise, I continued my studies and completed a BA (Hons) in furniture design at the University of Central Lancashire, graduating in July 2000. Upholstered seating has come to the fore, my work is ergonomically designed to be comfortable, to stand alone in space and create visual interest. It is a combination of organic line combined with the geometric, using the craftsmanship and the honesty to materials shown by the arts and crafts movement. I find seating to be a marvellous area to work in.

The image of Ki (pictured above) was used on the cover of the literature for the New Designers 2000 exhibition at the Business Design Centre London.

Other Galleries in Scotland & The Lakes

Open Eye Gallery
75-79 Cumberland Street
Edinburgh
EH3 6RD
Tel: 0131 5571020
Email: open.eye@virgin.net
www.openeyegallery.co.uk
Open:
Mon - Fri 10am - 6pm,
Sat 10am - 4pm

Gossipgate Gallery
The Butts
Alston
Cumbria
CA9 3JU
Tel; 01434 381806
Email: kempseys@gossipgate.com
www. gossipgate.com
Open: Daily Easter - October 10am -5pm
Winter daily until Christmas but weekdays
afternoons only.
Closed Jan - mid-Feb, then weekends only
until Easter.

Automata available through Hitchcocks'

10 Chapel Row, Bath BA11 1HN. Telephone: 01225 330646
Website: www.hitchcocks-bath.co.uk
Please telephone for opening details

Above: Opi
Left: John Maltby
Right: Robert Race

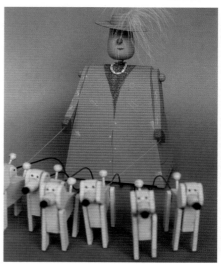

Above: Neil Hardy
Left: Melanie Tomlinson
Right: Ian Mackay

384

Automata @ Hitchcocks'

Signpost – to new makers

c/o Craft Galleries, Burton Cottage Farm, East Coker, Yeovil, Somerset BA22 9LS
Tel & Fax: 01935 862731 Email: cm@craftgalleries.co.uk Website: www.707.co.uk/craftgalleries

For the first five editions *Craft Galleries Guide* concentrated on the promotion of galleries and their makers, not individual makers without a host gallery. To mark our 10th anniversary we are experimenting with a new idea, 'Signpost'.

The idea came about with the publication of the resource book Second Steps - A Guide to Careers in the Craft World, now in its second edition, through which BCF Books has built links with many new makers.

The majority have just left college and are working hard to set up small businesses following their chosen craft. It seemed a logical step to help promote them through this Guide, and I hope that readers will find it a beneficial addition to the book.

The venue for the Craft Galleries office, host for Signpost makers

This selection of work provides a shop window for gallery owners and private buyers to discover new talent, perhaps even commissioning a piece of work from someone who may one day become a famous name.

As a result I hope that some may appear in the next edition, hosted by one of the participating galleries, established as a regular supplier, so helping the gallery, the maker and the potential buyer.

Enquiries:
Any enquiries concerning the new makers should be addressed to the Craft Galleries office, details above.

New Makers

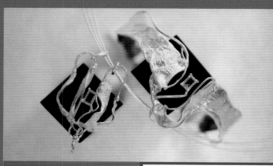

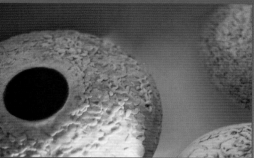

Signpost

A selection of work by new

makers not yet showing

regularly with

participating galleries

All enquiries through the Craft Galleries office

Mixed Media & Textiles

| 1 | 2 |
| 3 | 4 |

Mixed Media
1. Emma Hamer
2. Hesta Singlewood
Textiles
3. Trish Coady Clements
4. Carol Ballard

Pam & Paul Biddle

Textiles

Maggie Hollinshead-Beach Bag & Detail

Josephine Jeffers

Jenni Cadman

Jewellery

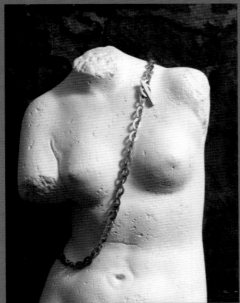

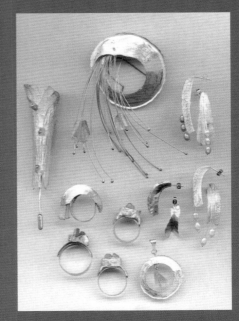

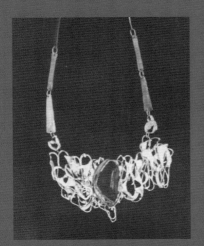

1	2	3
4		5

1. & 2. Hannah Elizabeth
Stamper
3. Gabrielle Tetley
4. Jane Mills
5. Suzanne Calderhead

Jewellery, Silversmiths & Sculptor

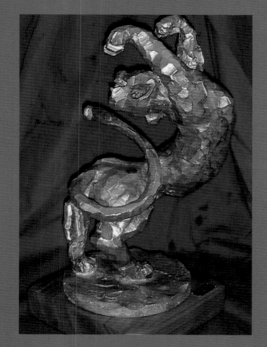

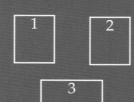

1. Brendan Jowett
Sculptor/Silversmith
2. Tara Coomber
Silversmith, Goldsmith
& Jeweller
3. Pamela Campanelli

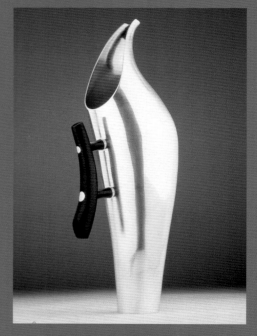

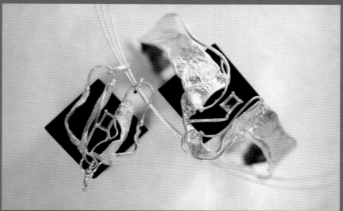

Glass

1. Mandy Clapson
2. Matthew Persson
3. Sophie Mortimer
4 & 5
Lisa-Michaela
Rabone

Matthew Persson

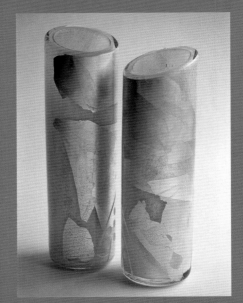

Etchings, Prints & Furniture

1. Natasha Kumar
2. Janet Jordan
3. Richard Pearce

Sculptural Ceramics

1 & 3. Ed Silverton

2 & 4. Sally Dunham

Sculptural Ceramics

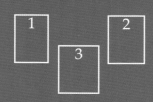

1. Lesley McShea

2. Dan Crawford

3. Ailsa Josland

New Makers

Sculptural Ceramics

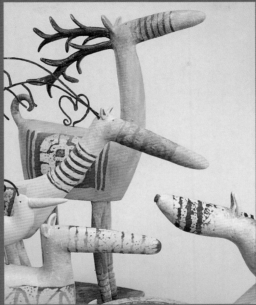

1. Paul Wearing
2. Claire Ireland
Photo: Kit Young
3. Carol Bones

	2	
1		3

Ceramics

Above ,centre & below : Helen D. Evans

Marion Valder

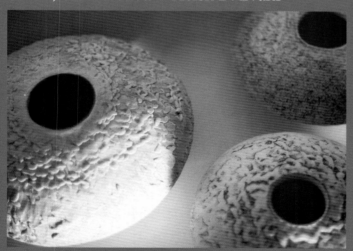

Sally French

Martin Auery

Ceramics

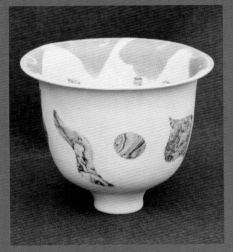

Jane Hoyles

Judi Swift

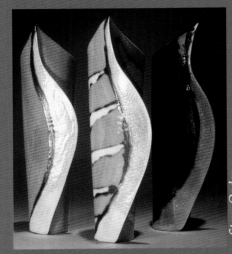

Steve Ogden

Kerry Cox

Joanna Sancha

Gordon Murdoch

New Makers

Ceramics

Karen Macdonald

Rebecca Harvey

Graham Murrell

Nick McKenzie

Katherine Winfrey

Independent Craft Galleries Association

Selected Galleries not dependent on public funding
For further information see www.icga.co.uk

Alpha House
Sherborne, Dorset
01935 814944

Argenta
Fulham, London. 0207584 1841

Artizana
Prestbury, Cheshire
01625 827582

The Bank Gallery
Chobham, Surrey 01276 857369

Bettles Gallery
Ringwood, Hampshire
01425 470410

Bowie & Hulbert
Hay on Wye, Hereford
01497 821026

Candover Gallery
Alresford, Hampshire
01962 733200

Cecilia Colman Gallery
St. John's Wood, London
0207722 0686

Church House Designs
Congresbury, Bristol
01934 833660

Eton Applied Arts
Eton, Berkshire 01753 622333

Facets
Dartmouth, Devon
01803 833534

Fenny Lodge Gallery
Fenny Stratford, Milton Keynes
01908 639494

Ferrers Gallery
Staunton Harold, Leicestershire
01332 863337

Godfrey & Twatt
Harrogate, North Yorkshire
01423 525300

The Gowan Gallery
Sawbridgeworth, Hertfordshire
01279 600004

Hitchcocks'
Bath, Somerset 01225 330646

Hitchcocks'
New Alresford, Hampshire
01962 734762

Hugo Barclay Gallery
Brighton, Sussex 01273 321694

John McKellar
Hereford. 01432 354460

Lesley Craze Gallery
Clerkenwell, London
0207608 0393

Montpellier Gallery
Stratford-on-Avon, Warwickshire
01789 261161

Old Chapel Gallery
Pembridge, Hereford
01544 388842

Pam Schomberg Gallery
Colchester, Essex 01206 769458

Porticus
Llandrindod Wells, Powys
01597 823989

Pyramid Gallery
York, North Yorkshire
01904 641187

Robert Feather Jewellery Gallery
York, North Yorkshire
01904 632025

Simon Drew Gallery
Dartmouth, Devon 01803 832832

St James's Gallery
Bath, Somerset 01225 319197

Derek Topp Gallery
Matlock, Derbyshire 01629 735580

Traffords
Stow-on-the-Wold, Glos.
01451 830424

T.H.MARCH
━━ INSURANCE ━━

Craft Galleries Insurance

Introducing an exclusive insurance scheme specially
designed for Craft Galleries

For full details please contact:

Hare Park House, Yelverton Business Park, Yelverton, Devon PL20 7LS
Tel: 01822 855555 Fax: 01822 855566

The Inspirational and the Indispensable

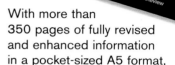
For more than 50 years, **ArtReview** has been at the centre of the visual arts in the UK.

ArtReview celebrates and champions all that is good about contemporary art, and our aim for the magazine is to make art accessible to the widest possible audience.

20% DISCOUNT FOR CRAFT GALLERIES READERS

ArtReview is the only magazine that supplies price guides alongside features, profiles and reviews, appealing to the collector as well as the exhibition visitor.

In-depth news coverage provides our readers with an essential insight into the UK art scene.

Plus, a monthly calender and comprehensive listings helps you to plan an itinerary for the month ahead.

Usual one year subscription price £38. **Craft Galleries Guide price £29.50**

With more than 350 pages of fully revised and enhanced information in a pocket-sized A5 format, **Art World Directory 2002** is the guide you can't be without. Where to go, where to buy, where to get advice and much, much more.

"Extremely useful" – *Anna-Liza Singh, Beaux Arts, Bath*

THE DIRECTORY SECTIONS INCLUDE:

- Advertising Services
- Art Book Publishers
- Art Bookshops
- Art Consultants
- Art in Country Houses
- Art Management
- Art Societies
- Artist's Index
- Arts Councils
- Auction Houses
- Calendar of Exhibitions
- Commercial Galleries
- Conservators & Restorers
- Fairs & Festivals
- Fine Press Publishers
- Framers
- Education

- Gallery Space for Hire
- Information Services
- Insurance
- Internet Galleries
- Marketing Services
- Packers & Shippers
- Print Galleries
- Print Publishers/Dealers
- Public Art Agencies
- Public Galleries
- Public Relations
- Regional Art Boards
- Sculpture Parks
- **PLUS NEW CRAFT SECTION**

To subscribe to *ArtReview* or order your *Art World Directory 2002* call **0207 246 3370** NOW!
Or mail your order, enclosing your remittance payable to *ArtReview*, FREEPOST, London EC16 1DE

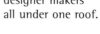

The Craft movement™

Ceramic Review

THE INTERNATIONAL MAGAZINE OF CERAMICS

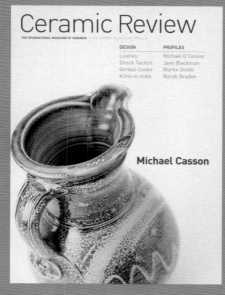

Ceramic Review

THE INTERNATIONAL MAGAZINE OF CERAMICS

DESIGN
Lustres
Shock Tactics
Gordon Cooke
Kilns in India

PROFILES
Michael O'Connor
Jane Blackman
Martin Smith
Norah Braden

Michael Casson

Ceramic Review

THE INTERNATIONAL MAGAZINE OF CERAMICS

Kevin de Choisy

DESIGN
Aesthetics
Donyatt Kilns
Mural Project
Paper Bonfires

PROFILES
Paul Philp
Andy Goldsworthy
Adrian Sassoon
Kathryn Hearn

GLAZES
20 PAGE GLAZE SUPPLEMENT

Ceramic Review

THE INTERNATIONAL MAGAZINE OF CERAMICS

DESIGN
Colour & Fire
Ash Glazes
China and Japan
Woodfired Kiln

PROFILES
Kyra Cane
Ashraf Hanna
Wouter Dam
Ewen Henderson

Marcus O'Mahony

Subscribe now and receive one copy FREE*

[7 issues instead of 6]

*New subscribers only Offer ends 31.12.02

Take out a **DIRECT DEBIT** subscription AND GET A FREE CERAMIC REVIEW BINDER WORTH £7.95. New subscribers only

SUBSCRIPTION RATES

UK	1 year £34.00	
	2 years £64.00	
Overseas	1 year £39.00	(US$70)
	2 years £74.00	(US$125)

Circulation Dept Ceramic Review
FREEPOST 25LON14688 London W1E 7DR
Tel 020 7439 3377 Fax 020 7287 9954
e-mail subscriptions@ceramicreview.com
website http://www.ceramicreview.com

Ceramic Review, the international magazine of ceramics, offers a wealth of information. Packed with practical advice, it carries details of new and stimulating processes and techniques, as well as profiles and reviews. A visual treat with excellent full colour illustrations of ceramics from the UK and around the world. A great source of reference.

INDICES

Index of Advertisers

Index of Advertisers

Makers Index

Index key: red letters indicate makers' medium. The following gallery index numbers (NOT page numbers) relate to the other galleries, participating in this book, with whom they exhibit. The red page number shows the makers' main entry, or photograph. A second page number (prefixed with P) indicates they have an extra photograph on that page.

C = Ceramics, E/P = Etchings & Prints, Cl = Collage, F = Furniture, G = Glass, J = Jewellery, M = Metalwork, PM = Paper Mache, Ph = Photographs, SC = Sculptural Ceramics, T = Toys, Tx = Textiles, W = Wood, B = Baskets

Key: **Maker's name** - Medium - Numbers of other Galleries where work can be seen - Page number

Key: **Maker's name** - Medium - Numbers of other Galleries where work can be seen - Page number

Key: **Maker's name** - Medium - Numbers of other Galleries where work can be seen - Page number

Key: **Maker's name** - Medium - Numbers of other Galleries where work can be seen - Page number

Key: **Maker's name** - Medium - Numbers of other Galleries where work can be seen - Page number

Key: **Maker's name** - Medium - Numbers of other Galleries where work can be seen - Page number

Key: **Maker's name** - Medium - Numbers of other Galleries where work can be seen - Page number

Key: **Maker's name** - Medium - Numbers of other Galleries where work can be seen - Page number 419

Galleries Index

Key: **Map reference number - Gallery -** Media stocked *Page number*

Key: **Map reference number - Gallery -** Media stocked - *Page number*

Key: **Map reference number** - Gallery - Media stocked - *Page number*

Key: **Map reference number - Gallery -** Media stocked *-Page number*   425

Craft Galleries Guide

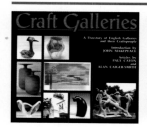   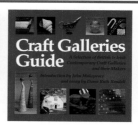 

In the last two editions I included the following answer to this often asked question,

"Why do we need a new edition of the Craft Galleries Guide, won't it just be the same as before ?"

The Guide has become a naturally evolving publication, some galleries have chosen to take space in every edition but hosting different makers. Others have decided to take a year or two out, at one time or another, returning with a fresh selection of makers.

Combined with the introduction, in each edition, of others who have never participated before (including brand new venues with innovative ideas) the result is a fresh selection of good quality galleries.

P.S. This year it is certainly not just the same, there are many new makers showing their work and over forty new galleries.

I believe that the Guide has now found its level and is unlikely to grow much 'fatter'. However the content continues to grow in diversity and I hope that the next edition, will surpass all the others. If the well established galleries (who have expressed intent to participate again) come in alongside more new galleries who were too late for this book, comprehensive cover will be achieved.

If you would like to order back copies (all available except the blue, third edition) or be placed on the mailing list (which gives you the opportunity to order at pre-publication prices), or take part in the next publication, please fill in the enclosed postcard or send you name and address to:

**Craft Galleries, Burton Cottage Farm,
East Coker, Yeovil,
Somerset BA22 9LS
Email: cm@craftgalleries.co.uk**

Exotic elephant by Helen Johnson

Acknowledgments:
This book has now definitely become a team effort.
I would like to thank the following, without whom it
would have taken even longer to compile:
Emma Brown for her enthusiastic help with research,
indexing and proof reading. My son Adam for his
advice over design elements and cutting text to the bones,
wherever possible.
Alan Bruce for drawing the local maps, Paul Bastin
(I.T. Force) for his invaluable computer help and advice
and Jean Bastin for word processing the text.